# PRECIOUS LIVES

Margaret Forster was born and brought up in Carlisle. She is the author of many acclaimed novels, biographies and memoirs, including *Have the Men Had Enough?*, *Lady's Maid*, *Mothers' Boys*, *Shadow Baby*, *Elizabeth Barrett Browning*, *Hidden Lives* and *Rich Desserts and Captain's Thin*. She is married to writer and journalist Hunter Davies and lives in London and the Lake District.

## ALSO BY MARGARET FORSTER

### Fiction

*Dames' Delight*

*Georgy Girl*

*The Bogeyman*

*The Travels of Maudie Tipstaff*

*The Park*

*Miss Owen-Owen is At Home*

*Fenella Phizackerley*

*Mr Bone's Retreat*

*The Seduction of Mrs Pendlebury*

*Mother Can You Hear Me?*

*The Bride of Lowther Fell*

*Marital Rites*

*Private Papers*

*Have the Men Had Enough?*

*Lady's Maid*

*The Battle for Christabel*

*Mothers' Boys*

*Shadow Baby*

### Non-Fiction

*The Rash Adventurer: The Rise and Fall of Charles Edward Stuart*

*William Makepeace Thackeray: Memoirs of a Victorian Gentleman*

*Significant Sisters: The Grassroots of Active Feminism 1838-1939*

*Elizabeth Barrett Browning*

*Daphne du Maurier*

*Hidden Lives*

*Rich Desserts and Captain's Thin: A Family and Their Times 1831-1931*

### Poetry

*Selected Poems of Elizabeth Barrett Browning* (Editor)

# Margaret Forster

# PRECIOUS LIVES

VINTAGE

Published by Vintage 1999

2 4 6 8 10 9 7 5 3 1

Copyright © Margaret Forster 1998

The right of Margaret Forster to be identified as the author of
this work has been asserted by her in accordance with the Copyright, Designs and Patents Act, 1988

First published in Great Britain in 1998
by Chatto & Windus

Vintage
Random House, 20 Vauxhall Bridge Road,
London SW1V 2SA

Random House Australia (Pty) Limited
20 Alfred Street, Milsons Point, Sydney
New South Wales 2061, Australia

Random House New Zealand Limited
18 Poland Road, Glenfield, Auckland 10,
New Zealand

Random House South Africa (Pty) Limited
Endulini, 5A Jubilee Road, Parktown 2193,
South Africa

Random House UK Limited Reg. No. 954009

A CIP catalogue record for this book
is available from the British Library

ISBN 0 09 927574 0

Papers used by Random House UK Ltd are natural,
recyclable products made from wood grown in sustain-
able forests. The manufacturing processes conform to the
environmental regulations of the country of origin

Printed and bound in Germany by
Graphischer Grossbetrieb Pössneck GmbH

# List of Illustrations

# Prologue

'THERE'S A DEAD dog down there,' the woman said to my father. 'Don't let the little lass catch sight of it, it's nasty; don't take her along the river bank, mind.' We were on a narrow path which led from the road to the river Caldew. It was fenced on both sides with wooden palings, loosely strung together with thick wire, and between these struts dandelions and nettles, growing in the rough grass, poked through. My father stopped, to let this woman pass. He stood with his back to the fence and ordered me to do the same. The path was very tight with barely enough room for one person to walk. She would have to squeeze past us as best she could. She had a dog of her own, a scruffy brown terrier, straining at the leash and whimpering. 'She's upset,' the woman said over her shoulder once she was through the gap we'd created; 'she got a fright, seeing that dead dog.' My father started walking again, still in the direction of the river, and I followed. Behind us we heard the woman shouting, 'You should turn back! There's a dead dog down there, I told you! You shouldn't let the lass see it! It'll upset her! Cover her eyes when you get there, any road!' This last instruction was very faint because by the time she gave it she was nearly at the other end of the path and we were nearly at the river.

My father hadn't spoken, either to me or to the woman; he hadn't reacted at all to this information about a dead dog. He always ignored strangers. Whatever they chose to say to him, he ignored them, giving no indication he had even heard them. Not a muscle moved in his face as he stared beyond them. Only if he was particularly irritated by being addressed would any sound escape his compressed lips and then it was a whistle, slow and tuneless. But now he was not whistling. We walked on, my steps attempting to match his, but he turned his feet out slightly and this was difficult for me to copy. We were now walking along the broad, grassy margin bordering the river but there was no sign of a dead dog. All we saw were ducks. We'd come equipped to feed them and I was carrying a paper bag full of crusts. I started tearing these crusts up and throwing the bits of bread, and the ducks squawked and fought over it until it was all finished.

We walked on. No dead dogs at all. I wanted to ask my father where he thought this dead animal might be but I didn't. My father did not like chattering and he especially did not like chattering which consisted of questions. He wasn't prone to speculation either. If there was a dead dog, we would come across it; if there wasn't, if it had been a figment of the woman's imagination, or if it lay in the direction we had not taken, we wouldn't. That was all there was to it – nothing to talk about. So I turned it over in my own mind, all the time scanning the river bank and hoping we would find the corpse of the dog. About half a mile along the bank there was a little spur of land sticking out into the river. The dog was lying on the muddy slope facing us. It was a black dog. The water was lapping over its partly submerged legs, the slight swell only sufficient first to cover the legs up to the knee joints and then recede to just above the paws. Across the dog's throat was a dark red gash. No blood was flowing; it was only sticking there, matted in the fur around the neck. We stopped. We stared. My father grunted. He liked things to come to pass: a dead dog had been promised, a dead dog had been found, everything was now satisfactory. 'Dead,' he said. I thought it might be considered permissible to ask a question. 'Will it be buried?' I asked. 'Might be,' my father said, 'when the farmer finds it, if a fox doesn't eat it first.'

I was fairly sure foxes did not eat dogs. I was only six, but even so I felt there was something wrong with this suggestion. Foxes ate chickens. Lions ate dogs, maybe, but there were no lions in Carlisle, not even in a zoo, because the city had no zoo. But I hesitated to challenge my father, who did not take kindly to correction or contradiction. We continued on to Cummersdale then, and when we reached the textile factory we turned and began walking back. This was the prescribed length of the walk and it never varied. It was raining slightly by then and as we passed the dead dog again I said, 'The poor dog will get wet.' 'Don't be so daft,' my father said, scornfully: 'there's nowt poor about a dead dog. It isn't poor, it's dead. Dead as a doornail. It can't feel a thing. No need to feel sorry for a dead dog. It's had its chips. Finished.' It was a veritable speech. Excited by this unusual flow of words from him I said, 'What about a dead person?' 'What about them?' my father said, growing annoyed. 'They're dead too, if they're dead. Like the dog. If they've popped their clogs, they're dead. There's nothing anyone can do about it.' He was walking faster and I was half-running to keep up. 'What about heaven?' I panted. 'The heavens are going to open any minute,' my father said, neatly turning the real question into a query about weather. 'We're in for a soaking. Your Mam won't be pleased.' We hurried on, down the narrow path again, into the road and along it, and there was the woman who had warned us about the dead dog putting her dustbin out. She saw us and shouted, 'Did you see it? You didn't let the little lass see it, did you? It would upset her, I told you . . .' The rest was lost as we rushed up the hill past the cemetery. 'Upset you!' my father muttered. 'Damn silly woman – as if the sight of a dead dog would upset you. You've got more sense.'

We were drenched by the time we'd walked across Dalston Road and up Dunmail Drive over to Orton Road, where we lived then. My father stopped when we reached our gate. 'No need to mention dead dogs to your Mam,' he warned. I understood perfectly why not. My mother's response to anything whatsoever to do with death was not my father's. She *would* get upset, even over a dog. But in that respect I was like my father. I wasn't frightened by the word 'dead'. I was interested, curious. Everything to do with dying was secretive and talked about in whispers, whispers which I tried hard to hear. It was the same with being born. This subject, too, was shrouded in mystery. It was equally hard to understand both – how life started and how it ended fascinated me but no one was prepared to enlighten me about either. My mother was emotional about births and deaths but my father was matter-of-fact. He appeared not to be afraid of death. It was just something inevitable. He had no religious beliefs, unlike my mother. He never went to church or said his prayers. There was no hint in anything he said or did that he thought of life as so precious that the thought of it ending was terrifying.

At this time, he was forty-four years old.

*

On Whit Monday, three years later, when I was nine, my father took me to climb Catbells, the fell above Derwent Water. We left the house very early to catch the bus to Keswick. It was a magnificent May morning with the kind of faint mist hanging low over the trees which always signified a good day to come but, although confident of sun, we took our raincoats with us. We were going a long way, after all, almost forty miles into the hills of the Lake District, and we wouldn't be back until late. We had sandwiches wrapped carefully by my mother in greaseproof paper, ham for my father and cheese for me, and biscuits. Beer and lemonade we would buy later, in Keswick.

Before we went to the bus station, we stopped at a telephone box. My father produced a slip of paper and some pennies from his pocket. 'Ring this number,' he said. 'It's the doctor's. Tell them to send him to 84 Richardson Street for your grandma. I'll keep watch.' I didn't even query these instructions or ask what he was keeping watch for. He didn't like telephones whereas I longed to have one in our house. He kept one foot in the door of the phone box while I rang. I delivered the message, pleased to have pressed button 'A' at the right time to speak, and when the doctor's receptionist asked why my grandma needed the doctor to visit I turned to my father, who was listening intently through the slightly open door, and passed this on. 'Because he's been sent for,' he said, angrily. 'She might be dying.' I repeated this, wondering why my father was so cross. I hadn't known my grandmother might be dying. It seemed good news to me. My mother had been at my grandparents' house all the day before. I'd heard her say to my father that his mother was very poorly and would need Dr Stevenson the next day, but I hadn't realised 'very poorly' might mean dying. As we went on to the bus station I started to ask my father about this turn of events but he shut me up. 'Don't spoil the day,' he said. So I didn't, though it did strike me as unfair that he was going off for a day out while my mother was going to spend it yet again with his perhaps dying parent.

The bus we caught was a double-decker and we went upstairs and sat at the front. It seemed a long and bumpy ride, with the bus going very slowly, its top deck brushing sometimes quite dangerously against the branches of overhanging trees once we were out of Carlisle and on the narrow roads of the real countryside. A double-decker was a cumbersome vehicle for such roads and its progress was occasionally unsteady as it lurched round corners, but we were always braced for the sudden interruptions in its speed. My father, looking ahead, could always predict when the nature of a bend meant the bus would have to brake sharply and throw us sideways and he'd tell me to hold on to the bar in front. I'd stretch out my arms to their full extent and just manage to do this. 'Good lass,' he'd say.

That was all he said. As usual, there was no talking, except if he pointed out such sheep, cows or birds he decided were worthy of comment.

Arriving in Keswick was exciting. It was so different from Carlisle, much smaller, the streets much narrower, and it was all grey, built of grey stone and slate, whereas Carlisle had mostly sandstone buildings. It had a different atmosphere too, full as it usually was of climbers and walkers dressed in all the appropriate gear and giving to the place a permanent holiday air. But in fact the streets that day were almost empty. We were so early, as we walked through them to the lake, that the shops which sold mountain boots and ropes and rucksacks were not yet open. It was becoming warm, the mist gone, and the sun beginning to blaze from a thrillingly blue sky such as we'd rarely seen in Keswick. There would be crowds later but we were ahead of them, ahead of all those still in their bed-and-breakfasts, and youth hostels and caravans and tents. The road to the lake was almost deserted and when we reached it and went to the kiosk where tickets for the steamers were sold it wasn't yet open. 'First in the queue,' my father said, with immense satisfaction. He hated queues. He had no patience and could not queue. We were also first onto the first steamer of the day (except it wasn't a steam boat, though called that, but a motor launch). Again, we sat at the front. The seats were hard and uncomfortable, just three slats of varnished wood with high backs to them. The boat ride across the lake to Nichol End was even bumpier and noisier than the bus had been but we loved it. Ahead of us, as the boat ploughed its way on, with masses of spray, between little islands we could see blue-black mountains silhouetted against the brighter blue of the sky. My father pointed and said, 'That's it, that's the one, that's Catbells.' I couldn't believe we were going to climb so high.

But it didn't take long. My father led the way along a wood-land track and through a meadow and then we were at the foot of Catbells. He pointed out the path, and I was off, way ahead of him in minutes. I didn't keep stopping to admire the view, as he did, and so I was soon at the top, panting and hot-faced and longing for my lemonade which he had in his raincoat pocket. It seemed to take him ages to arrive, wiping the sweat from his brow and scarlet with effort, and then we spread both our coats out and he lay full length while I immediately drank the lemonade (which was disappointingly warm and flat and not at all thirst-quenching). Picnic over, I was ready to go down, but my father seemed to be asleep. I wandered round the area of the summit, looking down at the shimmering lake on one side and into the densely green folds of the Newlands Valley on the other. Beautiful, but I was bored now. I wanted action. From behind the handkerchief spread over his face my father told me to settle myself, he was in no hurry to go down. 'It might be the last time I ever climb up here,' he said. I was puzzled. 'Why?' I asked. 'I'm getting on,' he said. 'I might not be able to manage it. This might be the last time before I go.'

Go? I knew what he meant. My mother, with her ever-present intimations of mortality, talked like that all the time. He meant he might die. He meant he might never climb Catbells again before he died. I couldn't see his expression, because of the handkerchief still over his face. Was he serious? But he was always serious. I sat down again and tried to wait patiently. Why was he suddenly sounding like my mother, with this uncharacteristic if oblique reference to dying? I wondered if it was because of my grandmother being apparently so near to death. Maybe everyone after a certain age started thinking about dying.

Eventually, he hauled himself up and we went down, slowly, in silence. He never did climb Catbells again but it wasn't because he wasn't fit enough. He could have done it easily at any time in the next twenty or so years, but somehow he just never did. My grandmother didn't die then either. She had another five horrible years, completely crippled with rheumatoid arthritis, to endure. We never discussed how my father felt about this.

When we got home that day my mother asked if we had enjoyed ourselves. 'Grand day,' my father said. 'Smashing. Everything went right, couldn't have been better.' My mother looked at me and I nodded. I wanted to tell her it had been such a grand day, such a smashing day, my father had thought about dying. But I didn't.

★

My father's father, George James Forster, died when I was seventeen and certainly old enough to appreciate the significance of this death. There was a funeral, with a church service (though George never darkened a church door in his lifetime) and then a tea at the Co-op. I didn't go to either. My excuse was that I was studying hard for A-levels and couldn't afford to miss a single lesson, and this was accepted. I quite regretted that no fuss was made about this, since I wanted the opportunity to make a self-righteous statement about feeling nothing for my grandfather, no grief whatsoever, and that therefore it would be hypocritical to go to his funeral. I was very hot on the evils of hypocrisy.

Coming home from school that day, cycling up the steep hill to our house, I saw my father waiting at the gate. He was very formally, very smartly dressed, still in his funeral clothes. We had moved from Orton Road and now lived, conveniently for funerals, in Richardson Street, bang opposite the cemetery. Our front windows gave us splendid vantage points for funeral processions, of which there were a great many in Carlisle in the 1950s. Carlisle people seemed to treat funerals with a Victorian intensity – lots of big, gleaming black cars, all crawling along bumper-to-bumper; masses of flowers, lavish wreaths and crosses; every single mourner in black, and many of the women

8

heavily veiled. I was fascinated by these spectacles and resented my mother closing our curtains out of respect, when I wanted to position myself in the window so that I could see everything. I was always curious as to who had died, and how, and what of, and would even go so far as to walk to the cemetery later on, to find the fresh grave and read the cards on the wreaths in order to work out as much as I could.

My father, when we were young, had often taken us for walks in the cemetery simply because it was more like a park than a cemetery if one could turn a blind eye to thousands of gravestones. He could. They disturbed him not one bit. He saw only the high standard of gardening and it pleased him. He admired all the bedding plants, the rows and rows of bright red geraniums and the pink and yellow dahlias, and the violently orange marigolds, all arranged in strictly geometric patterns. He approved of the brutally clipped hedges and trees lining the paths and he particularly liked the precision with which the whole cemetery was laid out, with everything neat and orderly. He made us walk properly in the cemetery, which is to say we were not allowed to run, or to walk across any graves, or to disturb any of the flowers. He didn't like me to look at the cards attached to the wreaths either. He said they were private. I said how could they be private when they were displayed in public, but he just said, 'Don't argue.'

So there he was, after his father's funeral, waiting at the gate. Funerals had never bothered him and I saw no reason why this one should have done. I got off my bike and wheeled it towards him. I didn't say anything. I didn't ask him how he felt, or express any concern, or enquire how the funeral had been (but are there different ways a funeral, like a party, can 'be'?). He opened the gate for me. 'Are you coming?' he asked. 'Where?' He glared at me, furious. 'You know where.' I smiled, I hoped derisively. 'You mean to the cemetery? Isn't the funeral over, then?' I knew perfectly well it was. I knew perfectly well he meant go with him to look at the grave and the flowers. 'Anyway, no,' I said, 'I'm not. What for? Why should I?' And I rushed quickly through the gateway and up the path. Behind me I heard the gate being slammed shut so hard the whole frame shook and clanged. I turned to see my father marching off to the cemetery gates shouting: 'Right! I'll remember, don't you worry! I'll remember this!' I laughed. He looked so ridiculous. Then I put my bike in the shed and went into the house, where I described this little scene to my mother. She was reproachful. 'That wasn't kind,' she said. 'When he's just buried his Dad.' 'He didn't care about his Dad,' I said, 'so I don't know why he's pretending now he's dead.' 'It's a matter of respect-for-the-dead,' my mother said, wearily. 'Well, I didn't respect his Dad,' I said, 'and I'm not going to start now. It's silly, stupid, all this respect for the dead stuff.' 'Oh, Margaret . . .' my mother said, sadly. I mimicked her tone and made an exaggerated face of distress, trying to make her laugh and failing. Often, I could make her smile by acting penitent, but not that day.

I made sure I was out before my father returned from his little pilgrimage. I went into the cemetery by the side entrance on Dalston Road. There was no fear of meeting him – I knew the route he would take and that he would have long since passed this point, the place where his own grandfather, after whom he was named, was buried. He always made us stop there and read the inscription so that we could marvel at this other Arthur Forster reaching ninety. He had an almost superstitious reverence for this gravestone, seeming to believe that if he read the name and the dates often enough he, too, would live until he was ninety. He would have passed it that day, on the way to the new part of the cemetery, up on the hillside, where his mother and now his father were buried, and as I entered by the side entrance he would be walking home down the main drive. I would not encounter him and thereby lose face. We were both very concerned about losing face in front of each other, but he need never know I had indeed come, if not to pay my respects to his father's grave then at least to look at the wreaths. There were only six, a poor show by Carlisle standards. One from each of his two sons, one from a surviving brother, one from a sister-in-law, and two more from people whose names I didn't know. Enough, just, to cover the raised hump of soil and grass sods under which the coffin lay.

All I could think of as I stood there was that I was glad my grandfather was dead. I knew 'glad' was a wicked word to use with 'dead' but that's what I was, positively glad. He was such a miserable old man, spending his days crouched over the fire in his gloomy, dark house. What had been the point of his continuing to live? Why should anyone be sad that it was all over? But my father was apparently feeling something, if only I could fathom what. Odd. I thought this very odd, and wished I could discuss his feelings with him. I practised asking him in my head but heard all too clearly the withering reply 'Don't talk daft.' So I didn't. I went home and said nothing. But I did find myself looking at my father after that and wondering if I would feel anything of what he had felt (even if I didn't know what that was) when he himself died. This event, his death, was something I'd wished for many times in the previous few years, but I'd just recently stopped wishing it. I didn't need him to die any more, because I was going to leave home and him soon, and so his existence was no longer of importance. The years of hating him were over. The sad thing was that I'd hated him with so little cause. He had never been cruel or violent. On the contrary, he had worked hard to feed and clothe me and give me treats. His sins were so trivial. I'd hated the way he shouted, his need to dominate, his scorn for books, his insistence that everything should be done his way. I'd hated the way he ate, his petty rules and regulations, his actual presence. Nothing to arouse hate, really. I was embarrassed to have to admit to myself how absurd my hatred had been. It was a relief to be done with it.

But all the same his death would not be something I dreaded.

*

It was a glorious summer's evening in London. My sister-in-law Marion had just come from work, straight to our house, straight into the garden, where she knew I would be sitting waiting under the pear tree with the chilled white wine and the Kalamata olives all ready for her. Every Wednesday she came and we both looked forward to it. It gave her such pleasure to sit in the cool of our shady garden and recover from her hectic day. She drank some wine, ate a few olives, sighed with contentment, and reached for her cigarettes. She lit one, head back, and inhaled deeply. 'Bliss,' she said. Not the wine, the olives, the garden, but the cigarette – 'bliss'.

Every now and again I went into the kitchen to baste the chicken I had in the oven. Whenever I came back out, there'd be another cigarette lit. In the winter, Marion never relished these pre-supper cigarettes so much. She was well aware that her brother, my husband, Hunter, loathed cigarette smoke and so she'd smoke only a couple then, sitting crouched by the kitchen door with it open a fraction, on even the coldest days. It made her feel furtive but she respected his right in his own home, and his need as an asthmatic, to keep his environment smoke-free. Until he left it at eighteen, he'd had to live in a smoke-filled house, where both his parents and his three siblings all puffed away, and he wasn't going to endure it again. But now, in the summer, outside, Marion could smoke as much as she liked and what she liked was a lot.

She sat and smoked, telling me about her day, which had been particularly fraught. She was a social worker, in Camden, and had had to see to the removal of an old tramp from a pavement. The tramp, a woman, had six cats, all of whom slept with her, curled up among her bundles of clothes and rubbish. The people living in the block of flats outside which she'd parked herself were complaining more about the cats than her. 'They want the cats put down,' Marion said. 'I mean, the idea, they're perfectly healthy cats. I'd rather they wanted her put down.' Then she laughed to show she was just being outrageous. 'Oh dear,' she said, 'the poor body's half dead anyway. She's got everything wrong with her, it's pitiful.' While she told me what she'd done about this case she lit yet another cigarette. Knowing I shouldn't, I pointed out she'd smoked more than usual. She shrugged.

It was silly to protest about her smoking, but sometimes I couldn't help it. It scared me. I kept reading about the proven dangers of heavy smoking, the sort Marion indulged in. She'd been one of those children who start cadging the odd fag very young, around eleven, and who by fifteen are smoking regularly. She was forty-one now and had been a serious smoker, on at least twenty a day, for many years. She loved smoking, adored it, and smoked with a passion incomprehensible to a nonsmoker like me. Often I'd asked her to describe what cigarettes did for her, but she was never able to explain the pleasure enough for me to identify it as anything I'd felt myself. Was it like drinking wine? No, it was not, it was better. Smoking apparently did wonderful things. It soothed her but it also stimulated her, and she loved the taste. She was never going to give it up. She knew of the dangers but she was prepared to take the risk, announcing that even if smoking shortened her life she would settle for that rather than give up.

She didn't, of course, believe it would shorten her life. Her mother had been a smoker and her lungs, when she died, in her eightieth year, of Alzheimer's, had been very healthy. But I'd read, that day, some new report in a newspaper about the rise of lung cancer statistics for women of Marion's age and I suppose this was what made me worry even more than usual about her smoking. I didn't want to nag her – it would do no good anyway – but I mentioned that I thought she had actually increased the number of cigarettes per day that she smoked. 'Oh, don't start that,' she said. 'You know what I think. I don't care if it kills me, I don't mind about dying. It's not that I want to die, but I don't really care – not enough to give up smoking, anyway.' We started to argue, which spoiled the evening. I said she wasn't thinking of the dying, the process, just of being dead. She wasn't thinking of those who loved her, who would have to watch her endure this and who cared about her continuing to live, even if she herself didn't hold her life as precious. I ranted on quite a bit and she groaned and asked if that chicken was ready yet.

After she'd gone, I went over and over what she had said about trading years of her life, if necessary, for the pleasures of smoking. She'd said everyone had to die sometime so why worry about it, but, although Marion was certainly not a thoughtless person, that seemed to me thoughtless. In the midst of life we are in death, yes, but I'd noted by then that the moment people actually were dying the struggle to hold on to life became compulsive and fierce. Life, which Marion could be so philosophical about when in no imminent danger of dying, became exceedingly precious the moment it was about to be taken away. The dying want every second of life, whatever the circumstances of it. Or else it is wanted for them.

It seemed to me there was something I could not quite grasp about that. I wanted to know why life remains precious to those whose lives seem far from being so to everyone else. What, when one is dying, does this value consist of? Within the same eighteen months I watched my father die of extreme old age and my sister-in-law die, aged fifty-six, of cancer (though not lung cancer). Their attitudes and their experience of dying revealed a kind of answer that was on the one hand consoling and on the other dismaying.

# I

MY FATHER, WHO left school in 1913, aged thirteen, was certainly not illiterate. He could read and write perfectly well but he did neither fluently. Writing, especially, he found difficult, something he had to labour over, with even a signature requiring concentration. Writing of any sort worried him, and so it was a surprise after he died to find he had kept a diary and had written in it every day. He may have kept earlier diaries but the ones which have survived start in 1969. He gave that one up in May. In 1970, he got to July before he stopped, but from 1971 he completed the entire year and as time went on wrote more, not less.

On 4 June 1990, my father recorded that he was eighty-nine and a half years old, but only did so in one of the two diaries he was in fact keeping, the *Expert Diary*, a gardener's diary published by D. G. Hessayon. 'Got out Bright and Sunny. Dismantled edge. Big job. Tidy up. 89 1/2 year old.' In his other diary (Nestlé's, given to him by my brother, who worked for that company) the entry reads: 'Bright and Sunny. Warm. Bit wind. Dismantling edge. Big job for me. All OK.' Two diaries filled in, with almost exactly the same mundane information, simply because he had been given two for Christmas and it would be a waste not to use both. I don't know what dismantling an edge means, though I expect gardeners do, but I know why he recorded a half-birthday: he wanted to reach ninety, like his grandfather. The nearer his ninetieth birthday came, the more impressed he was by his own age. It was hugely significant.

He was furious with himself on 2 July. 'Light showers. Mild. Cut grass. Front and Back. Had a Fall in Back. No Reason for it. Damage glasses. Worse. Eye. Bit blood. Pack up for the day.' Then he hid. He didn't want his kind, caring neighbours to see his damaged face. They would be concerned and might tell somebody, and somebody might call the doctor and the doctor might make him go to the infirmary, and he was not having that. So on Tuesday and Wednesday he kept out of sight, though he worried that this in itself would cause suspicion. He was a man of rigid routine. He shopped every weekday in his local shopping area, Denton Holme. He walked the half-mile there and caught the bus back, arriving home at twelve noon precisely. This shopping was important and people knew it was. Strangely, for a working man of his era, my father had always liked to shop. It was a task he was always happy to do for my mother and he did it well, going to the covered market to buy heavy foodstuffs so that she wouldn't be too burdened carrying them home herself. Once he'd retired and she had had her first minor stroke, he'd more or less taken over all the shopping. So the shopkeepers of Denton Holme knew him well. They knew he nipped into the betting shop after he'd been to the butcher's for his sausages and before he went into the bread shop for his teacakes. Should he fail to turn up for more than a couple of days, enquiries as to his health might be made – which they were. Mrs Nixon rang up on Wednesday evening to ask if he was all right. 'Grand,' he said, 'only I've been too busy to get out. I've been sorting bedding.' Explanation accepted, he was relieved. He'd got away with his Fall and by the next day the cut over his eye had stopped bleeding and the swelling was down. He could go out again, and anyway he had to because he had no bread left.

This episode did rather emphasise how low he kept his stock

of food and how shopping had taken on another dimension. In his extreme old age it provided the spur, indeed it fulfilled the positive need, to go out at all. It motivated him in a way he liked. Again and again I'd asked him to let me fill his cupboards with emergency provisions in case he became housebound, but he would not allow it. 'No! I have to get out,' he said. He accepted a couple of tins of Nestlé's food which my brother occasionally brought him, but he would not permit any methodical piling up of nourishing foods that would keep. This was why they knew him so well in the local shops and knew exactly what he bought and where. They were kind to him in unobtrusive ways. Realising that it was a struggle for him to load his shopping bag and hold his stick to keep his balance, the shopkeepers were adept at helping him. His worn leather bag was not very large and it filled quickly, but then he had not much to put in it, since he only bought two ounces of this and a quarter of that. Bread was purchased once a week, a large thick-sliced white loaf, and filled the bag, but then he bought nothing else that day.

He didn't attempt, after his fall, to go to town that Thursday, though it was his regular day for doing so. It was an adventure, by then, going 'up street' and he looked forward to it. He went to Marks & Spencer's food hall, where they sold plaice, individual portions, in breadcrumbs, and since first I'd bought it for him he'd become addicted to it. He only bought this fish and a bag of Devon Toffees. The price of Marks & Spencer's vegetables appalled him, and he still grew all he needed in his own garden. On his way to and from Marks & Spencer, he liked to take in what was happening in English Street. 'Ruination' was his description. He disapproved of the Town Hall being painted in a terracotta colour and saw no sense in pedestrianising the area in front of it – 'it's like the bloomin' Sahara' (the paving bricks used were rust-red and the space wonderfully large and open). The attractive benches dotted around were an abomination and only encouraged idlers to sit about. But he missed his weekly jaunt when he could not manage it, in spite of being spared the tension of getting the bus. He had trouble dismounting – the bus drivers often pulled up too far from the kerb for him to alight with ease and he would attempt to get them to correct their parking position, which could lead to heated exchanges of words. Then there was the performance over his bus pass. He always had it ready, but some drivers didn't bother looking at it and he insisted they should. So it was exhausting going to town, but it was also stimulating, and he missed it.

Three weeks after this fall, my father's sister-in-law died. Nan was eighty-two, seven years younger than he was. 'Nan died. Change in weather. Carlisle Races' he wrote in one diary and in the other, still without the slightest trace of any emotion, 'Nan died. Change in weather. Dull. Run to Caldbeck H & M.' So I and my family were staying in our cottage at Caldbeck, twenty minutes away in the northern fells, which is why I came to hear his comment that day on my aunt's death. 'She had it coming,' he said. 'She was a good age.' There was neither regret nor the smallest evidence of distress in this statement. He had never liked Nan and there was about him that day an undeniable and not entirely pleasant air of triumph: she was dead, he had won, he was going to make ninety. He didn't seem to regard Nan's death as heralding his own. There was no sighing, no shuddering, no intimation of his own mortality. Yet, obviously, if he thought Nan had died at a good age and that she had had it coming, how much more was he and did he? But he appeared quite serene and untroubled.

Both diaries reported that 4 December 1990 was an exceptionally fine, mild, sunny day in north-west England. What a blessing. It made my father's ninetieth-birthday lunch so much easier to organise and all the necessary travelling trouble-free.

My brother Gordon and his wife Shirley drove up from Surrey, and my sister Pauline and her husband David from Northamptonshire, without any worries about icy roads or snowstorms. Hunter and I were already in Loweswater, where we'd moved from Caldbeck three years previously, preparing the house for the big event. It only involved seven of us, counting my father. It had been agreed that since 4 December fell on a Tuesday, and because the weather could not be depended on, the grandchildren would all telephone but not come up. So it was going to be a small party but the preparations felt immense. Roast beef was called for, best sirloin, a huge piece, or the birthday boy would think nothing of the meal. Roast beef of Old England was what he wanted, with all the trimmings – roast potatoes, boiled potatoes, boiled cabbage and Brussels sprouts and carrots and, of course, Yorkshire pudding with gravy. My mother (who died in 1981) had made deliciously light Yorkshire puddings. Alas, she had failed to pass the secret on to me but I was going to have to try to imitate hers, or the disappointment – 'What, no Yorkshire pudding?' – would ruin the dinner.

I'm not much good at cakes either but luckily a professionally baked and iced cake was not just acceptable but preferred. It gave status. My father only ever ate sponge cake of the variety known as Madeira, and he didn't like icing, but for his ninetieth the cake must look impressive, so he conceded that iced the cake would have to be in order for his name and age to be written upon it in blue. Cards were of more importance than presents. Cards, to be, in his opinion, real cards, had to have verses – none of this 'left blank for your own message' cheating. I'd made mine out of blue cardboard using photographs of him which roughly corresponded to each decade. Arthur, aged twenty, on his motor bike on the Isle of Man (where he went for the TT races); Arthur, aged thirty-one, marrying my mother; Arthur, aged forty, standing by a machine in the Metal

Box factory – and so on. And I'd made up doggerel to go with each one which would pass muster, just, as verses. My present was a copy of *The Times* for 4 December 1900. He'd never in his life read *The Times*, but I thought he'd like the idea.

He arrived at midday looking incredibly smart in his best suit and with a sparkling white shirt to go with it and a new blue tie – but then he always looked smart. A little unsteady getting out of my brother's car but soon upright, trilby hat firmly on, bright blue silk handkerchief peeping out of his jacket pocket, shoes polished to army standards. No beaming smile on his face, however. No. Smiling was always a difficult, faintly embarrassing business. His lips could never learn the trick of opening up into a generous smile. If they attempted to, as they were then trying to, they wavered and quivered, resisting automatically the necessary abandon. But, 'Grand day,' he said, and, 'Champion,' and he nodded in salutation to each of us. No embraces, no kisses, perish the thought. He stood for a minute, surveying Mellbreak, the fell above Crummock Water which soars over our fields. The sun was full on it and every rock, every patch of green, was brilliantly lit. 'Grand,' he said again, and then was happy to be led into the conservatory, where the presents lay on the table. He settled himself in a comfortable chair and admired all the (hastily bought) plants but could hardly take his eyes off the view. The fells, usually so bleak at that time of the year, were indeed made soft and beautiful by the nature of that morning's sunlight and this was the best present of all. We were each thanked for our respective gifts – 'Thank you now, thank you very much' – and photographs were allowed. We opened champagne (which he didn't like but agreed was mandatory for the occasion), and then we trooped through to the kitchen for lunch.

Our table was unrecognisable, its battered wooden surface covered for the first time in its humble life by a rigidly starched pristine white cloth. There was even a linen napkin for each guest, ironed into triangles of geometric precision. There were flowers, blue cornflowers I'd managed to procure with great difficulty, in a crystal bowl (which once belonged to his mother) in the centre. The roast beef, mercilessly overcooked so that not a hint of pink flesh was visible when cut, was lying on a proper platter, a great oval dish of willow-patterned blue and white. The carving knife was for once sharpened to lethal efficiency and my brother carved with suitable skill and authority. The cabbage and Brussels sprouts had been satisfactorily boiled to eliminate any chance of crispness remaining and were piled in sodden heaps in tureens. The potatoes (roast) were browned perfectly and the potatoes (boiled) floury. The carrots, cut into chunks of the prescribed length (two inches), added a touch of robust colour. About the Yorkshire puddings it is better not to speak. I'd made individual ones, thinking I had a better chance of success, and not a single one had risen to the fluffy heights looked for. The gravy was in that quaint article called a gravy boat and looked suspiciously thin.

We ate. My father ate more than anyone. Gordon gave him three slices of beef and he requested another, to be cut from the top of the joint where the fat was thickest. He relished fat, all kinds of fat, and had tortured us for years with his sucking and chewing of it. I gave him two roast potatoes and two boiled, and he said, 'Put another of each on.' He said he would risk a Yorkshire pudding but he might not finish it, and he swamped it with gravy, saying, 'Is this gravy?' I apologised for it and he very kindly said I was not to worry, there was an art to gravy which my mother had possessed and I did not, it couldn't be helped. Such generosity. I was overwhelmed. He had seconds of the beef and then, after a short pause, we moved on to ice-cream. It was the only pudding he liked and he liked it plain, plain vanilla. The cake was lifted onto the cleared table and I lit the nine candles and we all sang: 'Happy birthday, dear Arthur, happy birthday to you.'

There was an odd sound. I couldn't at first identify it. As our singing, surprisingly lusty, tailed off, there was this strange, compressed noise, half sigh, half groan. My father was weeping. His head was bowed, his shoulders hunched, and he was weeping not extravagantly but quite unnervingly distinctly. Hardly had we all registered this than he had taken out a handkerchief (not the blue one in his suit jacket top pocket which was for show and never to be used, not even in emergencies such as this) and was blowing his nose vigorously. 'Damn silly,' he muttered, and: 'Don't know what's got into him. Ridiculous.' He took his spectacles off and held them up and peered at them, as though they might be to blame for such outrageous behaviour. Shaking his head, he put them back on and said, 'I'll have some more of that ice-cream with a piece of the cake when it's been cut.' I gave him a knife and he cut it, down through the 'A' for Arthur.

So it passed quickly, that one evidence of emotion we had ever seen him give way to. And we allowed it to, we encouraged the swift passing on to mundane matters, as relieved as he was that it was over. My father had never wept. When distressing things had happened – the commonplace tragedies of family life, the illnesses and accidents – he had always just grunted and said, 'Pity.' Even when my mother died he didn't shed any tears before us (though he may well have done in private). He looked stricken, but he didn't weep. In his diary for that day, he wrote, 'Lily died. 7.30 a.m. Sad' – and that was that. All his immense grief was rigidly contained before us. His concern when I went with him to the infirmary to see my mother's dead body was over a missing knife. He hid his distress behind his fury that according to him it had been stolen. This wretched knife was a special knife, fashioned to act as a fork too, made specially for people, like my mother, who had had strokes and could only use one hand. It was not on the list of Patient's Property we were given to sign before my mother's few belongings could be released. One dressing-gown, one pair of slippers, one bed-jacket, six nightdresses, one hairbrush, one comb, one pair of glasses – but no knife. My father was livid. He held this list in a shaking hand and concentrated enough to read out the small print at the bottom: 'I agree that the above list covers all the items deposited by me.' Waving the sheet of paper about he raged. 'It doesn't. There's no knife!' I didn't waste time trying to persuade him that it surely didn't matter when the knife was of no intrinsic value and in any case was only a reminder of a sad disability. I signed it myself, without his being aware I'd done so, in the privacy of the sister's office. He left the ward triumphant, convinced he'd stood up for his rights. The energy he'd used up, this forceful display of righteous indignation, had kept any tears at bay.

But now, on his ninetieth birthday, he had wept, if briefly. From happiness, I could only presume. After my mother died, when finally we were leaving him to go back to London, he said to me, 'I suppose I might see you all some time.' It was said as I was leaving his house, as I walked down the hall to the door, with him behind me. I turned and said, 'Whatever do you mean, you *might* see us, *some time*?' He mumbled, 'With your Mam gone . . .' 'What difference does that make?' I said sharply. 'For heaven's sake, we'll be coming all the holidays exactly as always.' But his thinking had been painfully obvious: our mother was the one we all loved, she was the draw, and without her we would discard him. We didn't, of course, but if it had gratified him that our attentions had remained the same, he never said so. I imagined that those few tears at his birthday lunch were because he felt valued for himself and perhaps felt fortunate. But perhaps not. Nobody was foolish or brave enough to ask him. His embarrassment was ours and we all conspired to get over it as rapidly as possible with much eating of cake.

The rest of the day passed in a haze of relief – it was over, he was ninety, the great event had taken place, the celebrating had been well and truly done. He sat in the conservatory all after-noon with his binoculars trained on the craggy end of Mellbreak while he followed a particularly huge bird, hoping it would prove to be an eagle (it didn't, it was at the best a buzzard). My sister and her husband took him home, stopping in Cockermouth, where the spire of All Saints was to be lit up in his honour (or anyone else's, if they were prepared to pay for it). It didn't light up very convincingly but my father, unusually, was prepared to be indulgent and told me later on the telephone that it had been a poor show but I was not to mind. In his diary, he wrote: 'Good day. Dry. Sun. 90 year old. At Loweswater for lunch. Margaret cooking good. G & S, D & P, H & M. And me, AF.'

We expected him to shift his sights to a hundred now he'd reached ninety, but he didn't. In fact, he seemed a little puzzled as to how to approach the rest of his life however long it turned out to be. 'I can't go on for ever,' he said, soon after, and I made the smart and silly rejoinder, 'I don't see why not.' It clearly fascinated him wondering how long he could indeed go on for, but meanwhile he carried on conducting his future around the demands of his garden. On 23 April 1991 he sowed three rows of potatoes and two rows of onions to feed himself for that year; on the 30th he planted six new rose bushes: Silver Lining, Tahiti Hybrid Tea, Colour Wonder, Fragrant Cloud, Sutters Gold, and Speraks Yellow. They would take at least three years to establish and flower to his satisfaction. On 1 June he bought a new raincoat 'to see me out'. Considering his old one had lasted twenty-five years, this was alarming. Life was clearly continuing as normal and no lack of confidence in it was being betrayed.

We had good outings with him that summer, all recorded as 'smashing'. The best of them were, as ever, to the seaside, to Silloth and Skinburness, lunching at the Skinburness Hotel.

There was a special thrill for my father in patronising this hotel, which he thought of as very grand. The manager, an affable fellow, very formally dressed, liked to go round chatting to patrons, and my father liked us to chat to him. 'You've been coming here a long time, I gather, Mr Forster?' he said, having been told this by Hunter (who was far too talkative for my father's liking). He grunted. 'You know this place well, do you?' the manager persisted. 'Should do,' my father said. 'Put the boiler in, didn't I? In 1921. No, 1920. Walked with it on my back from Silloth Station, didn't I?' Did he? The manager couldn't know, we couldn't know, but nobody dared dispute it. I actually didn't want to, though it sounded impossible. It conjured up such a magnificent picture: my father, the working man personified, staggering along the sea wall all the way from Silloth, a boiler *on his back*, bowed down with the weight of it, the waves crashing to the left of him, showering him with icy spray, the wind howling all around, threatening to knock him over, but on he goes, arriving at last, drenched and exhausted, at the posh hotel, making his way to the tradesman's entrance and being shown by some disdainful lackey to the boiler room, where he fits the new boiler . . . Really? Surely he meant he carried his tools on his back, or parts for the new boiler, and not an actual boiler? A boiler for an hotel would be enormous; he couldn't have attempted to lift it on his own, never mind carry it. But we all smiled and raised our eyebrows at each another and said nothing. It wasn't so much that we were being condescending, allowing him his unlikely story, as wanting him to be happy with his memory.

And being there did make him happy. He loved the drive there in our comfortable car, especially the moment when we turned off the Silloth road to follow the small winding road that led to the marsh and we saw the Solway across it. The landscape is so empty and lonely there, so flat and wide, that the eye can sweep across it uninterrupted until it meets the Scottish hills on the other side of the estuary. We always drove very, very slowly, not at all in a hurry to reach the hotel. But he liked going into the hotel too. Every minute change in its interior decor was noted and commented on – 'Hello! New wallpaper!' – as though it was revolutionary. He preferred eating in the bar (more stories about 1920) but on Sundays he quite liked the thrill of lunching in the dining-room with the sense of occasion this gave. He approved of its formality, the pale-green linen tablecloths and the crystal goblets and the china plates, but he didn't like the wickerwork chairs, which he said cut into his back. I said they looked pretty, though, and that always started us off on a discussion worthy of William Morris, of comfort versus art, of usefulness versus beauty.

Sometimes our outings were more adventurous. My father liked the old outings but he liked exploring too, especially if there was an object to the exploration. He liked it best of all if we were trying to find some place and got lost. One bitterly cold March day we drove to the Pennines in search of a restaurant we'd read about which was near Alston. He hadn't been anywhere near Alston for decades and he was all excitement as we started on the long climb up to it, reminiscing about how he'd toiled up once on his bike. It began to snow, great swirling clouds of snowflakes billowing around the car. My father loved it. The mild element of possible danger delighted him. 'We might get snowed in,' he said. I winced at the horror of that prospect – snowed in, with my father . . . On we went, the snow first lessening, so that we could see perfectly, then sweeping down again in thick gusts of wind so that visibility all but disappeared. It was hard to credit we were going to find any building at all, never mind anything as fancy as a restaurant. We reached Alston and then left it behind, pressing on into even more remote territory, still climbing, still pursued by snow flurries. 'Maybe we should turn back,' I murmured. 'Let's find somewhere to eat in Alston.' 'Turn back?' my father said, in tones of outrage. 'After we've come all this way? Don't be daft.' He was so content himself, secure in the front seat of our big car driving through this wild landscape. 'We can't give up,' he said, firmly, 'no good doing that. We'll carry on. We'll find it.'

And we did. A strangely dark house up a lane, the way down to it treacherous. There was no one else in this 'restaurant', which was really just someone's home. But once inside we sat very happily in a shabby, rather artistic sitting-room where there was a huge log fire and the owner, a woman who was both cook and waitress, served us the most delicious meal, steak so tender my father never stopped exclaiming and an array of vegetables of astonishing variety considering the time of year and the obvious fact that they had not been frozen. Her apple pie was sublime, the apples in quarters, firm but not hard, and the pastry light and flaky – oh, how we drooled, even my father who never touched puddings. We drank as well, which may have contributed a good deal to what followed. My father had two pints of beer, which he downed even more quickly than usual, and then, as it was so cold outside, a whisky. 'Grand,' he said, 'and you were going to give up. Never give up. Never-give-up.' 'Thank you, oh wise one,' I said. He sighed with what seemed like true happiness and then suddenly said, 'One day soon, I'll just pop off. Pop.' We laughed – it was impossible not to, he had said it in such a droll fashion, making a real popping sound, and he repeated it. 'Pop. I'll just pop off.' It was clear this is how death seemed to him, a matter of popping off, disappearing in a puff of smoke, all done in a second. He might not understand how this would be managed, but this appeared not to bother him. It would be arranged. All he had to do was what he called 'put my time in'. Life was nothing more than a sentence fixed by a hidden judge and it did not frustrate him not to know its length. It was not his to reason why. He had no religious faith whatsoever but that made no difference to his conviction that there was a plan for when he would die.

For a man of ninety years, his health was still good. His experience of doctors had been brief. He first went to his GP in 1916, when he injured his right knee in a motor-bike accident, but then it was eleven years before he troubled the doctor again with what was diagnosed as sciatica. In 1933, he had his ears syringed, in 1939 the doctor paid his first home visit to him when my father had influenza. He had no contact with any doctor during the forties and only one consultation in the fifties, about a sprained ankle. More bouts of flu followed in the sixties, but it was not until the seventies that his medical notes began to need more than two sheets of paper. He had still never been in hospital, though he had been there once for an X-ray. As far as he was concerned he was fine except for arthritis, which began to trouble him in his eighties. He'd had twinges in his hands and feet for years but he wasn't incapacitated by the arthritis as his mother had been. She ended up totally crippled but he remained mobile, helped by some medication. He was constantly on the move, walking a mile a day and gardening in all weathers, which probably also helped. Most winters he had at least one heavy cold, always entered in his diary as 'flue', but he didn't count that as being ill. It wasn't actually he who had 'flue' anyway. It was 'A'. Whenever there was anything wrong with him he referred to himself in the third person as 'A' or 'AF' – 'A. got cold', 'A. improving'. And he always did improve, rapidly, usually within three days. 'A. in bed' was followed the next day with 'A. up' and then 'A. out. All OK.' He simply went to bed with a hot-water bottle and a glass of whisky, and stayed there till he felt better, getting up only to go to the bathroom and to open and close the curtains so that nobody would suspect he was ill. Since one of us, his three children, rang every day at six o'clock in the evening he made sure he was briefly up then to take our call and then he retired to bed satisfied he'd fooled us. Afterwards, when he was better, he would tell us he'd been in bed ill and say, triumphantly, 'But I managed.' Managing was the purpose of life. And when he could no longer manage he'd just pop off.

At ninety, he visited his doctor's surgery only to collect his prescription for his arthritis tablets and for some others to do with what he referred to as 'the blood'. In March 1989, he'd broken his record of never having to go into the infirmary but he considered the record still stood because he was only there for a day while he had some kind of exploratory procedure to do with 'the blood'. It was an odd episode about which he was deeply secretive. His diary records the unprecedented fact that he called for his doctor twice in January that year and again in February, and the reason was 'BLOOD', written in capital letters and underlined. The first I knew about his alarm was when he rang me in March to say he had to go into 'that place' for 'an op, or something' but if all went well and he had someone to take him home and stay with him they'd let him out the same day. 'So I don't know what I'm going to do,' he finished in tones of the deepest gloom. I, of course, said I'd come and take him to the infirmary and stay with him. 'I didn't ask you, mind,' he said. Quite. So I went to Carlisle, wondering if I dare ring his GP and ask what was going on, only to be greeted on my arrival with: 'Don't ask the doctor anything. Don't you interfere. I know what's what.' I wished I did.

He was very nervous on the morning he was due to go for treatment (or investigation). He cut himself shaving, changed his shirt twice, put new laces in his shoes and then broke one tying it up. 'I suppose I'll have to take everything off, likely,' he said, face contorted in anguish at the awful prospect. I said yes, very likely. He sighed and swallowed, and said, 'Can't be helped.' We took a taxi to the infirmary and he sat staring straight ahead, failing for once to direct the taxi driver as to precisely which route he should take. I thought that once we had arrived at the day ward I might get the opportunity to ask what was going to be done to my father, but I couldn't ask in front of him, and after he had been admitted and I was on my own I could find nobody who knew. At any rate, a couple of hours later it, whatever 'it' was, was all over and he had come round from his first anaesthetic quite charmed with the experience. 'Count to ten, they said, and, blow me, I got to four and next thing I was awake and it was done.' We went home with him in high spirits and I cooked him steak because he'd missed his dinner and the anaesthetic, far from leaving him nauseated, had sharpened his already formidable appetite. 'Well, that's that,' he said, when he'd finished eating, 'over and done with. I thought I was a goner.' I wondered if it was all over, whether the problem of 'the blood' had indeed been solved, but since he was not called upon to return and was in due course given some pills to do with 'the blood' I presumed he was right and whatever was wrong with him hadn't been serious. But it seemed so ridiculous not to know what had happened, though he didn't think so. Ignorance was definitely bliss in health matters as far as he was concerned.

He took his arthritis tablets seriously, never failing to follow the instructions on the bottles. His prescription he regarded as a highly important piece of paper which he handled with something approaching awe. He called it his 'prep' and the handing in of this 'prep' and collecting of the pills it entitled him to was a solemn business. The chemist in Denton Holme got to know him very well. My father would not queue, so if there was even one person waiting when he arrived in the chemist's shop he'd turn round and leave. The chemist would offer him a chair to sit on and say he would only need to wait five minutes at the most, but, no, my father couldn't possibly wait. It was a waste of time. He had all the time in the world, but no, sitting on a chair for a few minutes in a chemist's shop was too much. Sometimes, during the five summer months when we were living at Loweswater and visiting him at least twice a week, he'd give me his 'prep' with instructions to be very, very careful with it and, once I'd handed it over to the chemist, equally careful with the pills he would give me in return. I was also honoured occasionally with the task of collecting the prescription itself from the doctor's surgery. 'You can get my prep,' he'd say, with the air of conferring a great favour – 'Put it straight in your purse, mind, not your pocket, take no chances.' It was a mistake then to make some mocking rejoinder about getting a Securicor guard to accompany me – prescriptions were like gold dust and should be treated as such. They were what kept him independent, or rather gave him access to the means which kept him independent.

There was no doubt at all that as he entered his nineties what made his life precious to him was his independence. He did not want to feel in need of anyone's support or help, not even his children's. He liked to rule his own life, to decide each day exactly what he would do and when and how. It was what gave point to his existence. Activity of one sort or another was the key to the pleasure he still took in life, though pleasure is the wrong word. He never acknowledged doing anything for *pleasure*. Far too frivolous. On the contrary, he was motivated by obligation, by things having to be done with no choice about it. He had to get up every day, didn't he? Well, then. And, once up, he had to wash and shave and dress and eat, didn't he? So. Yet in the carrying out of all these rituals there was pleasure of a kind, even if he denied it. The first thing he did when he got up was to go into his kitchen, open the airing-cupboard door, and switch on the immersion heater for the hot-water tank. He loved this heater, which he called 'the merser', and he got definite pleasure from switching it on – click – and he was gratified, his day had begun. He'd wait a moment or two, feeling underneath the lagging round the tank, over which his socks and underclothes were draped to air, until the first faint warmth began and then he'd go back to bed until he reckoned the water would be properly hot enough to shave. A miracle of science to a man who'd spent half his life boiling water in a kettle if he wanted it hot.

He shaved every day, another pleasure, or rather the smooth, clean face afterwards was the pleasure. Beards and moustaches were an abomination, a sign of laziness, slackness, or of being foreign. But then came the real thrill of the day: the Cooked Breakfast. It used to be bacon, egg, sausage and fried bread, but now it was just bacon and toast. Good, thick, fatty bacon, though, from the butcher's in Denton Holme, cut under his own eyes from a big joint and not any of that hopeless packaged stuff with all its flavour lost inside its plastic shroud. Three slices, fried until the fat oozed, then slammed between two slices of heavily buttered white toast – oh, and a generous dollop of HP sauce. He always used the same frying pan and if some of the bacon fat remained after the bacon was lifted out then so much the better. He left it there to congeal and start the next day's bacon off nicely. He took his huge bacon sandwich through to his living-room and sat down to eat it at his table, spread with a tablecloth, keeping up the standards his wife had set. He had his *Daily Express* propped in front of him, leaning against the teapot sporting its woollen cosy. One cup of tea only, strongly brewed, with two sugars stirred into it. Grand. It set him up for the day, was the most important part of that day. He never, ever, started any day without his cooked breakfast. On the day the hospital phoned to say his wife had died at seven-thirty that morning he went straight to the kitchen, cooked his bacon and ate it at 8 a.m. as usual, grief-stricken though he was. He had to have his breakfast, didn't he? Yes, he did. There was absolutely no question about it.

Nor was there ever any question about the shape of the rest of the day. Dishes had to be washed, almost before he'd finished eating from them, and dried and put away; clothes had to be soaked and scrubbed and then carried through into the garage (in which no car of his own had ever stood), where they had to be put through the mangle, then taken into the garden and pegged onto the clothes line, which then had to be hauled aloft with a long prop; shopping had to be done in Denton Holme, so it was on with his hat and coat and a firm grasp of his walking stick (only for use on such excursions) and off he had to go, at eleven o'clock, in order to get all his messages done and his bets put on and still be home in time for his dinner (bit of cold meat, bit of potato, another cup of tea) at twelve-thirty. Then a rest. A rest was not really in his plan for the day, it was not acknowledged as positively having to be allowed for, but it happened. A rest, a snooze, but only for half an hour, because he had to get into the garden to weed or dig, or cut the grass. In the summer the grass had to be cut every day so that it would not get too much for his old-fashioned mower and his waning strength. Then it was back into the house for his tea (a sandwich) so that he was ready to watch the Six o'Clock News on television and whatever programmes he fancied after that (sport, quizzes, gardening) until nine-thirty, when he had to have his supper (crackers and cheese) and go to bed, where he slept soundly and deeply.

He depended on nobody. What had to be done was done by and for himself. Life, his life, was about functioning on his own. Human contact and involvement were minimal. There was no need for them. He had his good neighbours to say hello to if he wished, he had shopkeepers to exchange the time of day with, he had his regular daily telephone calls from his children to keep him in touch. No friends came to see him. He had never valued friends and wasn't going to start now. His wife had been the one with friends. Every day, when she was alive, there had been someone dropping in, but she'd died nearly ten years ago and since then his diaries had recorded 'no visitors'. But this was not a complaint, nor was it noted sadly, not yet. If he wanted visitors he knew he could have them, but was still at the stage of not wanting them. They kept him back. They had to be talked to and listened to, and finally encouraged to leave if they were the stubborn type. Occasionally, an old friend of his wife's did think she should call in on poor Arthur, all on his own, and would ring up and suggest a visit, only to be told: 'I'm busy.' Should anyone turn up uninvited he was perfectly capable of keeping them standing on the doorstep until they became discouraged and left and never, of course, came again. The only exceptions to this were children. Anyone with a child was welcome. Then, he became quite sociable and ushered the child in (ignoring the adult). He liked children, especially the under-fives, and they liked him.

What he liked best was playing with them. In his opinion, children didn't need toys. Games could be made out of ordinary household objects and he proceeded to prove this with every visiting small child. Out would come his round, wickerwork peg basket and a pan and he'd start picking pegs out and throwing them into the pan and then, when six or seven had clattered in he'd put a lid on the pan and shake it violently before pouring them out and starting again. Children under three loved this and would immediately start to copy him and he'd cheer extravagantly as each wooden peg landed noisily in the pan. For older ones he had other entertainments. He'd bring out a leather pouch in which he kept old pennies and they were invited to scrutinise each penny, then put it on a pile according to its date, and soon they had a row of little towers balancing on the table. There was only one 1900 penny among them and the game was to find it. Then there was his bundle of knotted string which had to be unravelled to see who could get the longest length, and his box of postcards to be sorted into towns and countries, and his photograph albums in which babies now adults had to be identified, and his address book which popped open when each letter of the alphabet was pressed – oh, he was endlessly resourceful.

If these distractions flagged, he'd take the child by the hand into his garage to explore. He'd let them soak a towel in a bucket of water and then stand the child on a stool in front of his aged mangle and help them feed it into the rollers and turn the handle until the water streamed out. Children loved that. The compressing of the towel and the extracting of the water seemed a miracle to them unmatched by any modern washing machine, and they liked showing off their strength in the turning of the stiff handle, not realising my father was doing most of the turning. The pleasure he derived from their pleasure was visible and extraordinary and it created a bond between him and the children which other adults marvelled at. But his power over them vanished when the children reached puberty, especially the girls. Then he became awkward with them and critical, and he was inclined to label them 'spoiled' and separate himself from them.

This was how his life went on, his routine marking the days out and disturbed only when his family were staying nearby at Loweswater, forty miles away. Hunter and I were there for our five months each summer; Gordon and Shirley for a week in December for his birthday and a week in May; Pauline and David for three weeks at Christmas, two weeks at Easter, a week in October and very often a week in February. The grand-children came and went for other odd weeks, so that for three-quarters of the year he had family visiting regularly. But even then routines had to be observed. No one could call on him before noon – 'I'll be out. Don't bother' – and he didn't like outings or visits on Saturdays – 'It isn't convenient' (i.e. sport on television). He wanted everything organised round his routines and we humoured him, even when his routine didn't fit in with what we wanted. We drove obediently to his favourite places, with him directing. He couldn't read a map but he knew exactly the route he wished to take and it was 'turn right' and 'turn left, then left at the crossroads', until often we had covered a hundred miles and were exhausted but he was in his element. If he misdirected us it was quite likely to be because he intended to – he liked claiming to be lost, because this would extend the drive.

We always stopped for lunch in pubs of his choice, most of them pretty to look at and horrible to eat in. When my mother was alive there was none of this. Then, I would make the lunch in their own kitchen and the drives were in the afternoons and the meal we ate out was tea. She loathed pubs as much as my father loved them, but once she was gone his way was open to patronise all the pubs in Cumbria – and how we worked our way through them. The gloomier the interior, the colder the atmosphere, the more overpowering the smell of staleness, the greasier the lunch, the more my father enjoyed himself. He'd establish himself on an uncomfortable wooden chair and make me read the menu out loud, not because he couldn't read it but because he couldn't seem to take menus in: however simple – and pub menus were very basic indeed – they somehow baffled him. What he wanted to eat was his favourite dish: fried plaice with chips. If this was not on the menu there was consternation – 'Poor do, no plaice.' I'd suggest haddock, or cod, but, no, if he was going to eat fish it had to be plaice and not cod, battered or otherwise. Haddock was quite beyond the pale. It had bones. Bones might stick in his throat. He was not going to take the chance at his age. He might choke to death. The Queen Mother, his exact contemporary, had once taken a chance on haddock and look what nearly happened to her. I said I'd no idea what nearly happened to her. He expressed exaggerated surprise and said he thought I was educated and kept up with what was important in newspapers. Dear me, fancy not knowing a fish bone had got stuck in the Queen Mother's throat and she'd nearly been a goner.

We'd settle down to the awful meal with my father agreeing to have Cumberland sausage with his chips. While he concentrated on tucking in, I'd sit and wonder how buildings so attractive outside could be so ruined inside. In most of those where we ate, the old fittings had been chucked out and new ones put in. Stone floors had been covered with patterned carpets, stone walls plastered then wallpapered, old lamps replaced with strip lighting. Curiously, old prints and photographs survived and, though often garishly reframed, were the most interesting things to look at, a relief to the eye. Meanwhile, my father was finishing his pint and commenting on its quality. Some beers he detested. Jennings was one, which was unfortunate because Jennings is a Cumbrian brewery and ubiquitous in the county's pubs. Luckily there was no one to hear his opinion of the beer, because when we ate there, on weekday lunchtimes, there was no one else in these out-of-the-way pubs. The barmaid was always slightly aggrieved at having to go and stick whatever we'd chosen into a microwave, and my father would say, 'She's got a face on her, that 'un. She'll turn the beer if she isn't careful.'

Sometimes we were blessed, sometimes we hit on a pub where real cooking was on offer. This was usually in the Eden Valley where the catchment area included monied folk. My father loved this valley but he had no regard for the superior cooking. If the pub had also made an attempt at any kind of artistic decor, and especially if it had a garden with tables and umbrellas, it was damned for ever. It wasn't a real pub. It had lost itself. It was trying to be something it was not. He was against change. Life was about keeping everything the same. So, on the whole, we stuck to the dreary pubs and grew fatter and fatter, and felt more and more unhealthy as the summer went on. It was no good my ordering just bread and cheese – this annoyed him. I had to have something cooked or he was offended. Even refusing chips was an act of rebellion. If I asked for fish on its own and then picked the batter or orange breadcrumbs off it, he was displeased — 'Waste not, want not,' he'd say and shake his head.

The solution to this state of affairs was to have a picnic. Funnily enough, my father liked picnics, though we had rarely had them as a family when I was growing up, and even when we did they amounted to not much more than a few sandwiches and a packet of biscuits all wrapped in greaseproof paper and fitting easily into coat pockets. My picnics were something else and they amused him. For a start, I had a proper wicker hamper, large and oblong, the sort with cute little leather straps fastening the plates onto the inside of the lid, and compartments for bottles and cups, all lined with gingham material — incredibly pretentious, and I loved it. My picnics, even apart from the hamper, were sumptuous, with all kinds of cold meats, and often a whole roast chicken, and little tasty pies (kept hot in a special separate bag) and crisp salads (dressings in screwtop jars) and small sausages and french bread (in the hot bag too) and cheeses and masses of fruit (melon, cherries, strawberries) and beer and wine and coffee and tea . . . Oh, it was a sight to behold when the hamper was opened. I always spread a proper cotton tablecloth before I set out the plates (yes, china not plastic) and had real cutlery and napkins and glasses. There was a tartan rug, and some cushions for us to loll on, and a collapsible chair for my father. It was a great performance and he relished it.

Choosing where to have the picnic was a lengthy business in which my father and I conspired against Hunter, who was very easily satisfied and couldn't understand why we kept rejecting what to him were perfectly good sites. 'No, no,' we'd cry, 'not there. It's too bumpy . . . too much gorse . . . not sheltered enough . . . can't see the sea . . .' Because these picnics were always beside the sea, always. On hot, still days in June and July, out on the Solway Marsh, at the end of the marsh road past Bowness-on-Solway where there was absolute peace and quiet, not a sound to be heard except for the seagulls and nothing to interrupt the view all the way across the Firth to the Scottish hills.

'Champion,' my father would say, having eaten and drunk heartily. Then he'd whistle before falling asleep, briefly, only to waken and say, 'Champion', again. Contentment mellowed him and he'd call me a good lass. Now, if ever, he was surely near to philosophising about life in his ninety-first year; now surely if asked he could say what life meant to him, why it was still so precious, why he wasn't tired of it. But he said nothing and I asked nothing. He kept his thoughts to himself, either because he couldn't articulate them or because he thought that was where they belonged.

He was always reluctant to leave a picnic. As I began to pack up, he'd look astonished and say, 'Are we off? Already? Oh well, have it your own way.' 'Already' was after at least two hours. He'd grumble, just a bit, about having to get into the car and he'd say, 'That's that, then. Don't know when I'll have another picnic.' I'd say, 'Soon. The next brilliant day,' and he'd reply, 'There might never be another' (pause) 'or I might not still be here.'

Once we departed for London at the end of the summer there was, of course, no question of more picnics. He missed them, but missed even more getting out into the country which he loved and knew so intimately. My mother's death had released him from being more or less housebound, except for his short shopping forays, and for a while he'd tried to be adventurous and get himself out and about by bus. What he wanted to do, what would have satisfied him, was to go on a weekly Mystery Tour, but to his disgust the bus companies seemed to have phased Mystery Tours out — 'Nobody bothers any more about them without cars,' my father said. There was to be no more of the thrill of taking a Mystery Tour not knowing if he would end up in the Lake District or on the

Solway coast. All mystery had gone. Now, he would have to choose his destination which wasn't at all the same.

But after a lot of complaining, that's what he was obliged to do. His first choice would always be Silloth, by train, but Dr Beeching had axed the branch line to it long ago, robbing carless people like my father of easy access to their favourite holiday resort. My father had gone on that Silloth train all his life and the short journey, half an hour or so, had never failed to excite him. The train was always grossly overcrowded no matter how many extra coaches were put on the various engines – on summer weekends the platform for the Silloth trains would be literally packed solid with working-class people and their children. The fights to get on were alarming. My father had often travelled in the luggage van, thankful to get on at all, and he never minded the crush. He knew all the stops by heart, and exactly when to crane out of the window, as the train rounded the last bend, in order to see the church spire in the middle of Silloth. The engine would give a double toot at this point and everyone would swear they could smell the sea. As a young man he prided himself on being first off the train, jumping off before it had stopped, and racing ahead of the hordes to bag his favourite fishing spot on the sea wall. Later, encumbered by his children and a wife who thought it unseemly to rush in any circumstances, he'd been forced to shuffle along with the masses and he'd found it very frustrating.

The Silloth train no longer being an option, he had to condescend to go by bus or not go at all. He only did it once. He presented himself at 9.30 a.m. one September day, a Monday (so he hoped the bus would be empty and it almost was), at the bus station and was first on the bus. That pleased him. He hesitated only momentarily before choosing a seat on the right-hand side (the sea would be on the right when the bus got to the coast) halfway down, avoiding the seat over the wheels. He had a window beside him and was able to control the opening and shutting of it himself as well as be privy to a grand view when one appeared. He had his raincoat with him and his stick, but he didn't carry any food or drink. The bus was bound for Maryport via Silloth and Allonby and it would stop there an hour before returning to Carlisle, which would give him plenty of time to refresh himself at a pub.

The bus started dead on time – more gratification – and he enjoyed every single minute of the ride, even going through the city and passing the end of the road where he had once lived, in the days when he'd cycled everywhere. The bus was relatively new, the seats well upholstered, and the noise of the engine not too loud. There were only eight other passengers, all women, all sitting at the back, so their cackling hardly disturbed him. There was an irritatingly long stop in Wigton, but the rest of the journey was speedy, and when they hit the sea road the tide was in and the sun fairly making the water sparkle. He saw several fishing boats and a big tanker turning to go into the dock and wished he'd had his binoculars with him. Allonby was deserted except for horses galloping on the sands (where I had learned to walk). He had a pie and a pint at Maryport and a walk around – 'There's not much at Maryport, mind, not these days' – and then got back onto the bus. Someone was in his seat. A woman. He stood and glared at her and tapped his stick on the ground and 'acted dumb', as he put it later. She asked if she had taken his seat. He said she had that. She moved.

When he got home, he rang me to describe his day and say how smashing it had been and how he intended to take bus trips regularly, as a treat, and that he fancied Keswick the following week. But he never ventured forth on an outing again. I kept asking him why not and he said, 'Reasons'. These reasons remained undivulged but I suspect may have had something to do with his beginning to need to go to the lavatory very frequently, and his terror of an accident on the bus. He stayed near home after this, getting his fresh air in the garden, looking forward to being taken on outings when we came again, but not noticeably pining for them. They were not part of his routine, of his life, when he was on his own, and he coped. He was still remarkably fit for his age and proud of his independence even if his freedom of movement had become curtailed.

It couldn't go on for ever, of course. He might not have been waiting for a crisis, but we were, and in May 1992 it came.

On 25 April, my father spent a long afternoon in the garden, digging and weeding, pausing every half-hour to take a rest on a bench I'd persuaded him to let me put up against the garage wall. Next day, a Sunday, he walked his usual mile to and from the cemetery to visit my mother's grave, as he had done every Sunday since she had died eleven years before. My mother wasn't actually buried there, she'd been cremated, but we'd put her ashes under a sod lifted from her parents' grave and so he regarded her as being there. 'I don't know why I go,' he'd say, shaking his head. 'It's daft.' When he'd seen the fine grey-white ash after the cremation he'd been shocked and turned white and said, 'To think she's come to that.' But ever since, with the ash under the grass in front of the marble cross recording her parents' names and dates, he'd liked the idea of *something* being there and of being able to pay his regular respects. Besides, Sunday morning visits to the cemetery became another routine, another way of giving his week a structure. By then the walk was quite an effort, involving the return up a steep incline, but it was just this effort he enjoyed.

So he was fit enough that weekend but on 30 April he fell again. He was watering some plants he'd just put in, going backwards and forwards to the tap with an empty soup tin because he could no longer manage to use his watering can and keep his balance. He didn't really agree with watering – 'Folk water far too damn much' – but where new plants were concerned he conceded a little water was necessary. He tripped on the path as he was carrying the last lot of water. It was amazing he hadn't done so before. This path was made of concrete slabs which he'd laid himself, unevenly, many years before and which were now lethal for anyone the least bit doddery. Again and again we'd offered to re-lay this path, but it was the usual story – 'No!' and 'It'll see me out, don't you worry.'

This time, he didn't hurt his eye. In falling, he put out his hand to save himself and fell on his right wrist. The pain was intense but he struggled to get himself up from the path before anyone saw him and managed to hobble into the house. Luckily – or, in his opinion, unluckily – he had in fact been seen by his neighbour Mr Nixon, who came to check he was not hurt. 'I'm all right,' my father said. 'I'll manage.' He bathed his wrist in water as hot as he could bear and then he took two aspirin and rested. But the pain didn't wear off and he was awake all night. In the morning, he could do nothing with his right hand and it was very awkward frying his bacon using his left hand to hold the pan. Just as he'd finished eating his breakfast (though he'd felt sick and hadn't enjoyed it), Mrs Nixon came knocking on the door and he had to answer it. She saw how awful he looked and asked permission to call the doctor. 'Go on, then,' he said, grumpily, 'have it your own way.' The doctor came and, suspecting a fracture (correctly), said he would have to go to the infirmary. The obliging Nixons said they would take him, but, though grateful, this put my father in a foul mood. He made it plain that he was not going to 'stop in' even if 'they' said he had to. He was coming home, whatever.

He had always both hated and feared the infirmary and his, on the whole, tolerable experience in 1989, over 'the blood', had done nothing to endear it to him. This hostility dated from long ago, sometime in the forties, when he'd had some sort of accident at work and damaged his right leg. It was not broken but he could hardly walk and the pain was dreadful. Instead of going straight to the infirmary, or at least to the doctor (this was pre-NHS and would have had to be paid for), he insisted on being taken home. I remember him coming in just before I left for school, his face ashen, the lines of it set in a grimace as he tried to control the pain. My mother was full of commonsense as well as concern, telling him he would have to seek some medical advice, but he was adamant: he was not going near any doctor and especially not at the infirmary. A night went by as well as a day as he struggled to subdue the pain and recover, helped by doses of whisky and aspirin, but by the next morning the sweat stood out on his forehead and he couldn't talk, he was in so much pain. It was frightening to see the exercising of such will power and even more frightening to see it fail. My mother meanwhile took matters into her own hands and organised the one neighbour in all the area who had a car to come and take my father to the infirmary.

He was gone a very long time. I went to school, came back from school, and he still wasn't home. My mother was convinced he'd been admitted and was in the process of putting her coat on to go to the infirmary when my father walked into the house looking exhausted but triumphant. It seemed he'd been put in a cubicle when he arrived at the infirmary, and told to remove his trousers and lie on the bed. He'd obeyed, reluctantly, and eventually a doctor came along, examined him, and said the leg would have to be set in plaster, without explaining why. Someone else would be along soon to take him to the plaster room. But no one came along soon. Hours went by and the longer my father waited the more unhappy he felt about having his leg put in plaster. He wouldn't be able to work, and if he couldn't work he wasn't at all sure he would be fully paid and if he wasn't fully paid the rent and coal bill might not get paid . . . it was dreadful to imagine. So in this kind of mental turmoil, and still in acute pain, he made his mind up. He got off the bed, put his trousers on and limped agonisingly slowly out of the infirmary, almost fainting with the effort. But he wasn't going home, or to any other doctor. He was going to Geordie Long's.

Geordie Long was by occupation a barber, but was far more famous in Carlisle for being a bone-setter. He had a shop in Caldewgate, where he cut hair and shaved customers. Behind it, for those who wanted this additional service, he had another room, where he set bones. This had come about through cust- omers complaining about their necks aching, so while Geordie was cutting their hair he had begun to massage necks in an attempt to ease the pain; and he had discovered he had a talent for it. He had no professional qualifications whatever but grew so interested in the problem, not just of sore necks but of sore wrists, sore legs, sore backs, that he began reading up on anatomy in the library. Soon he was not only massaging muscles but manipulating bones – with a pull there and a jerk here he found he could sort out all kinds of aches and pains. He was still primarily a barber, but the queues were outside the back room where he did his bone-setting (he was always called that, a bone-setter, not a physiotherapist or an osteopath). He charged people half-a-crown, if they could manage that, but if they couldn't they were told to leave what they could afford on the mantelpiece. Everyone had complete faith in Geordie and never queried his lack of qualifications or worried about the safety of his methods. Unlike the doctors at the infirmary, he was a cheerful man, working-class himself and incapable of patron- ising anyone. He never claimed to cure people, saying only that he'd try to ease their pain, and always warned that whatever was wrong with them might not, in fact, be curable through his touch.

This was the man my father took himself off to. Somehow, he limped the half mile down to Caldewgate from the infirmary but collapsed as soon as he got to the barber's shop. The bone- setting waiting-room was crowded, as usual, but nobody minded when Geordie (who had always cut my father's hair) came out from his consulting-room – grand name for a bare room with only a high couch in it – and, seeing the state my father was in, took him straight in. What Geordie then actually did I don't know, and certainly my father never did either, but it worked. He apparently put his hands on my father's leg, felt it carefully over and over again, every inch of it, then he did what was merely described afterwards as 'this' and 'that' (which, seemingly, was excruciating and my father was ashamed to have to admit he'd let out a yell) and, hey presto, the leg functioned again. He invited my father to walk and he did, gingerly. The pain had not quite gone but it was a different and perfectly bearable pain and Geordie said it would soon go. He paid Geordie and left, arriving home to rage against the damned stupid doctor at that infirmary who would have had his leg put in plaster for weeks.

Ever after, the infirmary was a place where they tried to trick you and was to be avoided at all costs. The first question he always asked if anyone was ill was, 'Will it mean the infirmary?' To be ill enough to have to go into the infirmary was the worst possible news, but then all illness was bad news. Everyone feels this, of course, but my father felt it in an exaggerated way. He had no patience with illness. He resented and resisted it, seeing it as an enemy that had to be fought and conquered, if possible unaided. Anyone who liked to talk about their illness irritated him. He had no interest in symptoms and even less in treatments. He looked for the same kind of determination to deny illness in his children as he had himself. We all tried hard to measure up, but my brother, who was often ill as a child, had a hard time of it and so, later, did my younger sister. I pleased him most by failing to succumb, as they did, to scarlet fever and all manner of other childhood diseases. But when I was ten, my luck temporarily ran out and I had jaundice rather badly. He had no idea how to cope. I lay in bed for weeks, hardly able to lift my head from the pillow and constantly sick, and he said it was 'not like Margaret' in a disappointed voice. My mother was irritated, said I was just a child like any other child and I couldn't help being ill, for heaven's sake. She said he should show some sympathy. But he didn't know how to. In his lunch hour, when he'd cycled home from the Metal Box factory and had eaten his meal, he'd come upstairs to sit with me. I'd pretend to be asleep, embarrassed for him. I'd hear him coming up the stairs and I'd turn to the wall and close my eyes tight and breathe heavily. I knew he was sitting there, at my bedside, in his boiler suit but with newly scrubbed hands. He'd clear his throat. I'd stay still. Sometimes he pulled the blanket round me and tucked it in. Then, after a few minutes, he'd go. I'd hear him say to my mother, 'She seems to be sleeping nice. I didn't disturb her.' I imagine he sensed I wasn't sleeping at all, but he allowed me to pretend because it suited him. He cared, but he didn't know how to talk to a sick child. He hated to see me, usually a fizz of energy, listless and he didn't want to acknowledge I might be suffering. Illness, all illness, scared him and he didn't believe that involving himself in it, learning to understand it, would help banish his fear or at least put it into perspective. Disease could lead to death and there was no need to think about that.

All this, then, was the background to his usual avoidance of going to the infirmary or ever admitting he felt ill. But go he had to, on this occasion, with much sighing and muttering to the kindly Nixons about how his father had died there, his mother had died there, his wife had died there, and if anyone thought he was going to stop in there they had another think coming. He did not, however, need to stop in. The orthopaedic surgeon, who saw him in the fracture clinic, said he had a fracture of his distal third of ulna ('Double Dutch,' my father commented) and put it in plaster, but not a full-arm plaster. A below-the-elbow plaster was not ideal for his injury but in view of his age it was considered advisable. All my father cared about was getting out 'in one piece', as he put it.

Once home, he set himself to manage with one hand, thinking up all kinds of ingenious methods of continuing to do all the things he usually did. He wanted no social workers 'prying'. To all concerned, he gave the standard answer – 'I'm managing grand.' Maybe he wouldn't have managed if my sister hadn't come to help at first – to be greeted with: 'What are you doing here? I didn't send for you.' No, but she'd deduced the situation from a telephone call and decided to come. 'Well,' he said, 'you can make yourself useful and finish planting my gladioli.' She planted the flowers and then some vegetables and then she went home and we came up, conveniently, for our usual summer stay at Loweswater. Panic over.

By the time the day came for him to have the plaster taken off he'd become positively fond of the outpatients' department. He'd been there three times, to have his plaster checked, and was supremely confident by 12 June, loving the fact that he knew exactly where to go and what to do and what would happen. I was directed by him as though I couldn't read a notice or follow the evidence of my own eyes and, for a man renowned for being incapable of queuing, he settled down almost patiently when we reached the area where we had to wait to be called. I saw his eyes darting about, taking everything in, and though he initiated no conversation with the people either side of us (that would have been lowering his standards too far) he nodded when spoken to and managed to acknowledge various pleasantries.

I went in with him to watch him have his plaster taken off. I didn't want to, but he clearly thought he was offering me a treat so I had to accept. The doctor was a young woman. My father concentrated on her left hand. Confronted with any woman, he always subjected the third finger of her left hand to minute inspection: ring, or not? The doctor was not wearing a ring. I knew this would be commented on later and that it would be pointless telling him that the lack of an engagement or wedding ring did not necessarily signify what he thought it did.

'How are you, then, Mr Forster?' the doctor asked (pronouncing his name as 'Foster').

'There's an "r" in it,' my father said.

'I beg your pardon?'

'There's an "r" in Forster,' my father said, pronouncing it as 'Foster', as he always did, just as the doctor had done, without sounding the 'r'. My mother was forever telling him that if he wanted the wretched 'r' pronounced then he had to pronounce it himself. He never did, though he expected others to do so.

The doctor kindly didn't point this out. She smiled and apologised and got on with her job.

'We'll soon have this off,' she said; 'then you'll be as right as rain.'

'You hope,' said my father.

His wrist, his whole forearm, emerging from the plaster looked so frail, so desperately fragile, but he flexed his long, knobbly fingers strongly enough and the doctor was admiring. She said he would have to be careful, not to do too much with his right hand for a while, not to lift anything heavy or grip anything too tightly. The wrist would feel weak and there was bound to be some stiffness and loss of mobility at first, and some slight pain, but the fracture had mended remarkably well, which it often did not do in elderly people. To this my father said, 'I'm ninety-two' (though he was not, not until December). The doctor exclaimed that she couldn't believe he was a day past eighty and he smirked. He loved confounding people with his great age.

'Come back if there are any problems,' the doctor said.

'Oh, I won't be coming back here,' my father said. 'No fear of that.'

I couldn't imagine how he could say that, but he was

absolutely convinced he would never need to visit the infirmary again. His accident, the injury to his wrist, was merely an aberration, never to be repeated. He didn't even think about the possibility of this being the beginning of a whole sequence of calamities – no, it was the end. He'd made a silly mistake in allowing his wrist to be fractured and he would not make it again. On 15 June, three days after the plaster was removed, he was back in the garden, tidying it up. He walked carefully round the spot where he had tripped up (it was now precisely marked and cursed for ever), trailing his rake behind him. I sat on the bench and watched. He raked a flower bed, using his right hand without any care not to grip the rake too tightly, and whistled. He was home, back in his garden, back in his routine. He had survived. He might put nothing into words but his buoyancy after this wrist episode was visible: life was good again. It might be a battle, but then life had always been seen by him as a battle above all else, and the point was he was still winning. He had no intention of, or desire to, lay down his arms and surrender to old age and fractures and, ultimately, death.

But the next year, his ninety-third, saw a definite change in attitude. With it came the first hint of boredom with his life, imperceptible initially and then registered reluctantly. It was the garden that started it. On 11 March, he cut the grass front and back for the first time in the season and found it 'heavy going', as he dolefully recorded in his diary. It depressed him to have to acknowledge this. Then when he went to town the next day, he wrote afterwards, 'Glad to get home. A. so-so.' He struggled on, but preparing the ground for his usual vegetables and bedding plants became harder and harder. It distressed him to look about his garden and see the state it was in with the growing season not yet really begun. Weeds everywhere, soil not turned over, shrubs straggly . . . suddenly he was overwhelmed by the size of it. He couldn't keep up. Nature was getting ahead of him, everything was getting out of hand and he didn't know what to do. Mr Nixon was very kind and had taken over the trimming of the hedges, but he couldn't, and didn't want to, depend on Mr Nixon any more than he already did. He didn't want to depend on anyone – what kind of life would that be? A little of this worry seeped through into our phone conversations but whenever I said I'd hire a gardener to help him, dared to suggest it, he'd bellow, 'No! I'm not starting that game. I'll manage.'

Pride was saved by my nephew Simon, my brother-in-law Johnny's son, aged twenty-three and temporarily living back home in Rockcliffe, near Carlisle. He would go twice a week and do the heavy work, and I would pay him, but my father need never know that. He was fond of telling us how, when he was a lad, young folk had helped old folk (and he tolerated no cynicism about the reality of this) and he would see nothing suspect about a young man coming voluntarily to help him garden, especially one he'd known since he was born. 'At a loose end, is he?' he said when I tentatively mentioned Simon's willingness to garden for him. 'Send him along, then, and I'll find something for him to do.' If he was playing a game, my father played it convincingly. Simon, anyway, fully understood the delicacy of the situation and responded accordingly. He had actually never gardened in his life and hadn't the first idea what to do, but he was strong, willing and, most important of all, quite happy to accept my father's orders without question. He did what he was told how he was told. And he was not a chatterer. If asked a direct question, he replied, but he asked none himself, which was entirely to my father's liking. The two of them would have a break, sitting on the bench in the garden, and say virtually nothing to each other for the twenty minutes it lasted. These sessions gave new meaning to the phrase 'companionable silence'. Sometimes my father would fish a pound out of his pocket and send Simon to the nearest shop to buy a coke for himself and some beer for him. While Simon was with him in the garden he felt secure enough to garden and firmly believed he was doing most of the work himself. After the grass was cut for the last time on 25 October, Simon wasn't needed any more. Gardening was effectively over. He'd made it, another summer was over.

This was when 'Nothing Doing' began to be the standard entry in his diary. The winter approached and again and again he recorded 'Nothing Doing. Dark Soon. Long Day.' Not even the weather seemed worth describing in all the previously enthusiastic detail. A lot of sorting went on – 'Sorted Garage' . . . 'Sorted Drawers' – but not much else. He'd had to stop taking his daily walk to Denton Holme, unless a neighbour gave him a lift there and back, because he couldn't manage the whole distance and getting on and off the bus had become too perilous. He shuffled along instead to the Spar grocery at the end of his road and made of this a new routine. He couldn't make it to the cemetery any more so there were no more Sunday visits to my mother's grave. Going to town was out of the question, even given a lift. Mrs Nixon kindly got him anything he wanted from there. All his beloved routines, in fact, had either been wrecked or severely trimmed. He was restless and frustrated and, worst of all, bored. Even watching television had palled – 'Rubbish On', he wrote, and 'Bad TV'. And 'the blood' was back as a worry. On 28 April he referred to it mysteriously in his diary as 'A. had A Loss. But OK'. This 'loss' was of blood and it scared him. He was very much afraid that blood in his urine was a sinister sign and that it signified something rather more serious than a fractured wrist. But he didn't consult his doctor. He waited to see if this 'loss' would be repeated. It wasn't, to his relief, reinforcing his belief that if abnormalities were ignored they would go away.

But what didn't go away was this new boredom. Suddenly, he actively wanted visitors, to break up the monotony. Visitors, of course, had always been mere irritations. While my mother was alive, he had had to put up with them for her sake. Visitors were liked by women and he accepted that. But once she'd died, and he had discouraged them, he'd cut the few social contacts he had had other than his family. Now he wanted them restored. He was even aggrieved that these ties had been severed, forgetting he'd done the severing himself.

'I don't know what's happened to Mrs G——' he said. 'She hasn't come near for years.'

'And how often have you been to see her?' I asked smartly.

'Eh?'

'How often have you visited her?' I repeated.

'Don't be daft,' he said, angrily.

'It isn't daft. She's a widow, she likes visitors too, a bit of company, but you never think of visiting her, you just expect her to visit you.'

'I never said that. I just said she hadn't been near for ages.'

'Well, I'm telling you why. Visiting is a two-way affair. You can't expect visitors if you don't visit. It's no good wanting them if you give no sign you want them.'

'I don't want them. I never said I did.'

But he did want them. Complaining that he had no visitors was the only way he could bring himself to admit it. It was a weakness he'd never experienced before and he found that recognising it was uncomfortable. He decided it was his right, as a very old man, to be visited and in his head he began compiling a black list of those who, in his opinion, were failing in their duty. It infuriated him to learn that one nephew had had the audacity to drive through Carlisle on his way to Scotland and had *not* visited him. 'Scandalous,' he said. But when one cousin, also just on her way through Carlisle, this time on a long and tiring drive south, did make the effort to call, he was furious because her visit was so short. 'Twelve minutes!' he roared that night on the telephone. 'Twelve minutes, that's all she warmed the seat for! Haven't seen her for ten years and she turns up without a by-your-leave and stops twelve bloomin' minutes. Wasn't worth opening the door.' I asked if he'd offered his visitor a cup of tea. 'Tea?' he echoed. 'I'm ninety-three.'

Where once the ringing of the doorbell had enraged him, he now longed for it to ring. A phone call a day from one of us wasn't enough human contact. He wanted someone to keep him company on the long, dark, wet winter days, though on his terms. His two most faithful visitors were my brother-in-law, Johnny, and Marion's husband, Jeff. Both popped in as often as they could. Neither ever received any noticeable signs of welcome. 'Oh, it's you at last,' he'd say. 'I wondered where you'd got to.' Mrs Nixon began coming in for half an hour or so in the afternoon on weekdays, bringing with her a piece of delicious home-made cake, or a scone, for his tea, but very quickly she'd created out of her kindness a trap for herself. In no time at all he began to regard her visits as obligatory and she got the same kind of response as Johnny and Jeff if she failed to come – 'Where have you been, then? I waited for you all afternoon; didn't know what had happened.' When I tried to suggest maybe he was expecting too much of Mrs Nixon, who might after all have her own life to lead, he maintained, 'She likes to watch the racing on my TV. I don't mind – keeps her happy.' Poor Mrs Nixon was forced into feelings of guilt if she did not visit him every day and any remonstrations on my part were greeted scornfully with 'She's got nothing better to do' by my father.

Going into 1994, there was no more cheerful talk of just popping off. Instead, a siege mentality was setting in. He announced now that he was 'hanging on' and, as ever, 'managing', but the old defiance had gone. He wasn't as sure of himself, though there was still no suggestion that he wished he were dead – absolutely not. Nor was there any mention of possibly having to give up his own home. If he thought about this, he never confessed it. The game was one of stoicism, as it perhaps always had tended to be, though never played in such difficult circumstances. Whereas my mother had endlessly wished aloud to die, my father never did, not even now, at the mighty age of ninety-three. Such talk he rated as daft. It was pointless wishing to be dead. Your time would come when it came and that was that. It irritated him when my mother, or anyone else, wished for their own end. It was morbid and ridiculous. Death would come soon enough, they could count on that, so they should shut up.

By May 1994, he was frequently jotting down, 'A. off colour'. He could do even less gardening than the year before, but that summer he had Anthony to help. Anthony was a proper gardener, trained at an agricultural college, a farmer's son who lived near us at Loweswater and whom I'd discovered was currently going into Carlisle twice a week to study for another A-level. He was only too pleased to stop off at my father's and earn a bit of money helping. At first, my father was wary – this was no Simon, he knew nothing about Anthony – but after the boy's first afternoon he was thrilled. Anthony was apparently a wonder to behold, knowing everything there was to know about every aspect of gardening. He worked so hard and to such purpose my father was amazed to find himself telling the lad to slow down, there was another day coming. Like Simon, Anthony was not talkative but he was amiable and polite and took enquiries of the 'Are you courting?' variety good-humouredly. My father was intrigued by him – it was odd how, for a man so unsociable, he liked to find out about strangers if he could do it over a period of time and in his own way. They, naturally, were not allowed the same liberties with him. Anyone trying to find out anything about my father had always been given short shrift. But Anthony, not surprisingly, had no desire to cross-examine my father and came and went without any need to establish any but the most professional of relationships. He regarded my father as a character and left it at that.

So did most people, and my father liked the role. He certainly had no pretensions to being thought of instead as a wise old man. Old age, in his own opinion, had brought him no automatic wisdom. I once asked him if he thought he was wiser as an old man than he had been as a young man, and he said no, the world still made a monkey out of him. He'd worked hard and kept his nose clean and it had done him no good at all. Politics were beyond him and by then he was quite happy that this should be so. All politicians were out for their own good. When I protested that this wasn't true and cited examples he was derisive. 'Nelson Mandela? I'll tell you what, he likes his suits, cost a pretty penny of somebody's money.' It was no good reacting to this with anger or by trying to disprove the insinuation – my father was entirely cynical about the great and good. Nobody, in his twisted opinion, was ever motivated by the common good. 'Mother Teresa? She gets a rake-off somewhere along the line, likely.'

His grandchildren thought these kinds of absurd, illogical statements hysterically funny, but they weren't, they were perverse and bitter and sour. My father had cast himself long ago as the disadvantaged working man, endlessly exploited, never able to beat the injustice of the way life had dealt with him in material terms, always having to bow his head and put up with things. He was putting up by then with a life whose quality had been seriously eroded and which, it was beginning to occur to him, might go on too long. His urge to live was still incredibly strong – life was still precious to him – but so was his growing despair that he wouldn't be able to go on organising it as he had always done.

# II

THERE ARE SEVERAL entries in my father's minimalist diaries which record outings with my sister-in-law Marion, my husband's sister. Marion had left Carlisle at the end of the seventies, to go to London to live and work there, but she came back regularly. Whenever she did so she always managed to fit in a visit to my father and often took him for a drive and even treated him to lunch. He accepted her generosity and thoughtfulness as he accepted it from his own family – with occasional gruff thanks but no real appreciation of the time and effort involved. Anyone who had a car had it easy and should, according to him, take the car-less often and wherever they wanted to go: it was as simple as that. He'd tell me where Marion had taken him and I'd exclaim at the number of miles covered and he'd say, 'She wasn't pedalling.' No, indeed.

Marion was always amused by my father though she knew very well that he disapproved of her. She allowed him endless latitude, as she did all elderly people. She understood his attitude and shrugged it off – he was a victim of his generation, his class, and it was too late to re-educate him. She knew that, in his inflexible opinion, married women should stay at home and look after their husbands and there was no excuse for not doing so. They'd made their bed and must lie on it. Any suggestion that if this bed turned out to be uncomfortable it would be a good idea to change it for another was unacceptable. So for Marion to become a mature student at thirty-five and go off first to Ruskin College, Oxford, and then later, after a year back in Carlisle working, to leave for good to go to London, as a social worker, leaving her husband Jeff in Carlisle, was outrageous. My father never said so to Marion directly, but he didn't need to. 'Jeff managing all right, is he?' he would say to her, thinking he was being subtle, and Marion would say that yes, he was, and play him at his own game by pretending she didn't know what he really meant. She told him nothing about her life in London and neither did I. He had dark suspicions of her 'carrying on' but since he never directly voiced them it was easy to ignore his clumsy attempts at fishing for information. Marion would have been quite happy to tell him the truth, but she believed it would be more than he could handle and she thought the elderly should be protected from things they couldn't understand and which would upset them.

She even admired my father in a funny sort of way, admired his awfulness, his brutal outspokenness on all manner of subjects. She admired most of all his attitude to life, the way he got on with it and never moaned or groaned, the way he had no self-pity. She saw, by 1994, how he was declining and how hard it was proving for him to acknowledge his waning strength, and she admired his determination to maintain his independence. She dealt with a great many old people in her work and she thought my father's continuing interest in others remarkable. After a day out with him in the summer of 1994, she spent half an hour regaling me with accounts of things he'd said with such withering scorn that she'd burst out laughing, and when I'd protested that his remarks hadn't been in the least funny, she wouldn't have it. So Marion and my father had some sort of relationship, some kind of real connection with each other beyond the fact that she was his son-in-law's sister. She bothered about him, when even he had to admit that there was no blood connection, and therefore no positive duty.

Two years previously, Marion had thought she felt 'something' in her nose. Her GP could find nothing there, but referred her to a local hospital, where the nose specialist could find nothing either (and wrote to the GP saying so). But still Marion went on having the impression that there was 'something' there, high up on the right-hand side. After another year of worrying about it, she asked her GP to refer her to a specialist hospital. They found a small polyp, removed it, did a biopsy and pronounced it benign. But then, six months later, a visible lump had appeared in her neck and she had gone back to the hospital. When, in September 1994, I heard the shocking and completely unexpected news that Marion had cancer and I was forced to pass this horrible news on to my father – because it could not be concealed if I was to pack up early and return to London immediately – I expected him to show at least some concern. But he stayed true to form. 'She looked all right to me last time I saw her,' he remarked. It was said in an irritated tone, in an aggrieved fashion, as though Marion was trying to trick us all. Probably she would have laughed at this reaction, but I didn't. I wanted him to be sympathetic, and eventually he did manage: 'Pity. It's a pity. But there you are, nothing can be done.' And then he didn't want it mentioned again. He didn't want to hear anything about Marion's condition. He wanted me to shut up about it. I was being as bad as my dead mother, 'getting upset' when this did no good. The very mention of leaving Loweswater a month before we were due to enraged him. 'What for?' he asked. 'You can't do anything. She's got plenty of folk to look after her' (though he knew nothing about Marion's circumstances).

In fact, we didn't return to London just then. Marion was going back hospital for an operation (to remove the visible new tumours in her neck and investigate for any spread of the cancer cells to the lymph glands in the face) and then she would convalesce before starting radiotherapy treatment. It would make more sense for us to return just a little earlier than usual so that we would be there to help during the next stage. In a way, my father had been right: she did have enough folk to look after her and support her at the moment – a partner, Frances; a twin sister, Annabel, who rushed to her side (even though it was difficult because her husband has MS and needs constant care), and Jeff, who was ready to go at once. My father was pleased I was 'showing some sense and not getting carried away'. He asked occasionally how Marion was doing but hardly listened to the replies. It was easy enough to understand: if you're ninety-three and struggling yourself, the last thing you want to hear is depressing news about someone younger. 'It's cancer, is it?' he asked once, and I said yes. I'd told him it was. He drew a line under his throat and made a funny noise. 'What's that supposed to mean?' I said coldly. 'What do you think?' he said, scornfully. 'No hope, that's what.'

But there was hope, and we all had it, except for my father. The surgeon who was going to operate had described in great detail what he was going to do and had stressed there was no need to be pessimistic. This was relayed to me in one of the many telephone calls reporting Marion's treatment, and I wondered at the significance of 'no need to be pessimistic' as opposed, perhaps, to 'every reason to be optimistic'. But most of all I wondered about Marion's own attitude. The mental and emotional attitude of cancer patients is supposed to influence how they progress, or so I'd read (not that I believe it). I had worrying memories of that evening in our garden when Marion had professed indifference to death even if she didn't actually want to die. She might not turn out to be like my father, determined at all costs to hang on to his precious life, even now at ninety-three. Would she, in effect, give up, be resigned to her fate, and if she did would it make a vital difference? Or, in the face of imminent death, would she suddenly value life and fight tenaciously to hold on to it, just as my father was doing, if in very different conditions? Does everyone do that when life is threatened?

The operation duly went ahead and was, within its own terms, thought to have been successful. At any rate, it was over and Marion was recuperating, though finding it hard to be in a ward where other patients had parts of their face missing. It was impossible to look away all the time when eating meals at a communal table, and she was far too compassionate to do that, but being brave while confronted by such disfigurement was a strain. It made her wonder for the first time how disfigured she was going to turn out to be herself. Nobody had mentioned this. Nothing had been said about how she would actually look. She was annoyed with herself for caring – how could she care about her appearance when her life had been at stake? Was her face so precious to her? She wasn't particularly vain, but it was mortifying to realise how much she cared very much about not looking hideous. Surely being alive was enough without fretting about looks.

After the operation, when she was still bandaged, the surgeon had come to see her to enthuse about his own handiwork. It seemed he had had to negotiate a set of facial nerves which, if severed, would have left one half of her face permanently paralysed, but he hadn't severed any at all, hurrah. Marion thanked him and said she was pleased not to have a half-paralysed face. It was a while before she actually saw what she did look like. She knew she had to allow for the swelling and bruising, normal after such an operation, to subside, but even so she was dismayed at her battered appearance and the lopsidedness of her smile. Her mouth looked weird, she knew it did. But the state of her neck bothered her more. It was stiff, so stiff she had to hold her head oddly and could hardly turn it. It had never occurred to her that the removal of the tumours would affect the mobility of her neck. She was told her neck would loosen up in time and she would get used to the stiffness.

There was a great deal to get used to. All those who saw her – Frances, Annabel, Jeff – didn't care in the least how she looked. They stressed how little her appearance had changed, but then she'd known they would say that. Her own opinion was more important to her, but the other things she had to get used to soon overwhelmed her far more than her appearance. The awful dryness in her mouth was a torment. She claimed (rightly or wrongly) nobody had told her she was likely to lose most of her saliva glands. And she could taste nothing even when, with great difficulty, she managed to swallow any food. It seemed her taste buds, or most of them, had been further casualties. With her throat and the inside of her mouth in such a state telephone conversations were obviously out of the question, but I knew from everything Frances, Annabel and Jeff relayed to me that there was no indication whatsoever that Marion was going to be anything but the strong, brave person she had always been. There would be no giving up, no turning of her face to the wall. She wanted to live and would do anything and everything in her power to help herself do so. Whether she could be cured she couldn't possibly know, but if she could not be it would not be through lack of effort.

She'd had a lot of practice at making an effort and not giving in, which was why her earlier professed lack of concern about death had always seemed to me so out of character. She had never let illness of any kind get her down, though she'd never adopted my father's attitude of pretending it didn't exist. This would have been difficult because she'd suffered from acute psoriasis since she was seventeen. Eventually, steroid creams were prescribed to keep it under control, but once, while she was at Ruskin, she'd had an outbreak so severe she was hospital-ised. When I visited her, she looked like a mummy, entirely bandaged except for her eyes, nose and mouth. So she knew about having to endure a disease which, though not life-threatening, was a permanent affliction and she bore it stoically.

No one ever heard her moaning about her psoriasis, nor about the arthritis in her knees which started in her thirties. Like my father, she believed ailments were something which might go away if they were not talked about. She ignored stomach pains to such an extent in 1987 that by the time she was admitted into the Samaritan Hospital she was an emergency case, in urgent need of a hysterectomy, including the removal of both ovaries and her appendix.

That had been an enlightening episode. It revealed to me what a blessing it could be not to have much imagination. When I went to visit Marion in hospital she was astonished to find herself in post-operative pain. She said she'd never thought there would be any pain. In fact, she hadn't thought what such an operation would entail at all. It was a complete surprise to her. So was the surgeon's news that he was waiting for some test results to see if she needed further treatment. She thought that a funny thing to say, 'considering I've just had the treatment'. Never for one moment did she imagine that the fibroids they'd found could be (and indeed were suspected to be) cancerous. When she was told the following week that they were not, and she could go home, she was hardly aware of what a relief this was to the rest of us. This lack of looking ahead and imagining the worst had stood her in good stead, but it made it harder now that the worst, or what might turn out to be the worst, was upon her. The shock was all the greater for never having been fantasised. Observing her trying to adjust to the shock was a painful business – always held to be so strong, it was hard for her to show how much in need of support she was. She was the one who, all her life, had *given* support.

Marion had always seemed, to those who did not know her well (and to a few who did, or thought they did), quite self-sufficient, indeed almost tough, and certainly not a woman who had an awareness of an emptiness in herself, a hollow feeling, which she craved to understand and satisfy. To the world she presented a remarkably confident, even bold face, which was very convincing. I was convinced for quite a while. My first impression of her was of strength and also a touch of wildness – she looked as if she could say anything to anyone and I was wary (though I prided myself on doing exactly the same). She was seventeen then and I was eighteen. It was New Year's Eve 1956. I'd been brought home by Hunter for the first time, although we'd been, in Carlisle parlance, 'going out' for nearly a year. The house was crammed full of his Scottish family, and friends and neighbours, all celebrating Hogmanay in traditional style, with tots of whisky and Highland reels playing on the radio. The twins, Annabel and Marion, were not there when we arrived. They came in together, just before midnight, Annabel all smiles, Marion less animated and with a (to me, a stranger) more challenging look. We sized each other up and reserved judgement.

But it didn't take me long to work out how crucial Marion was to her family. She was her mother's chief support and her sick father's favourite (he had multiple sclerosis and was by then confined mostly to bed). She was her twin sister's protector and her younger brother's champion. Only Hunter, the eldest of the children, did not depend on her, except in the sense that through her he was excused from being depended upon himself. He had escaped, he was at university, removed from the strain created by his father's illness and his mother's exhaustion. The remaining family were close and absolutely devoted, but life for them, all their lives, was a struggle. Not enough money, not enough help, not enough space. To me it seemed that Marion ran that household. She was the only one who could deal with her father, who, because of his illness, could be angry and difficult and fly into rages. 'Marion stands no nonsense,' Mrs Davies would say admiringly. When her husband threw his food on the floor, saying (ludicrously) that he deserved more than mince considering all the money he brought into this house, it was Marion who swept into his room and told him that until he apologised the food would stay where it was and he'd get nothing else. She did it firmly, without anger, and unknown to him stood smiling sympathetically outside his door, waiting for the meek 'sorry' to follow, which it quickly did. Her mother would have cleared the mess up and brought fresh food.

It was Marion whom they all seemed to me to turn to, even though Annabel's role was vital too, and both of them shared all the domestic tasks. Marion was their spokeswoman, the one who could be depended upon to say what they wanted to say. So when she announced she was emigrating to New Zealand there was more frank disbelief than consternation. How could she possibly leave them? What would their lives be like without their precious Marion? But she genuinely intended to. Still the outsider, it was, for me, the first indication she gave that she wanted another kind of life and that she could only get it by tearing herself out of the heart of the family she loved so much and to whom she appeared indispensable. The plans went ahead. I listened to them, fascinated. She had the necessary medical and passed it. She filled in tons of forms and procured all the required references. Eventually, she heard that she had been accepted by all the various authorities for immigration into New Zealand. As her supposedly mad plan began to become reality, I watched her family and saw that still none of them thought for one moment that she would actually depart for the other side of the world. They couldn't afford to. Life without Marion would be insupportable. They made jokes about her going and laughed to show how ridiculous was the very idea.

Perhaps they always knew something I could not. Marion was emigrating with a friend – she hadn't quite the nerve to go alone – and perhaps they all knew that this friend would let her down, which she did. The friend became engaged and dropped out. Marion was obliged to abandon her plans. If she was devastated, it didn't show, but shortly after the collapse of this adventurous project she developed the psoriasis which was to plague her for the rest of her life. No connection was made at the time between its onset and the collapse of her hopes. Her break for freedom ended with a friend's engagement and she never tried again with quite the same determination. She was tied more securely than ever to her family, and to the life she had, and though they were sorry for her disappointment they were also, inevitably, relieved and glad for themselves. They were indulgent when she turned to Christian Science next, in search of a life change, even though they thought its teaching absurd (as all good Scottish Presbyterians would be bound to). If Marion wanted to try to overcome her psoriasis, and find whatever it was she was looking for, by becoming an adherent of a system that combated disease without recourse to medical treatment, then that was fine by them. They teased her only gently, affectionately, but they were not surprised when after a couple of years she gave it up.

All that was many years ago by the time she found herself in hospital again, but the habit of supporting those she loved had continued to be ingrained. Her father had died years before, and even her mother was dead now; her siblings were all married with partners to whom they could turn instead of to her, but still she was the linchpin of her dispersed family. She thought of them before she thought of herself, but now their dependence had to stop. She couldn't protect any of us from what was happening to her and we didn't want to be protected. We wanted to help, even if we were all woefully aware of how inadequate our help would be. Going back to London in October was a relief, for me, because it meant an end to the frustration of enquiries by telephone and, instead, some possibility of being actively engaged in helping Marion. I said as much to my father before we left – 'At least I'll be there, at least I'll be able to *do* something.' His reply was, 'When is Pauline coming?'

Once home, I was not prepared to keep all news about Marion out of my weekly letter to my father, though I never mentioned her in phone calls. The phone calls were always just chat about the weather and whatever was in the news, but the letters were a record of my week and no record could now be complete without mentioning Marion. But I didn't want to annoy or depress him, so I was restrained and careful and stuck to facts which told very little. I wrote that I'd been with Marion to the hospital where she was to receive her radiotherapy treatment, to see the doctor who would be in charge of it, but I didn't describe the visit. I didn't tell him of the misery of the visit, of the tension and sadness it generated. Such an airless basement we made our dispirited way to, such a dreary route down rubber-edged stairs and along low-ceilinged narrow corridors. And when we got there, to the waiting area, there were no vacant chairs or benches. For the first five minutes we were obliged to stand. Nobody looked at us, nobody stared, nobody showed any curiosity. They were all patients waiting for treatment, each withdrawn, some in what seemed a kind of trance, sitting with hands on knees or arms folded, staring straight ahead. Nobody spoke, nobody read. The only activity seemed to be looking constantly at wristwatches. A chair was vacated and Marion took it and got out her newspaper determinedly. It was hot, but she didn't take her coat off and neither did I. It would have felt too much like making ourselves comfortable for a long wait and we didn't want to acknowledge we might have to wait long; we wouldn't concede it was inevitable. Nurses came and went, calling out names. There were coughs and sighs, feet shuffled, chairs scraped, eyes were closed, heads tipped back. It didn't seem wise to look too closely at anyone, for fear of what might be revealed, for fear of having to confront abject despair. A great weariness smothered the room and gradually we were being suffocated.

Marion was sent for after a mere twenty minutes and we were led to the doctor's office. It was a small, drab room holding a desk with two chairs in front of it and one behind. We were invited to sit down but not to take our coats off. Time was precious: we mustn't be deluded into thinking this was going to be anything but a brisk five minutes. We were humble. We understood that, and we had prepared ourselves accordingly by making out a list of vital questions that Marion wanted answered. I had the sheet of paper in my pocket together with a pencil to write down replies. Whatever this doctor said, I was going to make her repeat it and then I was going to write it down, knowing as I did how memory could play tricks in cases like this where the listeners were so fraught. Marion had been worried about this. 'The doctor might not like it,' she'd said. 'The doctor can lump it,' I'd replied, and she laughed, hearing echoes of herself.

This doctor was a youngish woman. That must mean she was particularly brilliant, I thought. Hard enough to qualify as a doctor, doubly hard to have reached such a position in a London teaching hospital. But she certainly did not seem brilliant at establishing a relationship with a patient. She was perfectly pleasant but avoided eye-contact and never once expressed sympathy with Marion. Her attitude seemed offhand, almost flippant. Maybe this was a pose she'd perfected to cope with potentially emotional encounters; maybe she had to behave like that in order to get through these stressful sessions. At any rate, she plunged straight into an account of how the radiotherapy would be administered, talking rapidly and constantly opening and shutting the drawers of the desk, though never revealing what she was looking for. She sucked a mint during her homily, but at least offered us one each from the ragged packet. We politely declined. She said the air got very dry here. We agreed. She asked if there was anything else we wished to know which she hadn't covered. Anything else? I produced my bit of paper. We hadn't started yet.

One by one I went through all our queries, which were mostly to do with how Marion was likely to react to each session and how much pain or discomfort she would experience as the treatment continued. The replies seemed carefully non-committal, full of 'it depends on this' and 'it depends on that', and 'everything varies according to the patient'. Some could tolerate the effects much better than others, and so on. The doctor was beginning to sound quite up-beat until I moved on to the two questions Marion most wanted answered. The first was whether the doctor would give her a realistic assessment of the likely success of all this radiotherapy; and the second: 'Had there been, originally, a misdiagnosis?' The doctor swallowed the last sliver of her mint and sat up very straight. She picked up a Biro, drew a sheet of paper towards her and began to sketch something before turning the paper towards us, while still answering the first question (an answer so wonderfully vague and full of imponderables as to be useless). While she continued to talk rapidly, we stared at her diagram, unable to understand her drawing but understanding very well that she sounded defensive.

It was bothering Marion at the time that if the nose tumour had been diagnosed as malignant earlier, when she had first been sent to hospital – after complaining to her doctor of that 'something' in her nose – her life might not now be in danger. She knew perfectly well that blame was irrelevant now, but she wanted to know the truth. She also wanted to know if the initial excavation of the tumour had not gone far enough. The doctor's drawing was to demonstrate the normal depth of tissue removal and then how in Marion's case the malignancy had in fact spread deeper without showing any signs of having done so. 'Unless,' Marion said, quite sharply now, 'the surgeon had gone deeper.' The doctor said that there were no indications that he needed to. It was just bad luck. Marion said she might take this enquiry further. The doctor shrugged. It was up to her. She stood up, making it clear it was time for us to go. Out in the cold street, Marion seethed. She was sure a cover-up was going on. She knew it was tedious and pointless to persist in trying to establish the truth, and that she would waste a lot of emotional energy she could scarcely afford to spare in doing so, but she couldn't give up. It was her life and she wanted to know – even if it made everything worse – whether it had been put in peril through an oversight.

It was tempting to suggest that, as things now stood, there was no point in going backwards. The surgeon had already told her that the cancer had probably spread even before the tumour was found. But the exact sequence of events mattered to Marion and so it was impossible to dissuade her from beginning an investigation of her own, starting with the demand to see her medical notes. She talked incessantly of this, with rage, but then when the radiotherapy actually began she had no energy for it (though the correspondence with the relevant authorities still went on in the background). The sessions were an ordeal for which she was mentally ill-prepared, though she had technically been told what to expect. The worst part was the wearing of a mask made of some sort of see-through plastic which tightly covered her face leaving only tiny holes for her eyes and nostrils and mouth. Even having the mask made had been bad enough, but now, when she had to have it fitted, she felt so claustrophobic she was almost hysterical. It was always so fiddly to fit – it was marked with red, green and black lines which had to be in perfect position – and the nurses would fuss and fret over it until they had it on exactly right. Once it was on, the radiotherapy itself was quick, a mere few minutes, and then she was free, until the next day.

But very quickly she began to suffer from the effects and

much more severely than had been predicted. The roof of her mouth felt as if it had been scalded and swallowing was agony. Liquid she could manage, with difficulty, but solid food, however soft, had to be forced down. We dreaded watching her eat. Not a single sip or crumb could be got down without her face reflecting the searing pain. After nearly three weeks of this she was coming home each day from the hospital fit to do nothing but lie on her bed and weep. Yet she was not going to give up, absolutely not. She'd been told by the nurses that lots of patients receiving this kind of treatment gave up halfway. They simply didn't turn up one day – it was all too dreadful, surely life was not worth this torture. With three more weeks to go, Marion fully intended to continue, but she didn't know if she had the strength. Frances, with her all the time, was at the end of her own emotional resources. Together they were both near to collapse by the beginning of December.

The week of my father's ninety-fourth birthday (celebrated with my brother and his wife, who always went north for it), Frances went away for a short break, to stay with a friend, and Marion came to us. She was used to staying with us and had done so many times, so there was nothing strange about it for her. She was quite at home. But what was strange, horribly strange, were mealtimes. She was trying to make sure that the little food she managed to eat was as rich as possible in protein because she'd been warned she might have to exist on fortified drinks only during the last two weeks of the radiotherapy. There she was, the woman for whom it had always been a joy to cook, sitting at our table patiently spreading rich pâté onto minute scraps of soft white bread, diligently spooning mousses oozing with cream into her poor mouth, slowly ladling thick soups down her burnt throat and all with a look of terror on her face, anticipating the acute pain that every bit of nourishment would bring. But to live she had to eat and to drink. Life had to be worth the pain. Something that had once given her such

71

pleasure was now only a painful way of staying alive. And she wanted to stay alive at any price. How high could this price go? I had no idea, but watching her, watching the sudden collapses into tears after each meal was over, I wondered just how long even a determined person can go on, and why they would continue wanting to.

I hardly dared to mention the word 'hospice'. Hospices were for the dying. If I suggested Marion went into a hospice it would be interpreted as a sentence of death. But I knew hospices were not just for the dying. I knew, through a friend who worked in one, that they were also for respite care for those suffering from cancer. Patients could go in for a couple of weeks and come out again. I rang my friend and asked if there was even the most remote chance that the hospice where she worked in Hampstead, the Marie Curie Centre, would take in Marion so that she could survive the rest of her radiotherapy treatment. She said she was sure there was and would herself set admission procedures in motion if Marion was agreeable. I rehearsed what I was going to say, how I was going to explain the benefits of going back each day from the radiotherapy to a place where people would know how to look after a person in her condition. But I didn't need to recite my lines – both Marion and Frances burst into tears of absolute relief. They had a bag packed in a flash and within twenty-four hours Marion was settled into a room in the hospice with immediate advantage. Because of the angle at which she had to keep her head and because of the soreness of her neck, she hadn't been able to sleep. But once in the hospice a system of special pillows was devised which made her comfortable. It was all, in fact, a question of comforts – each one small but the sum total adding up to the feeling that she was in expert caring hands.

There were some treatments the hospice offered which were not small but quite large comforts. One was aromatherapy. Marion loved this. She had the kind of massage called *effleurage*, which consisted of the oils being applied with the flat of the hand, the fingers close together, the tips turned upwards, smoothing across her sore face and neck very, very gently. The room where she had the massage was warm, the atmosphere relaxed, and she lay on a comfortable bed covered with a warm towel, her eyes closed, trying to picture a summer garden or the sea, the Mediterranean, as the aromatherapist suggested. She loved the scent of the particular oils used – peach kernel, evening primrose, lavender, rosemary, geranium and bergamot. She felt soothed by the massage and, after it was over, for a while she would feel generally refreshed. She knew, of course, that this aromatherapy couldn't conquer the cancer but nevertheless it helped her to stay sane and calm, and that was important.

But hypnotherapy, also on offer at the hospice, proved even more important. Marion had always been attracted to the idea that the mind could control the health of the body (hence her early interest in Christian Science), and also to alternative medicines. Once she knew she had cancer she wanted more than ever to believe in anything that came into these categories and before her time at the hospice she had already experimented with acupuncture. For several weeks a man came to her home to administer it and also left her with various herbs which had to be infused and drunk as part of the treatment. I infused them when she stayed with us. They stank and tasted vile but Marion was still devoted to them and dutifully swallowed the concoction as well as having needles stuck in her. But then she'd caught this man appearing to smile when she winced with the pain the needles were causing her, and had told him not to come again. She was finished with acupuncture. It might work for others but she had no evidence it was working for her and it seemed ridiculous to add unnecessary suffering to what she was already enduring.

But hypnotherapy caused no suffering, and at first she really believed it was helping her deal with her fear and panic. She was taught certain mental exercises which she had to put herself through whenever she felt overwhelmed with despair, or so tense she wanted to scream. She didn't think she was actually hypnotised, but that she was brought to a state of semi-consciousness which made her receptive to suggestions that she should let her worries go. She said she felt dreamy and seemed to float away, though she knew where she was, and who she was, and was certainly not in any kind of deep trance, and that she liked this. The rest of us, sceptics all, were simply pleased she was finding any kind of relief. There were still three weeks of radiotherapy to go and she needed all the help she could get.

# III

M Y MIND, AT the end of 1994, was barely on my father. I
dutifully made the twice-weekly telephone calls, keeping
up the family rota we had established, and wrote my weekly
letters. But my thoughts were entirely with Marion. Pauline,
my sister, who herself had known Marion almost as long as I
had, knew this and understood perfectly. In any case, Pauline
regarded herself as the main one of us on duty, as it were, during
the winter months, because I was there to cover the summer.
She was ready and willing for any emergencies even if Marion
had not been so ill. At the end of the first week in December,
directly after my brother had been with him for his ninety-
fourth birthday – a quiet lunch out at a favourite pub in the
Eden Valley – and just as Marion went into the hospice, an
emergency arrived.

None of us was aware of it at the time, but throughout
November my father had been feeling ill, or rather 'A' had. He
stayed in bed a lot while 'A' was 'so-so', following the usual
routine of staggering up to take the evening telephone call and
conceal his condition. His voice did indeed sound fainter, but
when we picked up on this he'd say he had a slight cold but was
managing. Which he was, in a fashion. He was still slapping
bacon in the frying pan, still switching his 'merser' off and on,
still keeping all systems at go, but increasingly liable to collapse –
perhaps onto his tiled hearth, where he could have cracked his
skull open. He told only his diary that 'A' had 'Trouble. Water.
Colour Red' again. The last diary entry he ever made was for 7

December – 'Sunshine. Dry. Cold day. Waiting for Doc. Sport on Radio. A. not so good.' It was Pauline's turn to telephone him that day and, hearing the faint whisper of 'I'm managing', which was all he could produce, she was not fooled and did not hesitate. She went at once, suspecting this was the real crisis point we'd been dreading.

The doctor decreed my father would have to go into the infirmary. His knees were massively swollen, there was blood in his urine – his medical notes report him as telling the doctor his bathroom that day had looked like 'an abattoir' – and he was in urgent need of skilled attention. Pauline told me he was ashen and weak and without resistance. He'd had no energy to fight against admission to the infirmary. 'Push me over the edge of a cliff, then,' he'd said, 'and have done with it.' They took him to the infirmary in an ambulance. They carted him off to Ward 20, a fate he'd contemplated with horror. But Pauline's arrival made an enormous difference – in his words, she could talk to the nurses and set them right. Luckily, she didn't have much to set right. All my father's memories of what the geriatric ward of the infirmary had been like when he visited his dying father there vanished. Ward 20, for a start, wasn't a geriatric ward. It was a general male surgical ward in a new wing and he had his own little cubicle which gave him some privacy. Even better, it was near the sister's desk, where there were constant comings and goings, so he had plenty of action to watch. He settled in wonderfully well, against all expectations. Instead of being difficult or surly he was obedient and polite. The nurses liked him. He realised this and he behaved even better, discovering from some place deeply buried within him a charm never witnessed before. 'A' was a model patient with a model daughter constantly at his side, with flowers and letters and postcards arriving every day, and with a small but steady stream of concerned visitors. He was well looked after and well fed and perfectly comfortable. To his own astonishment, he found

himself quite content to lie there while his ailments were invest-
igated and, as far as they could be, treated. Sometimes Pauline
managed to wheel a telephone to his bedside and I spoke with
him and could hear how amazingly buoyant he sounded.

I never, of course, mentioned Marion to him now, and I
didn't mention my father being in hospital to Marion, just then.
Both of them had quite enough to do in focusing on hanging
on to their own lives without being called upon to have sympathy for each other. But if things were stable with my father
once he was safely in the infirmary, they were very bad with
Marion. The effects of the final stages of radiotherapy grew
worse and worse. Driving over to Hampstead to collect her
from the hospice and take her to the Middlesex Hospital, I'd
feel more and more apprehensive knowing the state she'd be in.
The driving itself was, for me, fearsome enough. I'd only just
passed my driving test that summer, at the mighty age of fifty-
six, and all the learning had been done on quiet Cumbrian
roads. Nobody suggested I should share the daily driving of
Marion to the hospital but I was determined to do it. I'd gone
out very early on a Sunday morning, practising the route, until I
felt I could cope, having memorised every one-way street,
noted every set of traffic lights. But it was fairly nerve-racking
for Marion, who had been driving expertly for thirty-odd
years, though she kindly professed complete faith in me. I made
her sit in the back at first, under some illusion that it was safer if
I crashed, but soon I'd demonstrated how careful I was and she
moved into the front, so we could talk as I made my slow and
stately way through the traffic.

What we talked about was never anything very much. It felt
cosy in the car, sealed off from all the noise outside and from the
December rain battering the windows. We chatted lazily about
this and that, just as we had always done, and because I looked
rigidly ahead, never daring to take my eyes off the road for a
single moment, there was an impression that everything was as

it always had been. I couldn't see Marion's bandaged neck, nor observe the misery in her eyes. She sounded as she always had done. But when I drew up outside the radiotherapy department, able to pause for only a minute or two because it was such a busy street, and watched her walk into the hospital I'd be overwhelmed by the pathos of her little wave and cheery smile, the smile off-centre because her mouth at one side was not quite so mobile, and I could hardly bear to see how her head suddenly bowed, as she disappeared. I drove home numb, imagining her putting on the cruel mask and lying under the huge machine. It was dreadful to think about and I thought about nothing else.

On the last day that I took her for treatment, I saw she'd been crying. She was ready for me, standing just inside the glass doors, muffled up in coat and scarf. She came out smiling as ever but her eyes were red-rimmed. I noticed her neck was more heavily bandaged than usual, and she said it was painful. The radiotherapy had begun to strip the skin off earlier in the week and at the hospice they were coating it with some special unguent, though around the wound left by the previous surgery it was still raw and bleeding. But she hadn't been shedding tears over her neck. 'It was just that I was thinking,' she said, as we drove off, 'how lovely it would be if tomorrow really was the end of it all, you know, of the treatment, and now I just get better and it's all been worth it. That was what I was thinking, and then I thought no, it isn't the end, it goes on, and nobody knows if it will have worked. And it just made me sad.' I knew, without needing to look at her, even if I hadn't been concentrating on the turn into Haverstock Hill, that she was crying quietly again. It was one of those terrible moments when to say nothing is despicable and to say anything is so hard. The natural reaction is to cry too, but that helps no one, it's an indulgence on the part of the listener which makes the sufferer feel worse. I wanted to stress that of course the treatment would have worked, and she mustn't think it might not have, but such unfounded optimism was offensive. Marion might need, and bring herself to accept, a small measure of reassurance but she would know that even this was given in ignorance. All I could think of to say was that at least this radiotherapy was over for ever: she would certainly never, ever, have to endure this again. 'Oh, I wouldn't,' she said. 'I'd rather be dead.'

After I'd dropped her off (no wave, no smile for once) I drove home thinking about what Marion had said, hearing her words about wishing this really was the end, over and over again. I backed the car down the mews lane to our garage, with difficulty, and then laboriously manoeuvred it inside. It took me three tries to get the car lined up so that the garage door could close, but finally I did it. Then I sat in the dark garage, unable to summon up the will to get out of the car. When finally I levered myself out I saw that I still hadn't parked as well as I could have done. The bonnet was practically scraping the metal up-and-over garage door and there was a yard's gap at the back. I could have left it, the garage was actually closed after all, but I wanted to have done the job properly. It had been repeatedly explained to me that parking cars neatly and well was all part of driving and I had to go on learning to do it until I could do it effortlessly. So I got back into the car, sighing to myself, thinking how I would always hate driving and everything to do with cars.

God knows what I did then. All I thought I had done was to take off the handbrake, prior to putting the car into reverse. But it shot backwards. There was a terrifying crash and suddenly I was showered with glass. I thought a bomb had gone off. I was transfixed, unable to move at all, my left hand still on the brake, my right on the wheel, but through the driving mirror I could see the garden – the garden! – so the back wall of the garage had gone. The back wall was gone and so were two sections of the roof. These had crashed through the rear window of the Ford Granada and were now lying on the back seat. Slowly, I tried to open the door of the car but it wouldn't open. I moved to try the passenger door, and at once more glass tinkled round me. The car seemed to shudder with every careful movement I made, but I inched across from behind the wheel and found I could, after all, open the other door. I got out and stared, appalled, at the wreckage. I climbed out of the garage through the massive hole in the wall – or what was left of the wall – and over the shards of the shattered terracotta pots once lined up along it. Behind me, there was the sound of splintering and I cringed as a big piece of wood, a strut running across the roof of the garage, gave way.

But the most terrifying sight was the back seat, with those concrete slabs resting on it. Anyone sitting there would have been killed, or at the least dreadfully maimed. Silly, morbid thoughts filled my head as I stumbled through the now dark garden to the house. Marion had sat there. Marion could have been killed. A stupid way to think – Marion would have got out first, once I'd parked, and she would never have got back in while I readjusted the car. But I couldn't stop those thoughts as I let myself into the house and slumped on a sofa. The irony of it paralysed me: what if Marion had been sitting on that back seat and had been killed on her way back from almost her last radiotherapy treatment. To have gone through all that, and then suffer death in two minutes. I couldn't get this out of my head, ridiculous though such pointless speculation was. I stayed motionless in the dark, without switching on the lights, until gradually I got a grip on myself, and started to worry instead about the damage I'd done. In the scale of things, a wrecked car and garage surely didn't really matter. I wasn't hurt, nobody was hurt, and that was all that mattered, wasn't it? It was merely an inconvenience and in no time at all would become a funny story. I could stand the jokes about my driving, couldn't I? Of course I could. There was no need to start turning such a mundane calamity into an event of sinister significance, full of omens, sent to show me how fragile life was . . . 'Don't be daft,' I could hear my father saying, and finally I listened to him.

Christmas Day was grim. Annabel and her family came on Boxing Day, as usual, but Marion was too ill to join us. She was in bed most of the time, feeling worse than she had ever felt even though the radiotherapy had ended. New Year was no better, because for the Davies family, being Scottish, it was the big festival of the year and not to be able to celebrate it appropriately was miserable. 'It might be my last, who knows?' Marion said. And what did I reply? That of course it would not be – the same old instinctive reaction of denial, the same refusal to contemplate the possibility of death.

After New Year's Day, it was three weeks before I saw her again. We went on holiday to the Caribbean, leaving my father in hospital and Marion still barely able to lift her head from the pillow. I expected bad news all the time but none came. When I telephoned the Cumberland Infirmary the nurses were delighted to take messages from so far away and my father loved their excitement. I didn't telephone to see how Marion was progressing, knowing there would be little to report and that it was enough strain for Frances to deal with the constant enquiries she already had. I lay on white, sandy, palm-fringed beaches and swam in turquoise waters and thought of the two of them all the time, my father and Marion, Marion and my father, ninety-four and fifty-five, both ill, both supposedly recovering, both obliged to wonder if they would survive another year. I should be in Ward 20. I should be in Marion's flat. But if I were, what would I be doing? Uttering platitudes, evading the truth. I could be there, bearing witness, lending support by my mere physical presence, a contribution anyone can make and which is not negligible, but Pauline was there for my father and Frances for Marion. This didn't excuse me, and in my mental ramblings I didn't try to excuse myself, but it made me feel a little easier.

For now, but only for now, for three weeks, I was the hedonist, thinking only of my own pleasure, but thinking, too, in endless clichés – life is short and sweet/ enjoy yourself while you can/ eat, drink and be merry, because tomorrow we die . . . It was my father's death I waited for. It seemed to me that if that call came which I anticipated, the telephone call saying he'd died in Ward 20, while I sunned myself and drank rum punches on a beach, I would be relieved. I longed for the release of it, as soon as possible.

But he hadn't died while we were away. On the contrary, he had improved in health and was almost ready to return home. In spirits, my sister informed me, a trifle wearily, he was his old self. She was amused but exasperated to tell me that he was making a big fuss, because he did not have a calendar for 1995. He'd driven her mad – 'Where is it? Margaret always gives me one, always. She won't have forgotten. It'll likely be in the house. You haven't looked properly.' Pauline, staying in our Loweswater house all this time, was obliged to say she had looked very thoroughly and there was no calendar to be found. I remembered buying it and wrapping it and leaving it for Pauline to take to him, but somehow it had vanished. Eventually, she had bought one herself, of the kind he liked – large, glossy, British Walks in lurid colour, the days clearly marked – and he'd grudgingly accepted it. He had to have a calendar so he would know where he was.

The calendar now became his diary, though until he left hospital he merely crossed the days off and wrote nothing in the vacant oblong spaces beside each date. He returned home on 24 January, his various immediate ailments relieved, his knees back to normal and his kidney infection cleared up. He was grateful for all the attention and care he'd received, and fulsome (for him) with his compliments; but he was eager to be independent again and carry on with the true business of life – with managing. Pauline and her husband, who had been so magnificently supportive, saw him into his bungalow and then it was my turn. I dreaded it. There I was, with my flash Caribbean tan, rested and fit after my wonderful holiday hopping around islands, and yet I dreaded catching a train north to visit my poor aged father just out of hospital. I couldn't use Marion's greater need as an excuse any longer. I had to go, so I went.

I walked from the railway station, as I always did, wanting fresh air and exercise after the train journey. It was bitterly cold, fine sleet driving into my face as I went over the viaduct bridge. I walked slowly to take longer to arrive. As I neared my father's bungalow, I saw him sitting in the armchair next to the window. Normally, he would have been on the look-out, and on his feet to get to his front door while I was still fifty yards away, but he didn't move. Maybe he was asleep. I hesitated about whether to use my own key (he'd always liked me to have his key even if I was hundreds of miles away) or ring the doorbell. I decided he'd prefer to open the door himself, so I rang the bell and waited. I heard him shuffling down the little hallway passage and fumbling with the door lock. There was a 'Damn!' I peeped through the letterbox and said, 'Dad, it's me, I'll use my key.' 'No!' came the command. 'I can open my own front door. I'll manage.' And eventually he did. 'You're back, then,' he said, by way of effusive greeting, and I replied in kind, as trained, with 'Yes, and so are you. You don't look too bad.'

Once settled back in his armchair, with the gas fire on full blast, he couldn't stop talking. Every detail of his stay in the infirmary was gone over, pouring out of him in a positive torrent of words, and all I needed to do was listen until it was time to make his tea. He said he didn't want much, he was still full after all the marvellous infirmary food – and he was off again, going over each and every one of the meals he'd had. We watched television, the sound ridiculously, and unnecessarily, high, since there was nothing wrong with his hearing. He just liked it loud. He said, at nine o'clock, that he thought he'd go to bed and I could put his electric blanket on if I liked. I went to switch it on, and stayed to check that the heat was coming through. His bed was so old, bought when he got married in 1931 and the mattress never changed since. It was of the flock kind and rested on coiled metal springs. Bits of flock leaked out of it between the ridges formed by two bodies lying there for so many nights. When my mother was still alive I'd wanted to make her more comfortable by buying a new bed, or at the very least a new mattress – but there had been a violently hostile reaction, and cries of 'This bed will see us out.'

The heat had come through satisfactorily. I pulled the bed-covers straight, so many of them, umpteen woollen blankets and an eiderdown and a counterpane, all blue. The bed, with its dark stained wooden headboard and footboard, took up most of the small room. There were only a few inches between one side of the bed and a vast wardrobe (in which one solitary dress of my mother's still hung, survivor of all the rest of her clothes which my father had systematically burned in his garden in his own version of a funeral pyre). On the other side, in front of the window, was a dressing table, its surface still covered with my mother's crocheted mats on which rested her hairbrush and jewellery box (though she never had any jewels). A small wooden chest of drawers, squashed into the corner near the foot of the bed, completed the furniture. I shivered, not just with memories of my mother lying ill there, but with genuine cold. There was no heating in this claustrophobic room. There was what was derisively called 'central heating' in the bungalow but it was of the hot air variety, blown through grilles and inefficient as well as horribly noisy. I'd wanted to take it out and install efficient heating but, again, was opposed. The only improvement allowed had been the addition of a storage heater in the hall passage. My father loved it. He maintained that with his bedroom door left wide open the heat from this heater warmed the room grand.

Not at 9.30 p.m. on a freezing January night, it didn't. The famous storage heater was of course stone cold, timed as it was to start belting out its heat in the early hours of the morning. At night, the bedroom was like an igloo, and passing from the fierce heat of the living-room into it was like passing straight from the tropics to Antarctica. But my father stood the exchange without complaint. Bedrooms in his life had always been cold. He duly went to bed, telling me that if I heard him making any noise in the night to ignore him. But he made no noise that night. I didn't sleep, so I knew. I lay and thought how awful this was, a ninety-four-year-old man dragging himself round each day, trying to keep his routines going, living by them, battling all the time with the constant erosion of his strength. What kind of life was it for him? How could he stand it? But at the same time I knew this was how *I* thought not how he saw it. He didn't seem to look at his life as I did. All his remaining energies went into 'managing'. He had no intention of giving up. The harder it became to manage, the harder he tried. And he was as obsessed with time as ever, keeping a close eye on his two clocks and his wristwatch and writing up each day on his calendar. Time was never just going to pass him by, certainly not.

I went out the next morning and bought a joint of best beef, sirloin, with plenty of fat round it – what else? There was no greater treat than the smell of beef roasting in his own oven, but I had grave doubts as to how I would cope with this ancient device. The oven practically exploded when I tried to light it and the roar of the gas was so furious it had brought him stumbling through to the kitchen to see what was going on. It seemed I'd been a fool. The way to light the oven was like *this*, not as I'd been doing, and Regulo 5 was obtained by turning the dial to Regulo 1. My mother, he said, had never had any problem and neither had he. He was clearly unsure whether he could safely leave me even when the gas had been properly regulated, but finally returned to his armchair after many instructions to baste the meat well. This was a daunting process. The oven door hung half off its hinges and the catch needed great pressure to seal the door. I dreaded opening and closing it, convinced I was going to wreck the oven, purchased in 1948 and still, in my father's opinion, as good as new. I wondered how it was that in my own house I managed regularly to cook huge meals for large numbers of people and yet I was now in a panic about cooking one meal for one old man.

Finding adequate saucepans in which to boil the carrots and cabbage and Brussels sprouts – for the meal would not be complete without these – was another difficulty. I tried to search for pans as quietly as possible, but my father heard me and came through once more to stare at me on my knees scrabbling around in the cupboard under the sink. He shook his head, exasperated. The pans he used were in the pantry. I'd seen these but there were only two; both were very small and neither had lids. 'Lids?' he echoed. 'What's wrong with a plate?' I thought there might be quite a few things wrong with using a plate as a lid on top of boiling water, but I didn't suggest any of them. In the end, I found three very old larger aluminium pans, two with proper lids. I scrubbed them out well and soon had the vegetables boiling merrily. That only left the gravy. Oh God, the gravy. Gravy had to be made my mother's way, as I'd tried to make it for his ninetieth birthday, but that involved the use of gravy browning. A spoonful of this was essential to mix with flour and then the residue of the meat juices. I had to ask him if he had a packet of the stuff. Triumphantly, he produced an opened half-finished  packet from the back of the pantry. I looked at it. I felt the packet. It was rock hard. 'Dad, this is solid.' 'Nothing wrong with it. You can manage.'

When we eventually sat down to our sumptuous dinner, the perspiration was pouring off me. We sat at a carefully laid table – tablecloth, place mats (views of hunting scenes), cork stand and woollen cosy for the teapot, china plates. The joint rested on the right kind of serving dish, which I'd found wrapped in newspaper dated 1972 on the top shelf of a cupboard. The vegetables were in a tureen, found in the same place. 'Grand,' my father said; 'everything right'. I carved the meat, inviting comparisons with my brother's carving abilities to my disadvantage, and doled out the rest of the food. My father tucked in, and I tried to, but only picked. 'Lost your appetite?' he said, his own cheeks bulging. I said I had, a little. 'All that foreign rubbish, likely,' he said. I agreed this might be so. He relished every mouthful of his dinner, especially the meat, chewed vigorously and the fatty bits sucked noisily, as usual. When he'd had seconds and finished he said, 'I won't have another roast meat dinner like that for a long time, any road. Once you've gone, I'll be back to normal. No roast joints then.'

Making that meal brought to an end the only meaningful, useful thing I could do for him. It had taken all morning and given me a reason to lurk in the kitchen and not to have to sit with him. I took a long time scrupulously washing and rinsing and drying and putting away all the dishes and pans. It was amazing, in fact, how very long I managed to make this job take. Then there was no escape from joining him in the hot living-room. It should have felt companionable, but it didn't. It never had done, either for me or, I was sure, for him. It felt awkward, the silence heavy. I'd exhausted accounts of my holiday and he'd exhausted descriptions of the infirmary meals. 'Put the TV on,' he ordered. I said there wasn't much on in the afternoon today, no sport, no nature programmes, but he said beggars couldn't be choosers and to put it on without the sound. Once it was on, once an old black-and-white film was flickering away, he seemed to relax. He fell asleep, slumped in his chair, almost immediately. I picked up a book. If I kept very still and turned the pages very quietly, he might sleep all afternoon. But he didn't. He slept for ten minutes at a time, waking repeatedly with a start, looking about him, looking at me with astonishment, sighing, looking at the television and then drifting off again.

At four o'clock, he woke up to tell me to close the curtains. It was still light, just. I said so, and he said, as he always had done (this was an old battle of ours), that he'd decide whether it was time to close the curtains or not. So I closed them. I made his tea, not because he actually wanted it but because he wanted the routine of it. Amazingly, he ate a sandwich and a piece of Madeira cake and was cross I would neither eat nor drink. Then the serious business of watching television began in earnest. Hours of quiz shows followed and if I failed to answer every question correctly, which I did, he professed surprise – 'Thought you went to Oxford.' Sneaking off into the freezing back bedroom to crouch in my bed, fully clothed and with a big scarf round my head, offended him greatly. I felt ashamed and guilty. I was rejecting him and his ways too pointedly and I shouldn't. So I came back into the living-room and counted the minutes till bedtime.

The following morning, I didn't just go out to shop. I went to do something I'd been putting off for a long time. I went to look at a nearby nursing-home, as a kind of insurance against my father's ever needing to live in such a place. I'd no intention of allowing him to go into any sort of institution but, absurdly, I felt if I went and inspected the most likely home the necessity of putting him into it would never arise. In fact, I'd more or less promised him it never would. To Mrs Nixon he had once confessed that 'they' would put him into a home if he couldn't manage. She told me this, as I'm sure she was intended to, and when I tackled him about it and told him he need never worry, that this would not happen, he seemed reassured. What I should have said was that I would try my best to see that it would not happen, but if I'd said that, if I'd qualified the reassurance, it would have amounted to no reassurance at all. I'd said it, and I'd hoped to mean it.

I still thought I meant it, but all the same I went to look at a home Pauline had discovered. I could hardly bear to make the visit. My father was a loner, a proud and independent man, who would loathe living among others. I knew that in these homes women heavily outnumbered men and so he would be not only appalled at the loss of his own house but at having to mix with women. They would embarrass him, make him feel permanently ill at ease. Death would surely be preferable to such a fate. I think I groaned aloud as I walked towards the place I was going to vet, which was on the far side of the council estate where we used to live. Our old house, once with its paintwork and windows gleaming under my father's care, once with the garden brimming over with roses and lupins, was now derelict. The windows were boarded up, the paintwork was peeling and the garden had been concreted over. It was the same depressing sight all the way through the estate until I reached the church, which was newly whitewashed, its grounds unexpectedly neat and well cared for.

The nursing-home was only a little further on, round the corner, but part of another estate, new and private, where there were attractive and expensive houses for sale. The home was at the top, but built in a dip. I stood hesitating, looking at it. It was a one-storey building, brick, with flower-beds already well established in front. It looked more like a small, modern hotel than any kind of institution, which was somehow hopeful. Appearances had always mattered to my father.

I went inside. The entrance hall was wide and light, with fresh flowers (at the end of January) on a table in the middle. The walls were freshly emulsioned, the floors squeaky clean. There were pictures and photographs everywhere and displays of mementos from earlier times – old lamps, railway memorabilia, boxes and posters. All the doors appeared to be open and there was an atmosphere of bustle, which seemed strange. There was no smell, except for a faint lemony scent in the air which might have been soap or something similar. I stood in the doorway of what looked like an office, and immediately the young woman sitting at a computer smiled and got up and asked could she help me – such a simple, obvious reaction but so cheering. I began to feel optimistic, as I was shown round, until we got to the main sitting-room. It was a pleasant room, large and airy, with french windows opening onto a small garden, but nothing could camouflage the depressing sight of eight very old, very ill people sitting there, three of them in wheelchairs. They all looked utterly pathetic and half dead. My father would go mad. He hated wheelchairs – 'damned things' – and was prone to saying outrageous things whenever he had to pass one in any kind of confined space – 'Shouldn't be allowed, cluttering the place up.' Asked how the poor occupants of the wheelchairs would then be able to get out and about, he would say, 'They should stop in bed in their condition, best place for them.'

I was taken next to see the individual rooms. They were small but not much smaller than my father's own living-room, and they each had a bathroom. He could bring his own furniture, or at least a couple of small items, and his own photographs and pictures of course. The home provided the bed (excellent mattress, much better than his own) and an armchair. The curtains and carpets were all fresh and pretty, the windows wide and with a broad view – but ah, the views. I realised at once that not a single window in this establishment had what could be called a view. There was nothing for old people, confined to their chairs and peering out of their windows most of the day, to look at. Built round a large area of grass, where nothing else grew (and there were as yet no urns of flowers), each room on two sides of the home had this emptiness for its view. One of the other two sides faced the front door, and the flowers, at the front, where at least there were some comings and goings to watch; and the other looked onto the gardens of neighbouring houses, but this view was interrupted by a big wooden fence. My father, if he was admitted – and I realised I was already thinking like this – would in any case have no choice of room. He would have to take whichever came up at the time. He would miss the view from his own living-room window horribly. There had not, to a less discerning eye than his own, been much to look at from it, but he had always seen a great deal during the hours he'd kept watch. Unlike the front windows of other houses and bungalows in his street, the window of his living-room was not shrouded in net or concealed by Venetian blinds. Nothing except glass came between him and his view. This was of his own front garden, where every blade of grass, never mind every plant and shrub, came under hourly inspection, and beyond that, across the road, a huge playing field between the backs of two rows of houses. This provided him with endless entertainment, watching children play there, and in November there was the bonfire to which he would drag over his own contributions.

But he saw more than the garden and the field. He saw such life as his street presented. Every inhabitant's routine was known to him and if it deviated from the norm this provided him with enjoyable speculation as to the reasons. No stranger could pass his window without arousing instant suspicion – he was a one-man Neighbourhood Watch. He knew every car, too, and if a car he could not account for appeared he took its number. One never knew. So this seemingly dull prospect from his window was, as far as he was concerned, crowded with action. To him, it was like watching a very quiet play without much plot and with no striking characters but a set full of subtle nuances which never failed to absorb him. The loss of this entertainment would be a blow made even harder to bear if it was to be replaced by virtual blankness. If only the place had not been built in a dip it would have had views on one side of hills and on another of a primary-school playground.

I didn't mention where I had been when I returned with

some shopping. My father was content to hear where I'd bought the fish and what the weather was like. The meal that day was simpler to prepare. I didn't have to tackle the oven, though I annoyed him by lighting the gas rings again with matches, because I couldn't get his so-called 'magic' wand to work. So it went on, for another day. By the time I did leave him, I'd had plenty of time to observe how unsteady he now was on his feet. Every movement was made by clinging on to the backs of chairs and then lunging for the next anchor. His bungalow was small and, of course, there were no stairs, but there were traps everywhere threatening his safe progress. We had quarrelled over the thick rug in front of the gas fire. Every time he went to put the fire on, or to regulate it, he stumbled over the edge of this rug. It simply had to be discarded, but he resisted any interference with it and it was so cruel to point out that if it stayed there he would surely fall again. He hated to think he would ever fall again. And it was more than that – this old, ordinary rug was part of his life, part of the comfort that his possessions gave him. Remove it and another little bit of himself, which he could ill spare, was taken away.

There were other traps but they were easier to deal with. Pauline had already coped with some of them. The telephone, for example. He'd always got up from his favourite armchair to answer it but she'd bought a small table to put beside his chair and altered the position of the telephone. It was now right next to him. She had failed, though, to persuade him to use his stick indoors as well as out. So did I. The stick was for outside and that was that. Well, he would surely trip without it and the only protection against the consequences of a resulting fall was the alarm system I'd set up some time ago. He wore the alarm button round his neck (or was supposed to) and if he fell someone monitoring the alarm would respond instantly and could speak to him while help was on the way.

It had already been tested before ever he went into hospital.

He'd fallen in his living-room and while he was lying on the floor, struggling to get up, a voice had said, 'I'm here, Arthur, don't you worry.' My father had been amazed, even though the system, and its workings, had been explained many times to him. 'No you aren't,' he'd replied, looking round the room, 'or I'm a Dutchman.' He was annoyed, not relieved or pleased, when someone duly arrived to help him up. 'Who gave you my key, eh?' he'd said. He hated strangers having his key. It was an infringement of his independence which he deeply resented.

But it made me feel a little better about leaving him. So long as he wore the alarm (doubtful), at least I didn't have to envisage him lying for hours with a broken leg. Otherwise, there was not much else I could do to protect him. His pantry was now well stocked (he absolutely would not have Meals on Wheels). His clothes and bedding and towels all clean, enough to see him through till Pauline came again. The Nixons would pop in, Johnny and Jeff would call, the daily telephone calls would go on. But as I set off to walk to the railway station and he stood at his window and waved, nothing had ever seemed more wicked than to leave him to fend for himself, even though that was what he wanted.

My father's life might not seem precious to me but his welfare was, so long as it continued. I wanted him to be as content and comfortable as it was possible for him to be. But if so, why was I not taking him to live with me? I never contemplated it. I didn't think up convincing excuses either, of the he-wouldn't-be-happy-away-from-Carlisle, or my-house-isn't-suitable variety. No; no excuses. I didn't want him, it was as brutal as that. I would do anything to avoid it. Only evidence of his ill-treatment would have forced me to such a step – then, I would have had to rescue him. But all my thinking was directed towards another solution, if he proved unable to manage any longer. I could try to set up a support system within his own home. His bungalow had two bedrooms. One of them could possibly go to some kind of companion. But would he tolerate this? And would anyone be able to tolerate him? We'd operated such a system in London for my mother-in-law, but it had only worked, when it did, fitfully, because we lived in the same street and could supervise, and Marion had actually lived in the same house, in another flat, as her mother.

It was what I should have done, but I hadn't. I left him, knowing my frail father would be lucky to go on managing until we arrived in May when I would be near enough to look after him if he collapsed again.

How long was this going to continue?

When I returned from visiting my father, Marion was making wonderful progress. It was thrilling to see how well she had recovered from the radiotherapy, how completely she seemed restored to life. But eating went on being something that had to be done with determination, with soft foods still her staple diet, and she could taste very little. It became a challenge cooking for her. Could any taste get through to her? Coriander did. Soup so heavily laced with the strong herb that nobody else could bear to eat it delighted her – more than anything, she wanted to be able to enjoy food again.

I don't know why it surprised me so much to realise how important food was to her. Hadn't she always been the most enthusiastic eater of anything I'd cooked for her? And whenever she'd returned from holidays abroad it wasn't the scenery or the weather she'd described first, it was the food, especially if she'd been to Greece. She loved Greek food and would rave about an especially rich moussaka or particularly tasty stuffed vine leaves. But in spite of this I hadn't appreciated that food, and shopping for food, constituted one of her chief pleasures after smoking. Now when the thought struck her that she might never be able to enjoy roast potatoes again, she could become upset – with so few of her saliva glands working, the consistency of potatoes was hard for her to masticate and her taste buds didn't react to them. I couldn't credit that out of all her misfortunes the inability to relish roast potatoes counted as a tragedy – it just seemed ludicrous and I could hardly take this lament seriously. But it wasn't ludicrous. Food mattered. Of the lesser pleasures in life, in a list of all the things that made it worth fighting for, food was very important. She could do without reading, without walking, without driving, without travelling, if she had to, but she dreaded having to do without the pleasure of food and wine.

But, eating apart, everything was going well. None of us held our breath in quite the same way and we dared to speculate that Marion after all had a long life yet in front of her.

# IV

THE DAY AFTER I returned to London my father fell yet again. That was it. Pauline went up immediately, but this awful version of leapfrog couldn't go on, we'd agreed. My father had tried so valiantly to go back to living on his own after being in hospital, and he had failed. But would he acknowledge that he had? Pauline had the dreadful task of trying to find out. As gently as possible she talked to him, and to everything she said he replied as he had done before, but this time with more emphasis, 'Put me on a cliff and push me over.' Meanwhile, before any decision was made, he had to go back into hospital, where they were going to investigate to see if he had coeliac disease which would explain his diarrhoea and the weakness which had led to the latest fall.

This time he wasn't in Ward 20. He was in Ward 16, a general geriatric ward arranged on the old layout of long rows of beds – no cosy little cubicle for him to make his own. He reacted badly to the lack of privacy and to the absence of the kind of interested attention he'd enjoyed before. Depression set in quickly in spite of Pauline's devoted attendance and Gordon's visit. 'Get me out of here,' he began begging, and after ten days the hospital authorities began to say much the same thing. There was nothing they could treat him for. The presence of coeliac disease was not proven, but the gluten-free diet he'd been put on had cured the diarrhoea and resulted in some weight gain. His blood pressure and heart sounds were normal. They needed the bed for someone who had treatable symptoms. But where was he going to go? Not back to his bungalow. I hadn't set up the wonderful support system I'd envisaged, with a live-in carer. He would have to go into a home, into the home Pauline and I had inspected.

How very naïve of us to think it would be as simple as that. While my father became more and more disorientated, a nightmare sequence of negotiations began, with social workers, with the matron of the home, with the hospital. Money featured heavily. We were warned, when we were already well advanced in our arrangements with the home, that if we took my father there without the agreement of the local authority in charge of such decisions, he might not be funded. He had no money of his own, which we had thought meant he was the responsibility of the welfare state, but it seemed the choice of home was not his alone (or rather ours, because he was past choosing). And that is what happened: the local authority chose another type of home for him. A residential home was perfectly suitable, they said, and he didn't qualify for the nursing-home we'd chosen. Fine, I said, I'll pay the difference. No, they said, you must pay it all if he goes there. In a rage, I said I'd take this to arbitration. I hated doing this, especially since I could afford to pay for him and was willing, but my brother and sister objected strongly to my doing this – *they* could not afford to contribute, but more important to them was the fact that my father was fully entitled to be cared for by the State, from whom he had taken so little.

Pauline patiently explained to my father, in one of his increasingly rare lucid moments, that he was going to convalesce in a very pleasant nursing-home. She showed him a brochure and he said he'd give it a go, he just wanted out of hospital, she could take him now. But she couldn't. I had been on the telephone for hours every day trying to organise his transfer, but what I hadn't realised was that the vacancy there had been filled in the meantime and that in any case my father had first to be assessed as suitable. There followed a terrible day when the matron visited my father in Ward 16 and found him so confused she wondered if senile dementia had set in. If so, he'd have to go to the Alzheimer's wing of the home, and that wing was full, with a long waiting list. Desperately, I pleaded the effects of hospitalisation as the reason for my father's apparent confusion, assuring the matron that once he was in a different environment he would be back to his sharp self. Pauline and I both stressed that there had been no sign whatsoever of dementia up to now and so, doubtfully, the matron agreed to give him a trial when there was a vacant room . . . which at the moment there was not.

Marion, who was staying with us again for a weekend, guided me through how to handle this. As a social worker herself, she was well acquainted with the rules and regulations governing the financing of care for old people like my father who had no money of their own. With her help I set about going to arbitration (and, after many months and an appearance before a tribunal, won my case). And meanwhile a person in the home we had selected died, and on 22 February my father was moved into it by Pauline and her husband. They had first furnished and decorated this room with such skill and attention to detail that it was almost a replica of his living-room, minus the fire. His precious bureau was there, in prime position facing the armchair. It was only a cheap article, made of a wood little better than plywood which had been varnished to look like something superior, but it held all kinds of memorabilia my father valued and loved looking through on wet afternoons – a great mess of photographs and postcards and bills and certificates, and any letters he had failed to tear up and throw away (mine arrived every week on Tuesdays and were torn up on Wednesday unless they somehow escaped this rigorous tidying up). He invested this humble, unlovely bit of furniture with some status and had always polished and dusted it enthusiastically. But none the less it was now patchy and faded-looking, the little brass handles dulled and forlorn. Once my mother had cleaned them with a toothbrush dipped in Brasso and rubbed them till they shone.

On the walls of his new room were all the pictures he valued most, though not always for their artistic merit. There was an oil painting of a village in the Lake District which I'd given my mother years ago and which had always hung over the fire (slowly melting the paint); a print of a Gainsborough beauty (my mother had admired the real portrait in Kenwood House and the print was a birthday present); a watercolour of a road leading to the sea (place unknown, but the painting had been bought on a rare holiday my parents had taken); an oil painting of our house in Loweswater, and another of my father himself. The family photographs, a grand total of thirty-one, were all fitted into the remaining wall space or decorated the long window-sill, the top of the bureau, and every other available surface. What a show of deep family solidarity it was — weddings, christenings, degree ceremonies, the lot. There was his own television, given to him by Gordon and much bigger than the ones the home supplied, and there were two mirrors and several jugs and vases for flowers. There were flowers already in them, early tulips and daffodils. 'Good,' he said, as Pauline took him in: 'flowers. From Margaret, likely. Where's the letter?' It was a Tuesday, so there had to be a letter. Moment of panic, but then it was found, resting on the pillow.

So there he was. In a Home. It had happened. He hadn't just popped off. He was ninety-four years and two months old and he hadn't popped off in time to escape a fate he had never thought would be his. He hadn't been pushed over a cliff either. He was alive, but dependent on others. Did this mean, was it going to mean, that life was not therefore worth living? Would he metaphorically turn his face to the wall and give up? Of course not. He set himself to adapt, to carry on the long tradition of managing, and he did it so successfully that the matron, who had judged he might be senile, was astounded. 'He's marvellous,' she confessed at the end of the first week. 'He just gets on with it, and the men don't usually – they moan and groan and don't settle like the women do.'

He had imposed his own routine at once. Not being able to find an immersion heater to switch on first thing for his hot water had puzzled him, but when he discovered that hot water came out of the tap all day anyway, he was content. He shaved himself, no bother, dismissing all offers of help scornfully. Not then being able to find a kitchen and his frying pan was far more of a worry, but once he'd been directed to the dining-room and given his first breakfast, his anxiety vanished. What a feast was laid before him – not just bacon, but fried egg and sausage and fried bread and as much toast and butter as he could eat. He had to admit it beat his own breakfast. He had to admit it beat Ward 20's. The only drawback was having to eat it in the company of those he referred to with chilling accuracy as 'slaverers'. He maintained he was surrounded by them, folk who couldn't speak or eat properly, folk with spittle drooling out of their mouths: slaverers. But he wasn't going to let them ruin such a magnificent breakfast. He just kept his eyes on his full plate and ignored them.

Breakfast over, he walked back to his room, quite pleased with the exercise. It was foul weather that first week, raining heavily outside, and he knew that if he'd been in his own bungalow he would have been a prisoner, unable to walk anywhere or see anyone. The walk to and from the dining-room interested him, though he was careful not to betray this. He had to go through the main entrance hall and there was always something going on – visitors arriving and departing, people delivering things, a bit of life in general, a feeling of being at the hub of something. Then there were the offices to peer into. The matron (or home manager as some called her) had one office, the secretary another. The doors of both were almost always wide open. My father could see the matron sitting at her desk, usually on the telephone. She was quite young and wore ordinary clothes, which he didn't quite approve of (any kind of matron should be in uniform), but she was cheerful and pleasant and always acknowledged him with a wave, which actually made him move on as quickly as he could – he liked to think he was invisible. It was a nuisance that on the next stretch back to his room there were often two or three of those damned wheelchairs in the way, but a hard push was enough to send them flying satisfactorily in the opposite direction to which he was going. If someone was in them, of course, this tactic was no good and he had to brace himself to pass them. The old folk sitting helpless in these wheelchairs looked pathetic – he hated the sight of them and was never going to be coaxed into joining them in the communal sitting-room. He'd rather be dead. Every time he passed this room he averted his eyes. The place and its occupants made him shudder.

But he was intrigued by the nurses' desk, and behind it their small staff-room, opposite the sitting-room. He liked to pause here, before the last corridor to his own room. This was where the nurses and carers reported to, where they answered the telephone, and where they were given their briefings at each change of shift. He was curious as to how everything was organised and liked to listen, if he could, to instructions being given. He wanted to know why some of the women wore blue uniforms and some pale green, and who was superior to whom. He slowly took in the differences (blue was for qualified nurses, green for carers with NVQ certificates) and learned names. Every hand was duly inspected for rings, every head of hair for signs of being dyed, every face for the presence of spots (and every spot was a barnacle), every body for being over- or under-weight, every ear for rings and piercing. It was sport, of a kind.

Back in his room after all this stimulation he was admittedly at a bit of a loss, but then he acknowledged he had been for some time now in his own home, ever since he'd had to give up the daily routine of going shopping to Denton Holme. He'd been restless, mid-morning, for a couple of years, but then he'd usually managed to think up some job in the garage. Here there was no garage. Worse still, his tools were missing. This shocked him. Where were his tools? He demanded them loudly; he wanted his screwdriver in particular, to fix a loose catch on his window. If he didn't have his tools, how could he see to anything that needed to be mended? He had made them himself when he was an apprentice, and they were of excellent workmanship and durability. The most complex of them was a vice, very finely finished and inscribed with his name. Then there were his chisels, his thread gauge, callipers for measuring circular objects, and the screwdriver he wanted so badly. These tools, which he'd had for eighty years and used constantly, all had his initials or full surname engraved on them. What he'd forgotten is that he'd given them to Pauline's husband, who he knew would use and treasure them. David was a skilled handyman himself (though not a professional) and when he'd admired these tools my father had said he could have them, because he didn't suppose he would need them where he was going. But now he did need them, and on bad days there was the faintest suggestion he'd been tricked into going into a place where his garage and his kitchen had been stolen from him. He also complained that he had been promised he would be surrounded by children. Nobody of course had promised this, but the brochure Pauline had shown him had a photograph on the front of an old man in the home being visited by grandchildren, and my father regarded that as a guarantee.

There was nothing to do but sit in his chair and read the *Daily Express*, or the *Cumberland News*, and mark any horses he could bet on. But that was another problem: how could he put bets on, stuck in this place? We'd anticipated this and when we'd had a telephone installed by his bedside, we suggested he could do it by phone. We'd make an arrangement with a bookie of his choice. He was offended at the very idea. His betting was private. It was between him and the bookie, or whoever was behind the glass partition in the betting shop. He said he would manage. Maybe he did. Maybe he co-opted one of the nurses or carers or a visitor into putting bets on for him, but if so no one confessed. The deviousness of this, if it happened, would appeal to him – the swearing to secrecy, the whispered instructions, the furtive giving of money. He had to have some excitement to make life worth living.

There was none outside his window. No trees, no shrubs. He looked across to the dining-room and soon had worked out the significance of various movements within it which indicated that lunch or tea was about to start, and this gave him some satisfaction, but otherwise there was nothing doing. He lamented the absence of birds, which was one thing at least we could rectify. A bird table was put in front of his window and nuts and grain bought, and now he had a little entertainment. He counted and identified all the birds that came and sent the staff (whom he had a bad habit of calling 'the servants') out to spread more food and refill the water container. They were not allowed to do it on their own initiative – they went only when he sent them and had to do precisely what they were told. All phone calls to us now began with descriptions of bird life and what a blessing that was.

Lunch, the main meal of the day, came before he was the least bit ready for it. He went obediently enough at first to the dining-room to eat it but didn't enjoy it. There was too much food, all delicious, but after his big breakfast he had no appetite. He was glad to get back to his room, where he promptly fell asleep in his chair. When he woke up, the rest of the day wasn't too bad. Nurses and carers came in and out, bringing freshly laundered clothes and taking away dirty ones, bringing his medicines, and so on. Their standards amazed him – 'One spot of gravy on my shirt and they bloomin' have it off me.' He protested this was ridiculous but nevertheless he was impressed and he liked always being spotlessly clean.

His room was equally pristine. Every day the carpet was hoovered, the surfaces wiped, the bathroom scrubbed. No dirt had a chance to take hold – 'There's not a speck of dust to dust away but they never stop.' Daft, all this excessive cleaning, but it gave him the opportunity to interrogate the cleaners. He talked to them all and luckily they were amused and even glad – not many of the patients engaged them in any kind of conversation, either because they could no longer speak, after strokes, or they were too ill and didn't have the energy, or simply because they had no interest in life any more. My father was becoming popular after the first week and his room a place where the staff chose to hang about and chat. And, of course, Pauline had made it attractive, his room, in contrast to many of the other rooms which lacked all his personal clutter.

The man next door to him had nothing decorative in his room. He had the furniture which the home provided and that was all. His walls were blank, his windowsill bare. He'd been put next to my father in the hope that the two of them would become friends and give each other some welcome companion-ship. They didn't know my father. Friends? What for? The whole concept of friendship had always been beyond him. He was deeply suspicious, even embarrassed, at the idea he should make a friend. At his age? When he was a young man, before he got married, he had sometimes knocked about in a gang, especially with other lads in the Boys' Brigade, but not often. He met men in the pubs, once he was working, and in the Working Men's Conservative Club later on, but they weren't *friends*, they were just people he acknowledged out of habit. That was as far as friendship needed to go, in his opinion. His wife had been his friend, the only one he ever needed, and when I was young I was a friend in the sense of being his chosen companion.

His neighbour, it seemed, had come in to my father's room to introduce himself, eager to initiate a friendship. My father was actually irritated – 'Fellow comes in here, says his name, and gives me this magazine about birds, says I might like to look at it, says it might help me identify birds on my table.' He snorted with derision at this point and repeated 'Identify the birds!' I asked what was wrong with that. 'What's wrong?' he roared. 'What's wrong? What's right, more like. I should hope I haven't got to ninety-four year old without needing a book to show me the difference between a bluetit and a robin. Identify the birds!' I didn't dare ask what he had said next to his unfortunate would-be friend, but he told me anyway. 'I sent him packing. "Thank you very much," I said, "but I can identify birds, no bother." And then, if he didn't go and leave his bloomin' magazine behind. Well, I'm not taking it back. It's his fault. He needn't think I'll come running. The servants can take it back.'

The staff, also treated to this impossibly perverse reaction, laughed. Like Marion, they found most outrageous things my father said funny. He was a character, awful but original. I went to see the man next door myself, taking the offending magazine, not to apologise for my father's behaviour – that would have been too ridiculous – but to chat and thank him. He was a kind, gentle man, a Bible open on his knee and a prayer book on the table beside him. Whereas my father had from the beginning kept his door wide open, this man kept his closed. I was told he rarely had visitors – since he had had no children and there were no surviving family members – and even more rarely went out. But he was apparently quite content and the staff were fond of him even though he lacked the amusement value of my father. There were two other men in the home then (against sixteen women) but they, alas, came into the cruel category of slaverers and no attempt was made to make friends of them either by my father or his neighbour. Apparently they had tried to talk to my father at meals but he had told them straight out that he couldn't understand a word they said – 'Sorry, lads, but you've lost me.' When they persisted in trying to communicate he had pretended he was deaf, pointing to his ears and shaking his head in a parody of deafness. So the staff quickly gave up hopes of introducing him to the hitherto unsampled delights of male bonding. He had made it horribly obvious he had no interest in any other patient.

Yet this was not quite true. He discovered that an old neighbour of his, a young woman at the time she had lived opposite him in the 1940s, was also in this home and his curiosity was greater than his desire to keep himself to himself. He just wanted to look at her, as he put it, partly because he couldn't credit that someone more than thirty years younger was actually in the same predicament as himself. He had to have it proved, and so he got one of the nurses to take him along to this patient's room, to show him where it was. 'Come and get me in five minutes, mind,' he instructed her. 'That'll be long enough. Don't forget: five minutes, then you come and say I'm wanted, doesn't matter for what.' When the nurse dutifully collected him, he was clearly shaken by the state he'd found the younger woman in. She'd had a massive stroke which had left her paralysed down one side and with only parrot-fashion speech. 'It was no good talking to her,' my father later told me on the telephone. 'She couldn't say a bloomin' word back. She just nodded. They should have told me. They shouldn't have let me in for that. Bad. It was a shock.' I listened, sensing that the shock had been deeper than he made plain. 'She's had it,' he went on; 'no point in her carrying on, like that.' I said I supposed she had no choice. There was a moment's silence, a grunt. 'Pity,' he said, then: 'I won't go and see her again. She never came to see your Mam all the years she was ill, anyway – never came near.' 'So this is tit for tat, is it?' I said sarcastically. 'You're quits now?'

He ignored my tone. 'No point going, any road,' he said, 'if she can't talk proper. No point going to see her.' 'She can still hear,' I said. '*You* could talk to *her*, tell her things.' He didn't bother replying to such an absurd suggestion, and then one of the carers he was especially fond of came back on duty and he turned his attention to her. 'What have you been doing with yourself?' I heard him say. 'Your face is all red, you look like a beetroot.' I heard her laugh in the background, and then he laughed at his own joke, though it was difficult to appreciate what it was.

I knew this particular carer from my flying visits. She wasn't his absolute favourite, but she was one of the three he liked because they were young and lively. This one, so delighted to be told her face was like a beetroot, was only eighteen, earning £3.20 an hour for work which included cleaning up incontinent old people and feeding those who brought their food back up with more regularity than a baby. She lived in a village out on the Solway marsh and got a lift into work and a bus back, or the other way round, according to her shift. She was pretty and cheerful, always cheerful. It baffled me, this permanent cheerfulness. I thought how, in her situation, with no qualifications that could get her a better job, even if one had been available (which it probably was not in the current climate), I would rather have worked in a factory or a shop. The work there might be grindingly boring and equally low paid but at least I wouldn't be surrounded by dying old people. How did she and all the others stand the sheer depression and misery of it? It wasn't the sort of thing I could ask; not yet, not till I knew them all better.

On the second visit I made in March to see my father in the home there was the final clearing out of his bungalow to do before it was sold. Pauline had done all the hard work, disposing of the furniture except for a bed in the back bedroom where I slept. The living-room and the front bedroom were completely empty, suddenly looking twice as big, if twice as shabby. I hated being there. All the memories of the strained visits over the last thirty years oppressed me. They were all, except for the first five years, visits connected with illness of some sort, my mother's and then my father's. We'd bought them this modest little bungalow in 1967 when they were sixty-six and sixty-seven respectively and still fit and healthy. Then the strokes and cataracts and arthritis, and God knows what else, had begun, and I had no happy recollections of them here. Yet seeing their last home stripped and abandoned like this made it seem strangely precious all of a sudden – everywhere there were still reminders of how it had been cherished, the walls so regularly painted, the carpets renewed and the garden kept immaculate. The garden . . . It was unbearable to stand by the kitchen window looking at the lilac trees just beginning to bud, and at the ground neatly dug over at the end of last year and now waiting for my father's planting of potatoes and onions. All that care. All that work.

I was glad when it grew dark, and for once I pulled the curtains together as early as my father used to do. But that only made the suffocating feeling grow worse. The place was almost empty, but it felt as claustrophobic as ever. Listlessly, I wandered from small room to small room, drenched in the pathos of it all. Everything in these rooms – utility furniture, mostly – had been beautifully looked after but was worth virtually nothing. Awful saggy beds, sad worn armchairs with the fabric of the arms darned and patched. Not one item of value – except to them.

Out in the garage there was still his work bench and gardening tools and my mother's mangle. The garage had been his empire. My mother had rarely gone into it. There was an old sideboard there, bought for their council house when they married in 1931 and too big to go into the bungalow. It had held all my father's paraphernalia for serious maintenance work

– nails, hammers, saws, wire, screws, bolts, washers – all kept in little tin boxes, everything in its place and that place known only to him. It was always cold there, but he'd never minded, and rather dark because he relied for light on a small window, never opening the main up-and-over door. He whistled a lot in his garage, tunelessly as ever, but this was a dependable indication of his contented state of mind. Nearly always, even in these last difficult years, he had found something to do there, even if it was just shifting things about. He'd take pan lids and screw the knobs on tighter, or a curtain rail which was sticking and needed to be greased, and there were always the soles of his shoes to attend to. He had a cobbler's last and liked trying to mend shoes. What he'd enjoyed best was hammering metal studs called skegs all round the edge of the leather soles. These made a terrible noise when he walked, but he found the ringing of metal on the pavement reassuring.

Going into the garage was hard. There wasn't much there, apart from the sideboard and mangle. A box of his onions on the ground, half a sack of potatoes beside it. Two tea-towels pegged onto a little washing line he'd rigged up inside. The concrete floor was swept clean. There was no mess anywhere. Everything in and out of the bungalow, rooms and garage and garden, all so neat and tidy, everything so organised, no sign of neglect throughout. Life, for my parents had been *about* being orderly, never slacking, never letting things slide. There had been such pride in this.

I locked the door and returned to the kitchen to apply myself to the last sorting-out. I had put a large cardboard box on the floor labelled 'To keep', another beside it marked 'Jumble'. Going through the drawers and cupboards, the jumble box was filled in minutes – with dusters, tea-towels, aprons, shopping bags. I couldn't stand the sight of them, conjuring up, as they did, years and years of cleaning and shopping. The 'To keep' box remained empty. What did I want to take of all this?

Nothing. And yet there was the impulse to save something, and so I took a mixing bowl and some kitchen knives, and some pegs. Hardly anything. The remnants of my mother's wedding china had already been taken to Loweswater and so had anything else of sentimental value. I went to bed shuddering, though I wasn't quite sure what with. Revulsion? Depression? More like despair: despair that two long lives, one still going on, could leave so little behind in the material sense and yet so strong a presence.

I couldn't wait to get through the last night and escape for ever. This place needed to be claimed by some other spirit as quickly as possible and to vanish from my mind. I should have been doing this final clearing out when my father was dead. It didn't seem right to be doing it while he was still alive. But how alive was he? Leaving his own home, giving up his most precious independence, was a kind of death.

Not, though, the real death, just the awful beginning of it.

# V

IN MAY, MARION'S partner Frances went to Australia for a desperately needed holiday. Marion wanted her to go. She urged her to go, saying it made her feel less like an invalid, more as if she was getting back to normal, which she showed every sign of doing. She had put on weight, regained some energy, and was even contemplating a return to work in a little while. So Frances went and Marion came to live with us – she wasn't quite strong enough to feel she wanted to be alone, and besides she knew Frances would worry less and be happier about going if she came to us.

I loved looking after her. I liked taking her breakfast in bed (though her breakfast was a meagre affair since she still had such difficulty swallowing), I liked laying trays and putting jugs of flowers on them and all that kind of fussing, and it amused Marion. Taking the morning tray in, I never asked her how she felt. It was a dangerous question, one I well knew she found impossible to answer. How she felt was full of contradictions. She felt fine, but awful; she felt lively, but listless; she felt cheerful, but afraid. But it made little difference how she felt because she knew feelings were not necessarily of any significance. She had no doubt that whatever was going to happen would happen without her being able to control her fate. Like my father, she knew only how to accept, and to go on to the best of her ability. They were two very different people, of very different ages, in very different situations, and yet they had exactly the same attitude as they faced the prospect of death:

press on, keep trying, don't waste time wondering what is going to happen, and how, and when, because nobody can tell you. Don't moan, don't wince, don't beg for pity or sympathy, don't loll around weeping, and don't make others suffer because you are suffering.

But Marion did volunteer, at the end of her first week with us, that she felt quite hopeful that she was actually, and against all her own expectations, truly getting better. In fact, so much so that she decided to go on a little holiday of her own, to Carlisle, to stay with Jeff, and see her younger brother Johnny, and her good friends Dorothy and Dusty. She went by train (put on to it by me as though she were a six-year-old – I actually wanted to put her in charge of the guard) and enjoyed it. She and Jeff took drives to the coast and into the country, and she came back delighted with her own daring. Frances, returning from Australia, herself rested and refreshed, could scarcely credit the difference in her when she met her at the airport.

Leaving Marion when the time came for us to go to Loweswater for the summer was easy after all.

Once we arrived there, a new summer pattern had to emerge. My father had no complaints about the nursing-home, but he liked to get out of it more than he had ever needed to get out of his own home. Then, our outings with him had been about pleasure, entertainment, diversion; now, they were about something much more important: they were about preserving his identity. The expression on his face (a face usually devoid of expression) when we entered his room on each visit was strange. He was startled, disbelieving. Yet he always knew exactly when we were coming, to the very minute, because we pandered to his passion for precision by always writing down on his calendar the date and time of our next visit and by telling the staff for good measure. But, nevertheless, when he saw us he betrayed surprise and then massive relief. 'You've come!' he'd say, and I'd say of course we'd come, we'd said we'd come. Then he'd struggle to his feet, suddenly excited and in a hurry – 'Good. Let's get going then, sharpish.'

Sharpish it wasn't, though he tried hard. It was a slow and rather royal progress through the corridors. He had to use his stick all the time now, but refused to hold on with his other hand to the rails that ran helpfully along the walls. Sometimes the staff had draped small items to dry over these rails and he took pleasure in stopping to unhook them, saying, 'Dangerous'. Any danger was only in his own head, but we didn't bother querying this judgement. Passing the bathroom (the individual rooms had only basins and lavatories), he liked to stop and point – 'That's the bath. Grand bath. They dip me in, then I steep.' He said this approvingly, wanting us to be impressed. Any inhibitions he'd tried to cling on to about young women seeing him naked had obviously long since gone, though he did remark, 'They do everything for me, mind, everything, and them just young lasses, most of them, and not married either' – and then he shook his head, but more in apparent amazement than horror. He loved having proper baths again and would have been prepared to put up with any indignity to have them. In his own home, he'd stopped being able to get in and out of his own bath years ago and had been deeply dissatisfied with the all-over washes he gave himself at the sink. Getting into this bath was no problem – 'See that pulley? See them ropes? See that thing, that cradle thing? In I go, over I swing, in I'm dipped, and then I steep. Champion.'

We would pass the nurses' desk at exactly 2.30 p.m. when shifts were being changed, and one of the going-off nurses would call out cheerfully, 'Going out, Arthur?' He'd stop and glare and say, 'What does it look like? Why have I got my hat and coat on, eh?' Used to him by now, the nurses would laugh and then one would say, 'Going anywhere nice? Can I come?' My father would say no, she could not, that he'd had enough of her for one day and she could get herself home without wasting time chattering. He was always pleased with himself for this banter, and we'd proceed on our way again with him whistling.

Whistling would change to swearing when we reached the front door. 'Damned doors, damned stupid; they want seeing to.' They were double doors, one opening in, one opening out, and difficult to co-ordinate, entering or leaving. As I held them open for him my father banged his stick vigorously against each door to indicate his disapproval in case it had failed to register. But once in our car he was all contentment, sinking into the comfortable front seat with a great sigh of pleasure, and grunting with satisfaction when the engine leapt into life.

Where we went on our drives was no longer of such importance. He didn't try to get us to go to the Keilder dam or make tours of the lakes, for which we were grateful. Now all he wanted was to be out of the home and he didn't care where we went. So we did short journeys, of not more than twenty miles there and back, and sometimes on days of poor weather half that distance. If we went further, if we took him to his beloved Silloth, he fell asleep on the way back or, far worse for him, lost control of his bladder. This appalled him and it was no use assuring him it didn't appal us. His dignity had to be preserved and every strategy employed to make sure he survived each outing safely. 'Not too far,' he'd say, 'not for too long, or else.' No need to say more.

We went to the Solway Marsh most often that glorious summer of 1995. The nursing-home was right on the boundary of west Carlisle and, leaving it, we had only a corner to turn before we were on the road to the marsh villages and out into the real countryside. Every inch of that road was precious to my father and familiar to me. Here, he'd taken me on the crossbar of his bike to pick brambles in the fields and hedges where he'd picked them with his own father; here, he'd marched with the

Boys' Brigade on their summer outings; here, he'd seen a man rush out of the pub in 1914 shouting that war had been declared. Every mile of the way to Burgh-by-Sands and Port Carlisle and Bowness-on-Solway, the isolated and utterly tranquil villages strung out on the flat marsh road, was full of memories, all of them important to him.

We usually parked at Glasson Point, almost at Port Carlisle, the place where we often used to picnic and paddle. There were no picnics now. There was no point in having a picnic. He didn't want food or drink of any kind. He was still too full after his excellent breakfast. And he was reluctant ever to get out of the car – the struggle to do so was tremendous and exhausted him, so he preferred to stay in the parked car, looking towards the sea. He had his binoculars with him and scanned the horizon intently as though looking for enemy planes. Whether the tide was coming in or going out was of prime concern, but once that had been established he was content just to sit and look. What he looked at was the marsh itself, empty except for the odd bird, and then the sea, calm and grey here, and beyond it the Scottish hills with a vast expanse of sky over them. Peace and silence. It was a place highly conducive to reflection and contemplation, but whatever was going on in my father's mind remained there. He said nothing. I said nothing. Hunter got out and walked along the edge of the sea and then came back, and eventually we went home.

But home was not home, it was the nursing-home. Returning to it made me tense. Sometimes, my father would say, as we turned into the road where the home was, 'Where are we going now?' He'd ask in a tone of genuine bewilderment, and when I said we were going home, to his nursing-home, he'd make a noise of irritation at his own forgetfulness, berating himself for being daft. The moment passed. There were no sighs or moans. He knew his bungalow had been sold, his real home broken up, his boats burned. But he never made us feel dreadful for selling it, for doing this to him. There were no resentful remarks, no accusations, no recriminations. He accepted what had happened without reproach.

The next awful moment was the actual point of re-entry into the home, when we took him to his room and helped him off with his coat and went to get him a cup of tea. He was always so grateful, so full of thanks – 'Thank you now, thank you very much, thanks for everything.' And what did this 'everything' amount to? Very little: a matter of a drive to a pleasant place for an hour or so.

All summer we made these outings, twice a week, in the set pattern he preferred. His calendar was enthusiastically filled in even if the handwriting was faint and wavering – 'Good day. Run to Burgh' . . . 'Smashing day. Sun. At Bowness.' He was in good spirits, doing well, walking well, sleeping well. Life was worth living, however reduced in quality. Moving into the home had not been all loss after all. At the age of ninety-four, an unsociable man had discovered he could, if put into the right situation, be sociable. The staff spoke to him and he found it easy and even pleasant to speak back to them. He liked the company and appeared to thrive on it. His room had become a place the carers liked to linger in and the matron had begun to issue tactful reminders that Arthur was not the only patient, that there were others who would appreciate some attention. And my father hadn't just gained through having people to talk to – he'd gained better health too. So many minor problems had been sorted out and he felt the benefit. His diet was better, his feet more comfortable; his eyes (which had easily become infected) were clearer and his mouth less sore. Careful hygiene alone had partially rehabilitated him. For his age, he was in remarkably good shape once more.

This had been recognised by the doctors who had treated him at the infirmary and still visited him. They asked him if he'd be part of a research project, explaining that it was rare to find a man of his age in such relatively good condition physically and excellent condition mentally. They wanted him to come to a special clinic once a month and be examined and asked questions and weighed. My father was rather impressed by this emphasis on his own importance and had graciously agreed to attend the clinic. But he only went twice and then said he was being made a monkey of and wouldn't go again. This heinous offence, this making a monkey out of him, consisted of making him sit 'with a lot of old folk in wheelchairs' and of asking him questions he considered 'daft'. He'd imagined he would be treated as someone special and he wasn't. So he announced he was putting a stop to 'that palaver'. They'd had their chance. They'd mucked it up. If they tried to force him to continue to attend this clinic he would refuse point-blank. I was to be on stand-by to speak to the doctor in charge and tell him what's what. Rather to my father's disappointment, I was not called upon to do so. No attempt was made to persuade him.

He was in fine fettle by July. Clearly, he was still nowhere near popping off. Clearly, his life still had value and meaning for him.

I forget the exact date of the most distressing phone call I have ever received. It should be impossible to forget, but I have forgotten. All I can remember is that it was about a week before Marion's fifty-sixth birthday on 16 July. She'd been having more trouble than usual swallowing and some new lumps had appeared in her neck. First, she'd consulted the doctor at the hospice where she'd spent those three weeks during the radiotherapy treatment. He'd continued to be so good at soothing her fears and had always said she could come back at any time if she was worried. She had an excellent relationship with the hospice staff, whereas she had none at all with anyone at the hospital. But then the hospice referred her back to the hospital, suspecting there was a flare-up of the cancer, which would need treatment they might not be able to give.

The phone call was short and, of necessity, brutal. Frances could hardly speak, Marion did not want to try. The cancer was now terminal. There was no hope at all of curing it and very little of extending Marion's life beyond six months. Any treatment would be palliative, concentrating on relieving pain. The cruel surgery and the radiotherapy with its vicious after-effects had all been for nothing. Everyone was devastated. The telephone suddenly seemed an instrument of torture, used to induce suffering. This woeful news wasn't something that could be discussed or analysed – it just had to be absorbed. And then silence. Lots of phone calls consisting of one short sentence, then silence, until receivers were gently replaced.

We left for London at once, leaving everything just as it was, pausing only to ring my father's nursing-home to alert them to what had happened and then to ring him and repeat this. 'So you won't be in tomorrow,' he said. 'No,' I said, 'not for a few days.' 'But you'll be back?' 'Oh yes,' I assured him – after all, we would have to come back to pack up, if we decided to return to London for good instead of staying as usual to October. He cheered up at once. We set off on a roasting hot day. The whole of England seemed to be burning as feverishly as I felt I was. The hills either side of the M6 were brown with drought, the grass verges grey with dust. It was like driving through a foreign country, and when we reached London this impression grew. The city we crawled into had gone mad, abandoning any staidness it had ever had, any of its famous English reserve. The streets were crammed with people in shorts and beachwear, people wearing hardly anything at all, torsos slick with sweat, eyes blanked out with dark sunglasses. The pavements were crowded with tables and chairs, every café and restaurant spilling out onto them, and over the lot flourished great gaudy umbrellas with stripes and spots and abstract designs, all running into each other in a clash of furious colour. We drove through it all, hot and sticky and exhausted, in no state to visit a dying person, but we couldn't bear to waste time going to our own house first to shower and change clothes. We went directly to Marion's flat, in Crouch End, approaching it with eagerness but with dread. We were desperate to see her, but afraid of what we would see; we wanted simply to be with her, but knew there would be nothing simple about it.

The curtains were all closed tightly. Was this to keep out the sun, merely to shade the rooms? Ringing the doorbell felt like an act of violence. We heard it screech inside, though we had only pressed the button once, lightly. The waiting for it to be answered, for Frances to come and let us in, seemed endless and then, when she opened the door, not long enough. Foolishly, we whispered, asked how Marion was feeling. Frances shook her head, unable to speak. Everything was so quiet as we tiptoed up the stairs. Turning the bend, I saw that the sitting-room ahead was in virtual darkness, though it was mid-afternoon. Ahead, facing the open door, was a doll's-house. It was a lovely toy house, double-fronted, tall, with lights on in its windows. It glowed, and not just because it was lit up; it looked cheerful and welcoming. It was to be a present from Marion to her twin Annabel (who had always wanted a doll's-house as a child), for their joint birthday.

Marion was sitting in a wing armchair, her back to the doll's-house, facing the fireplace. She was absolutely still, her arms clutching rather than resting on the arms of the chair, her back ramrod straight. She looked as if she were in a trance and we hesitated to disturb her. It was awkward, trying to embrace her in an armchair, but we tried. She nodded, and said nothing as we made stumbling attempts at sympathy. She was far away, quite removed, yet rigid with self-control. There were no tears. Frances said Marion had been watching rugby on television. It was the summer of the Rugby Union World Cup and she had become engrossed in this competition, to everyone's surprise. Ever since the new lumps had appeared she had been watching the games and had her favourite players, most of them Australian. She hadn't the faintest understanding of the rules of the game, but as far as she was concerned these were irrelevant – numb with fear, it was the action she liked, the running and kicking and throwing, taking her away from her own frozen condition, immobile in her chair. The players were playing for her.

It was the following day before I was on my own with her. I was making the inevitable soup in the kitchen. She sat at the table, quite expressionless. I might as well have been with my father so far as any real communication went. Everything I found myself saying was banal and Marion didn't seem to want to say anything at all. Nothing could have been more different from how we usually were together. In the forty years we'd known each other talk had been the connection – talk, talk, talk, vying with each other, interrupting, ranging over every conceivable topic of personal interest. It hadn't all been chitchat either, not all of it that slip-slop of gossip said to be so beloved of women. A lot of this torrent of talk had been serious. Sometimes the content had been crucial to some decision one of us had to make, it had had far-reaching consequences. We often looked back afterwards and knew such talks had been precious and that without them things would have been different.

Once, staying in Marion's house in Carlisle on a visit to my sick mother, I was sitting feeding my youngest child, a baby of only three months, in the early hours of the morning, when Marion came into the room, bringing me a hot drink. She sat by the fire and watched me, the room dark except for a dim lamp. She'd always wanted children, but they hadn't arrived and here she was, aged thirty-three, watching me with my third. There was no bitterness about her childless state and certainly no resentment or jealousy. She loved my children without wanting them to be her own. But that day, as we sat in silence, except for the sucking sounds my baby made, and the splatter of the rain against the windows, Marion talked as she'd never talked about her own feelings of some lack in her life. Maybe it was lack of children, she didn't know, but she felt appalled at how little she seemed to have in her life. She felt she was wasting it; that life was not giving her any kind of fulfilment, but was just passing her by. She laughed as she went over her seventeen years of work as a clerk, most of it at Tyre Services, deriding the pointless tasks, so menial, that she carried out. She couldn't bear to think this was all she was ever going to do, this was her fate. I said she should leave Tyre Services and do something else, but she said it would only be jumping out of the frying pan and into the fire, just exchanging places of work but not the work, because she hadn't the qualifications for a better job – 'something else' was likely to be something the same for someone who'd left school at sixteen without taking O-levels.

It was the school's fault. I sat there blaming the school. Marion had gone to the Margaret Sewell School, the second tier in Carlisle's tripartite secondary-education system. Only the top percentage of girls who passed the eleven-plus examination went to the High School; the next lot went to the Margaret Sewell, which took pupils to O-level but not beyond, and the remainder to Secondary Moderns. From the beginning, Marion was not in the stream destined to take O-levels. She took shorthand and typing, at which she was never much good. No teacher spotted her potential, nor did anyone seem to care about her home circumstances, or make allowances for them. They didn't act as if they even knew (though they did) about her father being bedridden with multiple sclerosis, and her mother, often ill herself, struggling to manage and relying heavily on her twin daughters. When Marion and Annabel arrived at school late, without their dinner money or their PE kit, nobody ventured to wonder why; when Marion was difficult and cheeky, when she was found smoking, when she was inattentive in class, when she seemed to have no interest in lessons, reasons for all these things were never sought. Her mother wanted her, and all her children, to stay on at school and go on to Higher Education but, unsurprisingly, Marion could not wait to leave. She hated school. She was made to feel stupid and almost came to believe she was. And besides, her expectations were low. She believed that what a girl was destined to do was work for a few years then marry and have children. She had no ambition to make any other kind of life for herself.

But now, at thirty-three, she yearned to do just that, to make something else of her life. She was despairing of a future which held only more years at Tyre Services and of being a housewife. I was glad, listening to her, of the baby in my arms – attending to her gave me time to think, time to be careful about what I said. After a long pause, while we both sat staring into the fire, I asked what, in an ideal world, forgetting things like qualifications, she would like to do. She groaned, said there was no point thinking about that, the world wasn't ideal, but I urged her to play the game, to indulge me. She shrugged and smiled and said she supposed some sort of social work, helping families in situations such as her own had been, but without mothers able to hold things together. That, to her, seemed a worthwhile job. I said she'd be brilliant at it and she laughed and said, 'Fat chance!' I wished I knew exactly how anyone became a social worker, but I was at least sure the starting point would be O-levels. I hardly dared to suggest that Marion should leave work and somehow attempt to take a few O-levels. She'd been hopeless at school and she'd never done any kind of studying since. But I did suggest it and, though she said she didn't think she was capable, she didn't completely reject the idea.

A few months later, she startled everyone by leaving Tyre Services, with the backing of her husband Jeff, and enrolling at

Arthur Forster in his teens, serious and posed for a Carlisle photographer.

The roaring twenties – Arthur in his wilder days, on holiday on the Isle of Man.

Arthur with his wife Lilian, and friends.

At work (*right*) in the Metal Box
factory, Carlisle.

Arthur fishing at Silloth,
his weekend hobby.

Arthur, years later, holding forth on a picnic at Skinburness, 1983.

Twins, Marion and Annabel (5), with their brothers, Hunter (8) struggling with asthma, and Johnny (4).

Marion (*centre*) loved having her picture taken: in carefree times with Flora, Jake, Margaret and Hunter Davies.

Marion with her mother and niece Flora, Christmas 1983.

Arthur on one of his favourite outings to Silloth, Easter 1988,
with Margaret and his grandson Jake.

Marion, centre stage, with Flora, Hunter and Margaret Davies
(*Photo: Christopher Cormack*).

Arthur's 90th birthday, with Pauline, Margaret and Gordon,
and a copy of *The Times* from December 4th, 1900.

Marion (*left*) soon after she moved into her flat in Crouch End in 1987.

Marion (*centre*) with her mother and her niece Lindsey, Annabel's daughter.

Marion, 6 months
before she died.

Arthur, still looking strong
and determined at 91.

the local Technical College to do four O-levels. After a fairly agonising time learning to learn, she passed them and promptly went on to do A-levels, which she actually found easier. She was beginning to enjoy studying and was genuinely interested in the social sciences. Success in A-levels encouraged her to apply to do a two-year social-science course at Ruskin College, Oxford, and to everyone's delight (and astonishment) she was accepted. Life, after so long, had opened up dramatically, in ways other than educational too. Marion had married at the age of twenty-three. She loved and was attracted to Jeff, whom she married in good faith, never suspecting that her true sexual orientation was lesbian (though later she did realise there had been indications which she had failed to recognise). At Oxford, Marion was approached by a woman and surprised herself by having an affair with her. But she was still married to Jeff, and went on caring for him, if in a different way, and was deeply unhappy at the thought of breaking up her marriage and dis-tressing not only Jeff but her mother and the rest of her family. So after Oxford, the affair over, she went back to Carlisle, started work as a social worker, and tried to pretend everything was fine (though she had, of course, told Jeff what had hap-pened and lived with him now as a friend).

It was a miserable year. Her unhappiness grew and so did her frustration at all the pretence. She felt there was a cruel choice facing her: either she remained in Carlisle, playing the part of the good wife, stifling her newly realised sexual identity; or else she went to London, where she felt there was the best chance of giving expression to it, and in doing so hurt Jeff by exposing the reasons for her departure to family and friends. Finally, she decided life was too short and too precious not at least to try for self-fulfilment. She applied for, and got, a job in Camden, and we found a flat for her in our street.

I fear I may have influenced her to make that decision – 'fear' because by doing so I was causing such pain to Jeff. Without our finding a flat for her, and so reassuringly close to us, I doubt (and so did she) whether Marion would ever have managed to make the break. It took enough courage as it was for her to plunge into London life at the age of forty without her having to find the extra nerve to be entirely on her own. She told only her sister and brothers the real reason for leaving Carlisle and to everyone else, including her mother, said it was for career reasons. Since she had no intention of divorcing Jeff, and he had no intention of asking for a divorce, and since they remained so close, nobody questioned her explanation. People like my father may have remarked, 'A likely story!' privately, but nobody said anything to her.

The memory of my conversation with her, so long ago in the winter of 1973, which seemed to have started off such an unexpected chain of events, came back so strongly to me as I stood making soup in Marion's kitchen in almost total silence. Where was the talk now? The confidences? I wanted her to say something, anything, about what was in her head. I wanted to listen and respond. I wanted guidance from her. But maybe I should start the talking, confront the horror of this death sentence head on. I knew she despised those who were cowardly about facing up to tragedy. She'd always spoken with pitying contempt of those who shunned the dying. Someone in her office the year before had been diagnosed with Aids, and she'd scorned those afraid to touch him, making a point herself of a hug and kiss of sympathy. Perhaps, by docilely making soup, by not initiating talk myself, I was failing her. But how to begin? Where were the right words, the right phrases?

I sat directly opposite her while she tried to sip the wretched soup. Too hot? Too thick? Queries about soup, and she was dying. It was ridiculous. It was up to me to take the lead and say something of what I wanted to say. But what was that? What did I so badly want to say that she didn't already know? That I was sorry she was dying? For heaven's sake. It didn't help at all to be told the obvious — *sorry*, indeed. That I was sad, upset, distraught, furious? All about my feelings, and who wanted to know those? They were obvious, and irrelevant. I went on sitting there, while she went on slowly, slowly spooning soup into herself. I found myself blurting out in an attempt to start some real conversation that I imagined thinking about Annabel would be causing her the greatest anguish — her twin, to whom she was utterly devoted and who had such need of her. She nodded. I waited. 'I'll try a little more soup,' she said.

Had she disapproved of my clumsy attempt to get beyond pleasantries? I couldn't tell. There was just no real reaction. She gave the same impression of concentrating, of holding herself together, that had struck me the moment I saw her. Being on my own with her had made no difference. There was to be no talk. Talk was too tiring, too draining. She had Frances to talk to and that was enough. She had no desire to communicate with anyone else. As her life closed in, there was no room there for others. It was best to acknowledge this, and not demand any but the most peripheral place in her world. And besides, she was going back into hospital, for chemotherapy, as soon as they had a bed. The hospice had advised her to agree to this chemotherapy on the grounds that it could reduce pain and possibly extend her life, and its quality, a few more months.

So we went back to Loweswater until such time as Marion would be back home and we could be of some use in helping to look after her.

We were there another month. Every day I phoned Frances, every day the report seemed to be worse. Marion reacted badly to the chemotherapy, which gave her dreadful diarrhoea among other side-effects, and she hated the ward she was in. She had never, she told me later, seen such suffering and it almost unhinged her mind. For Frances, and for Annabel and Jeff, who also visited, it was terrible to witness her misery and discomfort and also her rage. The calm front she had presented previously, that air of control, cracked and she could hardly endure the treatment. When the first course of drugs failed to have any effect, she refused point-blank to have a second and third course even though she was told three courses were often necessary. She wanted to go home. She wanted to die at home. No life was precious enough to have to endure this.

So we made our preparations to return, which meant telling my father that instead of staying until the end of October we were going back to London at the beginning of September. It was like saying to him that Marion was more precious to me than he was – which was true, she was. But he expressed no resentment, made no more remarks about there being plenty of others to look after her, and he seemed affected at last, he seemed sad. 'Pity,' he said, but that was all. For our last outing, we took him not to the Solway Marsh or any of the other country places we'd been frequenting, but just round the city, round Carlisle. It was a slow trundling round the one-way system so that he could catch up on what was happening to the streets and buildings he'd lived among all his life. He'd always loathed the Civic Centre (but then everyone in Carlisle did) and relished bewailing everything that had been knocked down to make way for it, so we drove past it on our route through the roads where he'd once lived. He liked to stop outside the house where he'd been born (Sheffield Street) and where he'd lived till he married (Richardson Street) and where my mother had been living when he courted her (Bowman Street). Round and round we went while he peered at these houses, criticising the paintwork, exclaiming over new windows. 'Happy days,' he said, and I saw him trying to squint at the driving mirror to see if he could catch my expression. I knew he wanted me to challenge him, to scoff at the idea of his life in Sheffield or Richardson Street being happy. I knew he wanted me to remind him of how his father had beaten him, how he'd left school at thirteen and started work in Pratchitts (an engineering factory), how badly he'd been treated and how little he'd been paid . . . I refrained. If he wanted to describe these as 'happy days', it was fine by me – and in contrast to his plight now, stuck in a nursing-home and very frail, waiting to pop off, then of course his previous life counted as happy.

We arrived by our chosen circuitous route outside the Metal Box factory in James Street, where he'd worked more than thirty years. The building was blackened, the windows high up and dirty. But he'd once told me he'd always been glad to enter this grim-looking place of work. He'd been the first, every day, to clock on. Work, employment, were so precious to him. It defined his life, and his greatest dread was the prospect of losing it. I'd made a mistake, when I was growing up, to think his work was just something he was forced to do to earn his living and support his family. I'd thought it was like slave labour. I was wrong. He may have had no academic qualifications but there was skill and satisfaction in what he did, which was to mend machines. I'd been in this factory only once and it had stunned me, this place of hellish noise where he spent his long days. Dirty work, and often dangerous – no wonder that when he arrived home on his bicycle he looked exhausted, his overalls smothered in oil and grease, his hands grimy and his face streaked with dirt. I'd always known I had a cheek to call anything that I did 'work'.

On the way back to the nursing-home we passed the end of the road leading to the street where he had last lived, but we didn't include it in our tour. He didn't want to go anywhere near the bungalow in which he'd spent almost thirty years (the longest time he'd lived in any house and from which, he'd always maintained, he would only leave feet first and in a box). He never mentioned his bungalow except to ask if it had been sold for a good price, and he was pleased that it had. After that, as far as he was concerned the place had disappeared from his mind – it had literally gone from his life and he didn't want to find that after all it was still there.

'I'll be seeing you sometime, then,' he said, when we made our difficult farewells, and in the next breath, 'When's Pauline coming? When's Gordon coming? Put it on the calendar.' I did this and said if he needed us he only had to lift the telephone and one of us would come. 'I wouldn't do that,' he said, scornfully. 'I'll manage.' Then there was the uncharacteristic but now usual litany of appreciation, for all we had supposedly done, echoing in our ears all the way down the corridor.

Then we were out of the home; we had left him again. Each time we couldn't help wondering if this might be the last time. When a man was nearly ninety-five and perfectly likely to 'pop off' any minute, every farewell might turn out to be the final one. One man had 'popped' the day before. My father had reported this with some relish. 'Fell into his dinner,' he told us. 'Pity.' We weren't sure if the pity was for the death or the ruined dinner. And the week before, another patient had attempted to do his own popping and had failed. My father loved the drama of it. The poor man had tried to cut his own throat – 'Daft,' my father said. 'Fancy using picture glass! He'd have been better with a razor.' He shook his head. 'Any road, made a damned mess. Not nice for them young lasses to clean up.' Quite. The staff had tried hard, naturally, to shield the other patients from this catastrophe, but they hadn't managed to hide it from my very alert father. 'I knew what was going on,' he said, nodding his head with satisfaction. 'All running up and down and yelling for this and that. Pandemonium, it was, and I got to the door before they could shut it. Oh what a mess, what a carry-on. What the hell did he try it for? Beats me.' I didn't dare suggest that this man had perhaps tried to take his own life because it didn't feel worth having any more – he was ninety, I knew he had just lost his wife, and he had Parkinson's disease. 'Anyway,' my father finished, 'he's learnt his lesson.'

*What was the lesson, Dad?* That's what I'd like to have asked, but I would only have got a withering glare in reply. The lesson, I had to imagine, was that in my father's opinion it was not up to you to pre-empt fate. When your number was up, it was up — that sort of homespun philosophy. Attempts at suicide were an impertinence. My father might hate all religion and have no faith of any kind, but he clearly still believed in some immutable law of life which laid down a natural progression towards death that was not to be tampered with. Everything was somehow ordered, though not by any God. By whom, then? He had no idea, and wasted no time pondering.

So far, he hadn't shifted this point of view.

# VI

THE CHANGE IN Marion was remarkable. She was no longer sitting rigid and controlled, in a world of her own, but was back, not to her old self, how could she be, but to being with us all again, present, not suspended in some shadow world nobody else inhabited. She was alert and talkative, willing to relate the horror of the failed chemotherapy treatment and the relief of leaving the ward where she'd felt no connection with anyone even though she knew she, too, was dying. Arriving home, she'd felt better immediately, but what had actually produced such an improvement in her condition was the steroids. The hospice had prescribed them, to boost her energy, and they had had a dramatic effect. Nothing could change the terminal nature of her illness, but these steroids changed the way she felt. She was able to get up and go for walks and have some kind of normal existence.

She seemed so cheerful it was almost eerie. This, she said, was because there was no hope left. She felt calm, now that the turmoil of hoping was over. Hope had evaporated, once the chemotherapy failed, and she hadn't been sorry in the end to see it go, because as long as it had been around, hovering teasingly in the air, she had been disturbed. She thought there was no sillier phrase than 'Never give up hope', as though hope in itself was something solid and trustworthy. Equally annoying to her was the insistence on *fighting* cancer – she wondered why cancer seemed to be the only disease referred to as one that was fought, one that was invariably described in terms of a battle.

She was sure she had indeed fought, that there had been nothing fatalistic and defeatist about her attitude, but she objected to the idea of being conquered. Still, the suspense was over. She'd hated this suspense, always wondering if it would be at this check-up or the next, or the one after when the bad news would be broken to her. She'd thought she would have a couple of years left, and was sure she'd been promised them when she agreed to the surgery and radiotherapy, or at least a good chance of having them, but all that was over now. She had felt shocked on being told nothing more could be done, but once the shock passed she felt less exhausted. It was the hope, the suspense, which had been hard to endure.

She had, then, no hope, and yet one afternoon she laughed and said, 'I don't believe it, of course. I don't believe I am going to die soon.' I must have looked worried because she instantly went on, 'I mean, I *do* believe it, I know it's the truth, but it's just that it seems impossible. I believe it, and I don't believe it. But that's got nothing to do with having hope. I really have no hope.' There was nothing desperate about her tone of voice, nothing distressing. It was interesting her, trying to work out how her feelings seemed so contradictory. How could she at one and the same time believe and yet not believe she was dying? She rejected the suggestion that this might be because on one level she was not accepting the verdict – no, she was quite sure that was not the case. She simply decided that as long as she was actually living, breathing and eating and talking and walking, the impossibility of 'ceasing to be' was a kind of tautology. It was, she came to consider, in the nature of being alive to be unable to imagine being dead.

All this came out when we talked, and now we talked again all the time. Easily. Freely. Each day, I went over to Crouch End to be with Marion while Frances tried to go to work for a short while. Sometimes I went in the morning, sometimes the afternoon, and usually for two or three hours. If it was the morning, our time was spent in the kitchen. It was a small room, rather cramped because of all the stuff in it – a gigantic fridge-freezer, a washing-machine, a cooker and a boiler. Not much room to move about, what with all this and a table and chairs. To me, it was claustrophobic, but Marion preferred sitting there to the lovely, spacious, sparsely furnished sitting-room at the front of the flat. She looked thoroughly uncomfortable, perched on an upright wooden chair near the window, jammed between table and freezer, but she pronounced herself content there and it was hard to shift her. It was still early September and the wonderful summer went on and on – the morning sun poured through the window and the box of plants on the sill had to be constantly watered. The view from this window was neither pretty nor interesting. It was of back gardens and yards, all small, many overgrown and neglected, and of washing hanging out to dry, and of walls and fences. No people, no traffic. At least it was peaceful.

But views didn't matter as much to Marion as to some people. This was just as well. She'd never lived in a house or flat with what could be called an interesting view from any window and had never expressed regret about this. The windows of the council house where she was brought up were small and at the front looked out onto the identical drab houses opposite, their concrete-rendered façades long since blackened and ugly, and at the back onto a neglected small garden. The Davies children tried not to see it at all, constantly averting their guilty eyes from the grass their mother urged them to cut and the flower beds she pleaded with them to weed. None of them had green fingers, least of all Marion. A garden, to her, wasn't even something to enjoy looking at – it was a place to sit in to catch any available sunshine. Yet a couple of years before her illness, when she was living in the ground-floor flat below this one, which she and Frances had now bought, she had suddenly started trying to make the garden attractive. There had been a great deal of rushing backwards and forwards to garden centres looking for bargains, and a lot of huffing and puffing as she dug-in various plants. A clematis she put against the fence flourished and she was thrilled. The next project was what she grandly referred to as 'my rockery'. To everyone else it looked like a hopelessly untidy heap of randomly placed stones set in mud.

In her Crouch End kitchen I busied myself cooking or tidying up, and Marion sat there and smoked. If she had only months left to live, and if she was going to be receiving no treatment which could be made harder to endure if she smoked, then she wanted to smoke. It was a pleasure she had missed most bitterly. She could hardly taste the cigarettes since her taste-buds had been virtually destroyed, but she still loved to smoke again. On the table were letters and cards which flooded in by every post and which she enjoyed opening and reading. Every message of sympathy and concern meant something to her. She appreciated these signs that people valued her, which surprised me, though I don't know why. She was also not averse to visitors, though they had to be very carefully chosen. She said she only wanted what she mockingly called her 'loved ones' around her, but this inner circle could sometimes be breached. Arrangements were made if she gave the nod. Frances or I would be detailed to ring chosen visitors, and these privileged few would arrive bearing what they hoped were appropriate gifts. Opening the door to them, I'd see their hesitation, sometimes their apprehension, and always their anxiety as to how they should behave, what they should say. Especially what they should say. Visiting the dying is so very tricky, oh dear yes. There's not a single book of etiquette on how to be polite and say the right thing to the dying.

Marion liked, afterwards, to discuss how her visitors had felt. She was amused at how quickly they relaxed, once they saw she wasn't lying prone on a sofa weeping, once they saw she was composed. She made their visits pleasant. Something they'd dreaded became a pleasure. The conversation quickly turned to their own concerns, and Marion would listen carefully and, astonishingly, give something back. But she was tired afterwards. She had to prepare for each visitor by having a nap beforehand and needed another rest to recover when they'd gone. Conserving her new-found energy, which was mostly a steroids-induced illusion, was something she had to learn to do. There was not much of her precious life left so it must not be squandered. But she was determined not to spend whatever time remained just sitting about. She wanted to go out. In the early afternoons we went for walks. It was a great performance, the getting ready to go, the selecting of whichever jacket and scarf she would wear, the choosing of the shoes in which she would feel most confident. She needed an arm to link now, to steady her (her balance wasn't perfect) and so we walked very close together along the streets and at a slow pace.

Everything, absolutely everything, was worthy of comment. Marion had always been a great dasher – dashing here, dashing there, hurtling from one place to another and often going from front door to car without seeing anything. Now she scrutinised every house, every vehicle, every dog and cat. She stopped to admire bright scarlet geraniums in a window box, a new brass knocker on a door, a blue and white number plate on a gate. She'd lived in her street nearly eight years (she'd bought a flat there after she moved from our street) but knew few of her neighbours – it was a typical London street with an ever-changing population and most of its inhabitants were out at work all day. But occasionally she would see someone she vaguely knew and then she liked to stop and pass the time of day. When an Irish woman who lived across the road rushed across to ask her how she was, she was so pleased. The woman was friendly and sympathetic in the right sort of way – kind, gentle, cheerful with it. If an acquaintance clearly tried to avoid her she was pitying rather than hurt – 'Poor soul, they know no better.' She was parodying her mother, who had been fond of this remark, but it gave us an excuse to laugh. Marion had loved everything about her mother, but what she had loved most of all was her sense of humour. This was of the sardonic variety, occasionally verging towards the sarcastic. Human behaviour, with its absurdities and stupidities, was the main source of derision. Marion had endlessly laughed at her mother laughing, relishing the pleasure she so visibly and audibly derived from displays of the ridiculous. It was a Dickensian kind of humour (Dickens was Mrs Davies' favourite author – she could recite whole passages), dependent for the joke not so much on what was said as how. There was nothing inherently funny, for example, about Mrs Davies saying, 'Anyone seen my milkman?' and yet she'd collapse with laughter after she'd said it. This phrase came from observing an old neighbour of hers who used to say this at the same time as fluttering her hand near her cheek to draw attention to a ring she'd been given – 'Anyone seen my milkman?' meaning 'Can everyone see this diamond I'm flashing and are you all jealous?' Marion still used the phrase, murmuring it quietly whenever someone tried to conceal that they were showing off.

We walked round the block, literally. We turned left out of her door and down her long street, then left again into a short stretch where there were a few shops. One was a pretty little gift shop which also sold a few fresh flowers. Marion loved to look round it and always urged me to go inside. Her behaviour in this tiny shop was odd. She smiled all the time and went round and round in the confined space peering at the things for sale, lifting up all the bits and pieces as though searching for something in particular. The young male assistant, whose eyes had flown to Marion's neck wound at once, always politely asked if he could help, and his help was just as politely declined. He withdrew into a back room, trusting us entirely. 'What are you looking for?' I whispered to Marion, to be told, 'Oh, I don't know, just something, but I'll find it.' Candles were examined and sniffed, greeting cards held up and scrutinised, artificial flowers fiddled with, and still she went on searching. The shop assistant peeped round the corner occasionally and smiled too and raised his eyebrows questioningly at me, and I raised mine back and shrugged. 'There isn't any hurry,' Marion said. I agreed. I hoped she didn't think I was impatient, because I wasn't, I was just at a loss. I began picking up things myself in desperation. 'These are nice,' I said, holding out to her some wooden fruits impregnated with the appropriate oils to make them smell of their shape, of lemon and apple and pear. She sniffed – 'Oh yes!' she exclaimed. So I bought two wooden lemons and an apple and a pear and she was content. We could go.

We went to the café on the other side of the street. It wasn't really a café so much as a bread shop which had stuck a couple of tables and a few chairs outside, like so many shops during this amazing summer. We often sat there and had a cup of coffee, and Marion would repeat over and over how pleasant this was, how enjoyable. What a treat to be sitting in the sun in the afternoon having coffee, the height of bliss. We watched the Hoppa bus go by, we watched children coming out of school. We had plenty of time to sit and stare. Then, before we set off home along the other side of the block we were walking round, I was sent in to buy cigarettes and a copy of the *Guardian*, for whose Society pages Marion had once written a witty column. It had such a happy history, that column. Every one of those Wednesday evenings when Marion used to come, straight from work, for supper with us, she'd regale us with tales of the more extraordinary cases she was involved in and make us laugh as she described how she managed her team. Again and again we'd say this material was too good to keep to herself and that she should write it all down and offer it to some newspaper or magazine as a new sort of column. We coaxed and bullied her and eventually she got down to doing this in the summer of 1991. When she'd completed four columns she sent them off to the *Guardian*, who immediately accepted them and asked for more. Oh what rapture! There she was, by then fifty-two, someone who had never tried to write before, and now she was a *Guardian* columnist (though under a pseudonym, hiding behind the name Mary Black — Leader of the Pack — because she was worried about being sacked if anyone identified her).

She had changed all the names, of course, of both clients and staff, and altered locations and so forth, but essentially the columns were true to life. Even now, as we walked along she'd see people in the street who would remind her of clients she'd written about. 'Look,' she said once, nudging me as we made our slow way down her road: 'that woman's just like the one I called Mrs Brown. Remember Mrs Brown?' I did. Mrs Brown had made one of her funniest columns. She was a woman who'd come into Marion's office demanding a free bus pass. She'd brought her five young children with her, all of whom had run amok in the waiting-room. Marion had explained that a bus pass could only be issued under the Chronically Sick and Disabled Act to those who had 'a permanent and substantial handicap'. She asked Mrs Brown what her handicap was. Mrs Brown went into detail about all the operations she'd had. Politely, Marion explained that none of these qualified her as either permanently or substantially disabled. Mrs Brown promptly stood up, lifted her skirt, pulled down her knickers, and showed a large scar which ran from her navel to her pubic hair. She said she would like to know what could be more permanent or substantial than that. Marion gave up. She said she'd consult Mrs Brown's GP and let her know the result.

I'd forgotten what it was. Marion reminded me as we turned the corner, and 'Mrs Brown' disappeared. She'd met Mrs Brown on Brighton beach a year later, long after her request for the bus pass had been turned down. She'd moved to Brighton and was now the proud possessor of the bus pass Camden wouldn't sanction. 'I'm handicapped now!' she shouted to Marion as she ran and jumped around with her children on the beach. 'It's grand!'

It was sad to buy the *Guardian* on Wednesdays now and know there would be no column of Marion's on its Society pages. She didn't want to go into the newsagents herself in case she was jostled – it was a busy place at that time of day, full of school-children buying sweets – and so she stood leaning on the window, looking nervous, until I came out. Then off we'd go, on the last lap, passing a launderette where Marion knew the woman who worked there. She was from Pakistan and spoke hardly any English, but seeing Marion she'd dart out to say hello. The first time she did this her beautiful eyes widened and she pointed at Marion's neck – not covered that day by the usual scarf – and looked concerned, miming a question about what had happened to cause this wound, Marion smiled, and said, 'Nothing, it's nothing,' and patted her hand. But the woman didn't need any English to know it was not 'nothing', and ever after we had to go through the same poignant charade. It was tiring for all concerned, but as a sign of genuine concern it was uplifting.

The stairs from the front door to the first floor flat were at first no problem but then, as September went on, became something of a challenge. There were fourteen stairs rising steeply in a straight row to the first landing. 'Wait,' Marion began to say, 'wait'. I waited. We took her jacket off and hung it on a hook. She stood still, gripping the stair rail running up the right-hand wall, the very picture of determination. Slowly, she began to tackle these stairs, each foot having to be joined by the other before it was once more lifted. She made little puffing noises as each stair was negotiated and when finally she reached the top her sense of triumph was blatant, coming out in a great 'There! Done it!'

She went into the kitchen in such good spirits and celebrated with a cup of coffee and a cigarette. Soon, Frances would be home. 'Go home,' she would say to me, 'go on. I'm fine. Don't wait for Frances, get yourself home.' I never knew whether she urged me to go because she wanted some time on her own, or because it made her feel less of an invalid to be without anyone for a little while, or because she was concerned that I would be walking home in the dark if I stayed much longer. If it was raining she worried about me and wished I'd call a cab, and when I went striding off without an umbrella she was so anxious. She was never, ever, so wrapped up in her terminal illness that she lost concern for others.

On Thursdays, I didn't go to be with her. Thursday was Annabel's day. Her twin sister came straight from work, by train from Leighton Buzzard, and stayed the night. Marion, though longing to see her, would stress, every week, that Annabel must not exhaust herself – she must never think that she was obliged to come. She was under enough strain as it was, what with working and with looking after Roger, whose multiple sclerosis was so severe he could do little for himself. But nothing would keep Annabel away, and Roger himself urged her to go, understanding perfectly the incredible strength of the bond between these two sisters. So on Thursday, Annabel came, agonisingly hard for her, agonisingly hard for Marion, but it was precious time together. They both, fortunately, shared the same philosophy: facts had to be faced and as cheerfully as possible. Neither believed in burdening the other with her own despair and misery; neither went in for public weeping and wailing; neither bothered to curse fate, because it would only sour the months left to them.

It was strange, during this time, to witness the subtle change in the relationship between the twins, a change forced upon them by these new and distressing circumstances. Marion, always thought (though not always correctly) to be the stronger of the two, was no longer able to be strong in the sense of being the one upon whom Annabel could lean. In a way, it was a return to their very early childhood – their mother had told me how slow Marion was to learn to speak and how she depended on Annabel to interpret for her. The bond between them was as tight as ever, but naturally it was not the same. Marion was not able to be the protector, a role she'd come to fulfil as the twins grew up.

When they were children, she had literally fought anyone who threatened her sister, including their own older brother, Hunter. He was four years older than his sisters but easily beaten in any fight with Marion. He only had to push Annabel for Marion to be whirling at him like a boxer. In fact, she was so effective as a fighter that if he was involved in any scrap of his own outside the house he wasn't in the least embarrassed to enlist her aid. She took on adults, too, if necessary. There was one PE teacher who made her life, and Annabel's, a misery. Everyone hated this teacher, but the twins especially loathed her because she seemed to take a delight in victimising them. They never had their own PE kit (Davies finances did not run to one set of kit, never mind two) and were obliged to borrow from other girls who had the lesson before. This meant they were always wearing blouses and shorts too big or too small, and the teacher would look at them in disgust and hold them up to ridicule. But worse than that was her treatment of Marion. Marion had a badly injured arm, the result of a burn caused by pulling a pan of boiling water over herself when she was very young. The burn had shrivelled and twisted the skin the whole length of her arm. It was unsightly and she was acutely self-conscious about it, naturally preferring to keep it covered. But the teacher wouldn't let her. 'Short sleeves only!' she'd shout, and force Marion to expose her arm.

All this Marion put up with, but what she would not put up with was malice towards Annabel. Annabel once yawned at the start of a lesson (she and Marion had been up at six doing a paper round before school) and the teacher had told her to go and sit on the bench if she was so tired. This was tolerable for one lesson but ever after, week after week, the lesson would begin with 'Annabel Davies, on the bench!' She sat there, isolated and conspicuous, taking no part in PE or games or dancing. Miserable, and afraid of the teacher, she slunk to the bench when ordered until one day Marion had had enough. 'Annabel Davies, bench!' shouted the teacher, as usual, as though Annabel was a dog, and this time Marion shouted back: 'No! Don't go to the bench, Annabel!' Annabel froze, scared to disobey the teacher but automatically obeying Marion. 'Bench!' yelled the teacher. 'No!' yelled Marion. The whole class of twelve-year-old girls was mesmerised. Who would win? Suddenly, the teacher launched into the lesson, without Annabel having gone to the bench.

But later, as the girls queued up for showers, the teacher came down the line. When she reached Marion she drew back her arm to lash her bare thighs with all the force she had – at which point Marion seized her arm and heaved the teacher right round, pushing her off. Again, the class held its breath, and again the teacher did nothing. She, in turn, was now obviously a little afraid of Marion. Everyone, child and adult alike, became wary of her strength and of her fury when crossed. Annabel, smaller, slighter, more delicately boned, was clearly protected by her bigger, stronger, tougher twin. And though things changed once their lives separated, the rules of their relationship were set. Until now. It upset Marion to think she was failing Annabel and causing her such pain; but Annabel was determined to be resolute and show she cared more about supporting Marion than about losing support herself.

By October, we were all wondering just how many months were left. Time had become an obsession, naturally enough. So had keeping charts and making lists. On the freezer door, there was now a chart made by Marion listing all the varieties of ice-cream she'd bought (forty pounds' worth) and against each were ticks for how often she'd eaten them. She had become passionately interested in the consumption of the coffee ice-cream compared with the pistachio, of the chocolate over the maple-and-walnut.

Then there were the drugs. She was taking so many, and liked them all to be listed, with the times they had to be taken and the dosage beside them. After she'd swallowed each lot she would tick off what she'd taken. Frances was extremely efficient at doling out these drugs, and under her guidance so was I – there was no chance of mistakes, it was really quite simple. But not for Marion. She would get in a panic about whether she was taking the right drug at the right time and would hardly trust me or Frances to know the system. 'Fancy,' she'd exclaim, joking yet clearly meaning it, 'three of the greatest brains in Britain and we can't get it right.' But we always got it right. It was she who, losing control of everything else in her life, struggled to control this single aspect. The drugs were keeping pain at bay and they were keeping her mobile, so she felt that if they were not administered properly disaster would follow. So she sat hunched over the kitchen table, laboriously writing down yet again the names and dosage of each drug she took, the only way she could stave off complete disintegration.

But she was also, each day, jotting down thoughts and obser-vations and sometimes little verses she'd made up. She'd come late to writing, very late. She was over forty before she'd begun to try to write plays, and even older before she attempted any journalism. And when she did start, she was slow. One play had been produced at the ICA in London, and broadcast on Radio 4, but no others had followed, though she'd completed a second eventually. All her efforts had gone into her *Guardian* columns, but once she became ill these had stopped. I kept urging her to write but she said she didn't see the point any more: writing didn't attract her, it wouldn't give her any pleasure or provide any sense of release. She said she supposed that meant she wasn't a real writer, writing wasn't second nature to her, it wasn't in her blood, like it was in Dennis Potter's (who, at that time, was writing up to the very end of his life, and deeply impressed her). But nevertheless, she felt some sort of urge because there they were, her observations, her thoughts. She had a pad of A4 paper on the kitchen table covered with her scrawls – and they were scrawls; her handwriting was appalling. She had the most disturbed-looking handwriting I have ever seen. It gave me vertigo to look at it. I'd always longed to send a sample to a graphologist who, I was sure, would instinctively have recoiled at what was revealed. This writing of hers was backhand and loose, looking more like hieroglyphics than recognisable words, and it bounced wildly all over the place. But using her word processor was now beyond her – it sat, sadly, in the corner of her bedroom – so a Biro was the only option.

Sometimes when I arrived in the morning and was clearing the always cluttered table, I'd see a fresh page turned and a lot written down already. I'd ask if it was all right for me to read it and she'd say of course, it was nothing. But it wasn't nothing. It was often a touching stab at trying to make something of what was going on in her head, confessions of all the losses she was experiencing and would experience, little bursts of misery she was struggling to overcome, forlorn acknowledgements of the suffering she was causing others. She never wrote anything down when I or any other visitor was there, only when she was with Frances or on her own. She said she liked to write best early in the morning, when she first got up and was testing herself. If she could swallow her mushy Weetabix fairly easily it was going to be a good day and she felt up to recording whatever she was thinking. Once, looking directly at me after I'd read what she'd written that morning, she said, 'When all this is over, are you going to write about it?' I said I had no plans to. I reminded her that she knew books didn't start like that for me, they started with problems, with turning over problems. 'Well,' she said, 'isn't this a problem? Isn't dying a problem?' There was a sudden awkwardness, almost an embarrassment. 'Do you want me to try to write about it?' I asked. She smiled, and shrugged and said, 'If you like, if you want, sometime.' It was never mentioned again.

Three months had gone by since the prognosis in July that Marion had about six months to live. Did that mean there were only three left now? They'd said it could be more. Or less. But she still seemed, by mid-October, fairly strong and in good spirits. 'If this is dying,' she said, 'if this is how it is going to be, it will be all right.' She said she wasn't in what she regarded as pain (though I had the feeling others might) so much as some discomfort and she had morphine at hand for whenever this became too much. It was kept in a bottle — no, not a bottle, some sort of container beside her bed. It amused her to watch people looking at it and guessing what it was. 'It's liquid morphine,' she'd say, straight out. 'I can have as much of it as I want. Too much, if I like,' and she'd laugh. I asked her if 'too much' meant what I thought it meant. Did it mean she would drink enough to end her life if it became unbearable? She said yes, it did, and that she intended to do just that if the pain she feared began in earnest. She'd tell Frances first and then she'd do it. All she worried about was whether this would invalidate her life insurance. 'For God's sake,' I said, exasperated, 'who cares about life insurance?' 'I do,' she said, 'but if I'm in agony I won't.'

So that was clear, or so it seemed. There was after all a point at which life would no longer be precious enough to cling on to at all costs. It was a relief in some ways to know this, yet at the same time I saw a grey area opening up. How bad does pain have to become for death to be chosen, actually *chosen*, as preferable to life? And when it is reached, will control, the control to decide to use all the morphine, still be there? Or does someone else have to lift the bottle to your lips when you beg them? Problems there, indeed . . . But Marion was content to have made this decision and then to have set it aside. She was still getting up each day, still going for walks, still reading (though only newspapers now), still listening to the radio and to music on tapes. Television was no longer one of her small pleasures. She had no patience with it.

But a change was coming. I sensed it nervously. I more than sensed it. I was on the look-out for it, monitoring every movement she made, minutely examining her face and body for signs. Surely she wasn't walking up the stairs so well. Now, her 'Wait, wait,' took longer to end and the heaving up of her feet was awful to watch. She'd stop halfway up and had literally to be pushed on. But she was still keen to go for walks, though it was no longer safe for just one person to go with her. By the middle of October, it took two of us, one either side. The last walk I took her on by myself was very nearly disastrous. She said she didn't want to walk round the block. She wanted to go into Crouch End, shopping. She'd made a list and was quite feverish in her determination to get everything on it, especially the first and most important item, a Christmas present for Frances, to be hidden in my house and given to her on Christmas Eve by me, 'if'.

I wondered even before we set off if we'd ever make it to the clock tower and the main shopping area, never mind making it back. All the time we shuffled down the busy, noisy street I was on the look-out for taxis, noting minicab firms just in case. We went the whole length of Crouch End Broadway to Boots. It took ages, but Marion was bright with excitement. She wanted to buy ordinary things first, toothpaste and a face-cloth, and then some food, salmon at the fishmonger's next door and bread at the bakery opposite. People looked at us, or rather they looked, as we queued at tills, at Marion's neck. She wouldn't wear a scarf any more – scarves irritated her neck – and so the wound was visible, ugly and bleeding slightly, and the whole area round it massively swollen with new tumours clustering there. She realised she was attracting attention but she was impervious to the stares. She didn't see why she should hide what had happened to her. But I was glad when we were out of the shops and at last on our way home, though still without the most important purchase, that future present for Frances. Almost home, we went into a small shop that sold lamps. Success. She saw a beautiful Tiffany lamp and put a deposit on it. I said, 'Why only a deposit? Why not buy it now?' but she wanted to think about it. Annabel could come next day and buy it, if she decided it was what she wanted for Frances, and then I could pick it up (which is what happened).

On the whole, although she had always been the most generous of people in all the ways that matter, overwhelmingly generous with her time and concern, Marion had never been a great present-buyer. It was always a big deal for her, buying a present, hence the prevarication even now. The obligation to give presents on birthdays annoyed her. In fact, birthdays in general annoyed her, or rather the fuss some people (me, Frances) made about them did. It was almost the same with Christmas. 'I'm not giving presents this year,' she would say firmly. We would tease her, ask her if she would still be receiving them, and she would graciously indicate she would be prepared to. The children thought this hilarious. But on those rare occasions when she decided to give presents, they were always witty and fun, worth waiting for. Now, suddenly she wanted to lavish presents on all her 'loved ones'. Her delight in the choosing and giving was immense, almost childish in its intensity. One Thursday, Annabel was sent off by taxi to buy Frances a new tartan dressing-gown and Marion could hardly contain her impatience to see it unwrapped and worn and exclaimed over. Her nieces and nephews were astonished to benefit from this new largess – one got a suitcase, another a mobile phone, another kitchen equipment. She didn't have much money, but because she'd always saved she had more squirrelled away than anyone had thought – just small amounts here and there, now released to indulge her new pleasure.

She'd made her will back in July, the moment she was told her illness was terminal. She was particularly anxious to leave her financial affairs in perfect order. And she set about arranging her own funeral. It was beyond me how anyone could want to think about their own funeral, but Marion did. She was not religious but liked to describe herself, only half-mockingly, as 'spiritual'. Certainly, she'd spent her life searching for something but, apart from that adolescent flirtation with Christian Science, had never found it in any church. All the same, she wanted a church funeral and settled on the United Reform Church at the end of her road, a church she had never entered in her life. She contacted the vicar, who to her delight was a woman, and asked if she would come to see her, 'to discuss my funeral'. When the vicar came, Marion told her there were two things she ought to know in case either presented an insuperable problem to holding the funeral in the church. The first was that she had no belief in an afterlife; and the second that she was a lesbian, which meant that both her partner and her husband (whom she'd married before identifying her own lesbianism but never divorced, and with whom she was still friendly) would both be there. The slightly startled vicar said she thought neither factor presented any difficulty.

There were a couple more meetings with the vicar for Marion to outline her wishes in some detail. This detail occupied her for several weeks, as she read endless hymns and passages in the Bible which she thought might be appropriate. I was told not to 'give me that look'. I tried not to, but it was hard to hide the look of disbelief on my face. Funerals appal me. I think dead bodies should be despatched rapidly and without show. But Marion was firmly of the opinion that a funeral would help people through the immediate aftermath of her death, especially Frances and Annabel. She thought they'd find some comfort in the singing of hymns, the reading of verses and the general ritual of a funeral. And she admitted, on top of that, to feelings of pleasure at the thought of a church full of people gathered together to honour her passing. So she went on planning her funeral and I learned if not to banish 'that look', at least to keep quiet. Except about flowers. Marion's plans did not include flowers – 'Scandalous waste of money,' she said. On the contrary, I said, if she was going to have such a splendid funeral, not to have flowers would spoil it. And I wanted flowers: it was the only part of the ceremony I was in favour of. So she conceded I might put flowers of my choosing in the church, 'But only one lot, and not too expensive.'

All this had been done long ago, by the middle of October. The will, the funeral, both taken care of. There was nothing to do now but settle into waiting without knowing the date we were waiting for. Over and over again this consciousness of waiting, waiting, emphasised how precious every moment must be. But when this platitude is held up to the light, what shines through it? Nothing precious at all; just a void, an empty space which has to be filled. Thinking how to fill it panics people. How often the jolly question is put in an idle moment: if you had only six months to live, how would you spend them? And the answers are invariably banal, full of travel and excesses of high living. Marion would have liked to spend her last months travelling, but she was in no fit state to travel anywhere. She wasn't capable of flying to the Caribbean to laze on a beach and swim in turquoise seas – and, besides, she was dependent on so many drugs she would have had to take half a chemist's shop with her. So there was no room for flights of fancy like this. Home was where she had to be and facing up to the 'precious' nature of each hour was a curious problem. She didn't want to waste time, but what constituted waste? Was sitting looking out of the kitchen window for ages wasting time? Was lying on her bed listening to Anna Raeburn's radio programme wasting time? Was it scandalous, in her situation, with so little time left, actually to feel *bored*?

The time left might be short, but the days felt increasingly long to her. She began wanting new diversion. She was seized with an urgent desire to see her younger brother Johnny, and she issued a royal-sounding summons for him to come from Carlisle. He came with alacrity and spent the day with her; and she looked at him and listened and loved his being with her, and yet not a single emotionally charged word passed between them. It was the ordinariness of the encounter she wanted: she just wanted him to chat, about his family, about his work, about the new house he was in the process of buying. To chat, and to be near. When he came a second time, not even their parting, almost certain to be the last, was emotional. Johnny responded according to the family rules: 'Don't make a carry-on, keep everything light' – the way he had been brought up. Those hours he spent with his dying sister were infinitely precious to him too, but they had to pass gently. That was their value.

It was what we all had to learn. The time left would only be marred by any lunge into the kind of melodrama Marion had never condoned. However absurd it felt always to be talking about nothing in particular, it was this very nothingness that seemed to keep her on an even keel. Dying, she had no wish to launch into debates on great ethical issues. It was too tiring even to contemplate fathoming the meaning of life when she was so near the end of it. Nor, while it was still going on, did she wish to be asked what she had made of it. She just wanted to tick over, quietly, soothingly, with the strange new rhythm of her days interrupted only by the visits of those dear to her. Small comforts became huge ones – the newly changed bed, the fresh flowers. Constantly, people asked if there was anything they could do for her, *anything*, but there rarely was. Only if they were lucky (because people feel privileged to do something for the dying – it relieves them) was there a small service they could do, which was invariably something trivial, like finding a particular tape of music she wanted.

But the boredom which was not quite boredom, which was more of a restlessness, grew in spite of the permitted visitors. Marion wanted to go further afield, to different surroundings entirely, out of Crouch End, for more ambitious walks. Her walking was now so unsteady, and she had to get back up the stairs on her hands and knees, but she was emphatic: she wanted a much more ambitious walk than any we had been doing.

So we drove, Marion, Frances and I, to Alexandra Palace, a mile away in north London. It was a beautiful late October afternoon with a faint coolness in the air in spite of the sun. Marion was well wrapped up in her padded green jacket and warm trousers and very sensible flat black shoes. She was excited, her eyes bright with the adventure of it all. We parked by the palace itself and began walking along the broad tarmac area in front, Frances on one side of her, me on the other. She was walking more quickly than she had been recently, though with short, choppy steps; and we found she was pulling us along as we tried to slow her down to a more measured and less exhausting (for her) pace. Backwards and forwards we went, on the flat: quite enough, we thought. But Marion didn't agree. This was boring. She wanted to go further, away from the building. She nodded towards the paths on the other side of the car park, where the ground sloped downwards. We pointed out that if we went down, we would have to come back up, and that there were steps to negotiate, but she didn't care, she insisted we explore further.

It was certainly a prettier part of the park. Lots of shrubs, some trees, some late flowers still in bloom. 'Lovely,' Marion said, 'lovely. Look at the blossom coming out.' It was the end of

October, there was of course no blossom, but this wasn't a sign of poor vision or dementia. Marion had never had the slightest interest in nature and could hardly tell one flower from another. She'd often told me how she wished she could be transported, the way others were, by the sight of a beautiful landscape but though she could admire a view, could see it was indeed beautiful, it did nothing for her, as she put it. It was the same with art and architecture. Her husband Jeff regularly went into ecstasies over a painting or a building, but Marion just stared, said, 'Very nice,' and then felt wistfully that she was missing something. But now she was looking at everything in a different way and at last feeling something profound – amazement, it seemed to be, at how things grew. And in this realisation was some sort of comfort that it was so, this endless cycle of dying and being born again.

We reached the limit of the park itself. 'Further,' Marion urged. I said if we went further we would come to a very noisy, busy road. Reluctantly, she allowed us to turn back and begin the long haul up to the car. It was a struggle. When we reached the car, Frances and I were worn out, not with any physical exertion, but with worrying about whether we would ever get there. How cheerful and hearty we suddenly were, opening the car door with a flourish for Marion to get in. But she wouldn't. She was not pleased. 'I can't go home yet,' she said, a touch of panic in her voice. 'It isn't enough. I haven't had enough. I can't go back yet.' It must have been the steroids which gave her this illusion of ferocious energy – she was suddenly terrified of inactivity. In her mind she was running and jumping and her body was being pushed by her to do the same.

In the end, we persuaded her to go home and the crawl up the stairs used up some of the energy she felt so full of. But the next day there was the same frantic need to get out and about, to *do* something. I arrived next morning to have the newspaper grabbed out of my hand. 'Quick,' she said, 'what's on? I want to go and see a film, I want to take Frances to a film.' I began reciting what was on at the local cinemas – 'No, no,' she said, crossly, 'the West End. What's on in the West End? Look and see, help me!' Slowly, I sorted out the page with West End cinema programmes listed. How could she possibly brave the West End? But she was determined. She wanted to treat Frances, to take her to a plush West End cinema. It would be like old times. It was not at all like old times. I was not allowed to come, because this was to be a special outing for Frances; they would manage on their own without an additional minder. A minicab was ordered for the evening and Marion had a longer rest than usual in the afternoon in preparation, though she was in such a state of euphoria at the prospect of this daring expedition she couldn't sleep. Frances bravely faced up to the challenge this outing to the cinema would present – steps, semi-darkness, finding the minicab afterwards – and off they went, with me on stand-by to come at once if all these arrangements failed. Frances would ring me on her mobile phone, and I would swoop.

There was no need to, but the whole thing was a flop. Marion was bored after ten minutes. The film was *The Madness of King George*, widely praised, obviously hugely enjoyed by the rest of the audience she sat with, but dull and dreary to her. 'I'll want to see something better next time,' she said in disgust ('And next time,' Frances murmured, 'I'll need help'). But there was no repeat visit to the cinema. Instead Marion wanted to go shopping. She'd never been a lover of shopping (except for food) and was not a woman for whom the height of bliss was a trip to London's Oxford Street, but now she wanted new clothes and she wanted to go with Frances and select them herself. So the crowds in the nearby Wood Green Shopping Centre had to be risked. They were. She came home tri-umphant with a pair of tartan trousers and a new sweater. She suddenly looked so thin, in her new clothes. But she was so pleased with herself, holding her arms up to show them off and turning round slowly for me to get the full effect. So thin. How had I not realised that the weight was dropping off her body alarmingly? It should not have been a shock, but it was. After all, she was hardly eating anything, though making a great ritual of every meal, always sitting at the kitchen table as though about to have three courses.

This was the point, on her suggestion, at which her brother Hunter (my husband) interviewed her on tape. She said she had been surprised that no one seemed interested in the process she was going through, the process of dying. She wished she could meet other people, also dying, to talk about it, because it didn't seem right, or even possible, to talk about it with those who weren't dying. She didn't know if she had any thoughts on it worth preserving, but she liked the idea of trying to find out. And it would, she thought, amuse her; it would pass the time. She wanted to record something soon because she feared something might happen to her brain. Her greatest fear had always been that her throat would close up and she would choke, but one day that week she suddenly said to me, 'It could be the brain.' I'd had to ask her what she meant, since this comment was made in no sort of context. 'The brain,' she repeated. 'The cancer might get to the brain.' Curiously, this didn't seem to terrify her as much as the previous conviction that she would choke.

She was self-conscious, being interviewed on tape. I was not present, neither was Frances – it was just her, and Hunter asking the questions and pretending she was a stranger, which was how she wanted to do it. Everything he asked her seemed to startle her and the tape is full of long pauses. She is constantly exclaiming, 'Oh! Oh, I'll have to get my head round that, wait.' The waiting goes on and on, and often she's obviously forgotten the question. The answers, when they do come, are mostly flat and strained. She announces that a great deal of what she is being asked to go over is 'irrelevant'. This includes the whole history of her illness and of the treatment she was subjected to, and also the matter of whether she suffered a fatal original misdiagnosis – irrelevant, all of it. Nor does she wish to spend even a minute considering a question on the lines of 'Why did this happen to me?' Her attitude is 'Why not me? I'm not a teenager . . . Only a little bit of a normal lifespan has been lost . . . I've had fifty-six years – that's a life.'

It isn't until she is prompted to describe her current state of mind that the tape becomes interesting and her tone less constrained. She describes first how happy she felt once she was out of the chemotherapy ward and back home, free from pain and with a new energy once she was on the steroids – 'Such happy days,' she says, 'lovely, lovely days in my own house, being well looked after and showered with treats.' This she reckons went on about six weeks and then she began to think not only that she was perhaps *too* happy but that there was something odd about this happiness – 'How could I be happy when I was dying?' She says it didn't make sense and what was puzzling her also was another feeling, the sense that she was 'bored with good days'. This shocked her, and one morning, when she'd woken very early, at five o'clock, she got a pencil and started jotting down why there were in fact many reasons for *not* being happy. The tears had come quickly then, virtually for the first time in a couple of months. She reads the list, of what she calls 'losses', on the tape and her voice breaks – 'This is the sad bit,' she whispers. It took her two hours to write and by the end she felt different. She realises she'd concentrated so hard on being happy that she'd ignored her grief. She is aware of a change in her state of mind ever since she made this list, but she can't precisely describe it though she struggles to do so.

This leads her on, surprisingly, to claiming to be lucky she is going to die soon, at this particular time – 'If I die now, everyone is in a nice phase.' Carefully, she goes round most of the family, stating what she sees as each individual's alleged happiness. As a piece of self-persuasion it is remarkable, especially since she very noticeably skips over those 'loved ones' whose unhappy state is obvious to the rest of us. But no, she emphasises how good a time this is – 'It strikes me profoundly' – and even then says it makes her feel guilty – 'I feel guilty because I'm lucky leaving at such a good time.' Whatever disasters or tragedies are to follow she is relieved that she will not have to witness them. She gives the impression that waiting for her own death is becoming a worry, in case her rose-tinted view of the family's contentment fails her; and this leads her on, in turn, to the general tedium of waiting. 'What am I waiting for?' She has nothing she wants to finish or do, and envies Dennis Potter – 'He had so much to do in his last months, he was a man of zest, with a goal.' She has no goal and she'd like one. Suddenly, near the end of the tape, she says 'Dying isn't all it's cracked up to be.' Hunter protests that nobody said it was fun, and she explains, 'But it's made such a big thing of . . . it's always made to sound dramatic – all the talk of last words and epitaphs . . . There are very few deaths not read as dramatic, and mine is so *un*-dramatic.' 'Not to us it isn't,' Hunter says.

She was so disappointed with herself over this tape – 'I wasn't good,' she said. Hunter told her it wasn't a question of being 'good', it hadn't been meant as a performance, but she insists she hadn't done her thoughts justice. He told her he'd make more tapes, this would be the initial one, to build on, but another was never made.

From that moment on Marion's condition began to deteriorate. I noticed it the very next day. It was a sunny afternoon but she didn't want to go out. She didn't want to get dressed either. Frances had forced herself to go to work for a couple of hours and we sat, for once, in the sitting-room. Marion was in the wing chair, its seat padded with an air-cushion, and, though it was not cold, she had wanted the fire lit. It was one of those fake gas fires (which look like coal burning), newly installed in the Victorian fireplace. 'At least I've seen the fire on,' she said. There was a pause followed by, 'But I'll never see *Derby.*' She was almost in tears, but I couldn't help laughing. 'Derby!' I said. 'For God's sake.' But she'd been watching *Pride and Prejudice* and longed to visit Derby, where it was made. She laughed herself, but said it was stupid realisations like that which brought home to her most forcefully that she was really dying.

It was a strange afternoon. I read bits of the *Guardian* to her – she still loved newspapers but no longer actually read much of them – but she wasn't concentrating. 'I'll never know the end of all the stories,' she suddenly said. 'I'll never know what happens to the young ones. What will they become?' There was the same breaking of her voice as on the tape. Her three nephews and four nieces were so very dear to her. Maybe if she'd had children of her own she would not have had the time or interest to have been such an involved aunt, but, if so, her loss had been their gain. My children had seen the most of her because when they were growing up she had lived in our street, and she'd been intimately acquainted with their troubles and triumphs. She talked to them for hours, and they talked back (or in other words argued ferociously with her), and she never grew tired of them. And now, dying, she worried about them and couldn't bear not to know their futures. All I could think to reply was that nobody ever dies knowing the ends of all the stories.

She rarely referred directly to the future, to a time after her own death, but that afternoon she did. As I gave her a mug of tea she said, 'Do you think Frances will be all right?' Quickly, much too quickly, much too emphatically, I said that of course she would, she was young and attractive, she had a strong personality, and in time I had no doubt at all she would rebuild her life. 'Good,' Marion said, nodding, and then, 'Mind, I don't want her or Annabel going to pieces when this is all over.' She paused, and for the first time that afternoon she laughed. 'Well, at first they can, of course, but then no more weeping and wailing – it's stupid to carry on.' Extravagant tears always destroyed her. She thought that, contrary to popular belief, there was no release to be found in 'a good cry'. The times, the very few times, when she herself cried were awful because she so hated losing self-control. Crying was a messy indulgence she felt better without. 'It's no good crying' was an edict built into the very fabric of her life, echoing her mother's 'If I start crying, I might never stop'. Crying, she found, weakened her, made her feel ill. And other people's tears were a burden, because they made her feel she must comfort them and this used up what energy she had. If people were going to cry, she'd rather they didn't do it in front of her. These were the sort of visitors she wished would stay away.

She didn't want visits from those who were afraid, either. She sensed their fear and she didn't like it. It was better they didn't come. In fact, only a couple of friends reacted like this and her disappointment in them was far outweighed by the gratitude she felt when others were overwhelmingly generous and thoughtful. One young man, who had once been part of her social work team, invited her for lunch to his home and, knowing she would not be able to manage on her own, invited not just Frances too but me as well, and Annabel who was visiting her, and, because he was acting as chauffeur, Hunter. Her friend and his partner gave us a splendid lunch and devoted themselves utterly to Marion. She was so happy, that day, actually to be out to lunch accompanied by a (rather embarrassingly large) selection of 'loved ones'. It made dying so much less boring. Nobody flinched at the sight of her swollen face; nobody shuddered at the ugly neck wound; everyone was patient with her slow and slightly slurred speech.

This was almost but not quite the last occasion upon which she left home. A few days later, she went to Leighton Buzzard to visit Annabel and Roger, an expedition of heroic proportions. She wasn't really fit enough and right up to the last minute there were doubts as to whether she would be able to go. Every step she took was an almighty effort and she was mentally not exactly confused so much as lacking concentration. It was over an hour's drive there, over an hour back – too much for someone who had made no car journey longer than twenty minutes for months. But she was adamant that she wanted to go. She wanted to see Roger, who was confined to a wheelchair and for whom all travel was difficult, making it almost impossible for him to come to her, and she wanted to be in her twin's home one last time. Hunter took her and Frances in our car. The outing was more or less a disaster, straining all involved and leaving them on the edge of those tears Marion did not want. But she herself was said to be largely oblivious to the strain – she slept a great deal, even during lunch – and pronounced herself delighted with her day out. She'd achieved what she wanted, a little goal not on the Dennis Potter scale but nevertheless an achievement.

She never left her house again, never attempted the stairs. It was as if a drawbridge had been pulled up. At the beginning of November, we settled down for the final siege.

# VII

THE DAY AFTER the exhausting outing to Leighton Buzzard, Marion stayed in bed, to recover. Arriving in the morning to see her there, comfortably settled on the pillows, I felt such relief, but it was a guilty relief. It is so much easier for carers if the invalid is lying all neat and tidy in bed. It is when they are struggling to haul themselves up, straining to stand, to move about in any way, that their sickness becomes obvious and pitiful. Make them stay in bed and all kinds of pretences can be maintained. So many times I knew I'd urged Marion to stay in bed, to rest, to have a little sleep, thinking not so much that it would be in her best interests as in my own. But she had resisted – what was left of life was far too precious to waste lying in bed (and she knew in any case she'd be unable to move from it soon).

She had always insisted on getting properly dressed, when I had promoted the advantages of a dressing-gown, dreading for myself, as well as her, the ordeal of putting on clothes, with all the twisting and turning and stretching and bending of her poor limbs. Stay in bed, stay in your nightdress, stay still . . . and now she had little choice. Her bedroom became her world for most of the day. It was a small, square room at the back of the house, a room that was to have been her study when she and Frances moved in, just before her illness was diagnosed. There were two bedrooms upstairs but, once she could no longer manage the stairs, the study became her bedroom. Her bed took up a third of the space. There was a special mattress on it, which overlapped the base slightly and made the bed look bigger than it was, and a special wedge-shaped pillow on top of the ordinary ones. A table next to the bed, under the window, held all the many drugs she took, including the ever-available liquid morphine. On the wall above her head was a large framed old map of Cumberland and, facing her, taking up nearly all of the wall, an enormous oil painting of Hyde Park at a point near the Albert Memorial, originally given to me by the friend who'd painted it. She liked the colours rather than what was depicted. It was an autumn scene, all strong oranges and yellows and browns, the paint slapped on in huge lumps. It would have driven me crazy to have to look at this all day, but she found it somehow cheerful (and also liked the idea of having saved it from being sent to a jumble sale after I'd got tired of it).

There wasn't really room for an armchair, but we brought one into the bedroom so that we could sit comfortably during the long hours we were now going to be there. The chair faced the bed and the window, which was covered with a yellow blind. Most of the time the blind was down, since there was nothing much to see outside except the dismal backyards, and the light filtered through well enough. At least it was quiet there, which was lucky because noise of any sort had become anathema to Marion. She wanted everything to be peaceful and even the doorbell, or the crash of something dropped in another room, startled her. She couldn't cope with anything that violated the calm she liked, including the arrival of new people.

New people, unfortunately, had to be brought into this small room all the time. She had developed a pressure sore which needed to be dressed daily, so we were now on the district nurse's rota, and we had a Macmillan nurse overseeing all the treatment. The nurses were kind and efficient, but Marion found it hard to accept any of them. It was curious, Marion's slight antipathy towards nurses in general. Her mother had always wanted her to be a nurse – Marion was to be a nurse,

Annabel a teacher. But quite apart from the fact that nursing had never appealed to her (maybe she'd had enough, in effect nursing her own father during her adolescence) Marion would have been quite unsuited to conforming in the way the nursing profession requires. She would not have taken kindly to fitting into the hierarchy and working under sisters and matrons. There was an appealingly anarchic streak in her which showed itself in lots of trivial but telling ways, and which, if she had grown up in a different family and a different environment, could well have made her active politically.

This revealed itself quite early. She was never cowed by authority, though she defied it only in small ways and usually secretively. Once, enraged because her particular school was to celebrate the Queen's coronation not with a party, like all the other schools, but with the planting of some shrubs in the grounds, she wrote a letter of protest to the local Director of Education, asking him if he was aware of this unfairness, and pushed it through his letterbox at night. When the headmistress subsequently announced a change of plan, and said there would be a party after all, Marion claimed this as a personal victory. It gave her great pleasure to think how she'd challenged the headmistress (even if the headmistress was unaware of it).

This side of her character had made her a very useful and popular aunt. I always refused to write notes to teachers asking for my children to be excused anything at all if, in fact, they had no real excuse – certainly not, Mummy was much too law-abiding. But Marion would, without my knowing. My youngest only had to drape her loving arms round her aunt's neck and whimper that she hated games and hated the teacher and wished she could get out of the next horrible games after-noon, for Marion to say: 'Give me a bit of paper and a pen, petal.' Then she'd write a preposterous note, claiming some incomprehensible ailment as an excuse for my daughter not to be able to do games, and say, 'That should do it.' Apparently it always did. Maybe the teachers simply couldn't decipher Marion's awful handwriting. She'd join in a conspiracy with the children against teachers, expressing contempt for the majority of them, and finding few in her experience as a social worker with much understanding of children's backgrounds. Nurses were not as bad, but she was still suspicious of them and had no awe (as her mother had) of their qualifications. It was a case of 'So she's a teacher, so what?' and 'So she's a nurse, who cares?'

She would have preferred us to manage without nurses. The hardest for her to accept were the night-duty nurses who arrived to put her to bed (even though she was in bed most of the day, this still involved a routine of checking the pressure sore, remaking the bed and helping her to the lavatory). Theoretically, it should have been a boon, having these skilled helpers, but it wasn't. As with most such services provided by the local authority, there was no knowing when the help would arrive. We understood this and were grateful all the same, but gratitude could soon vanish. Going to answer the door on the second night, at about ten o'clock, I heard loud laughter and shouting on the doorstep. Well, why shouldn't nurses laugh and shout outside? But these two didn't stop as they came charging in. They rushed past me, clattering noisily up the stairs and calling out, 'Come to do the patient – where is she?' The tranquil atmosphere was shattered and tension of a kind we had tried so hard, and so successfully, to banish seemed to blast through the flat like hot air.

Frances was waiting at the top of the stairs, finger to her lips. 'Sssh!' she pleaded. The nurses stopped. 'Come to do the patient,' one said. 'I'm Frances, Marion's carer,' Frances whispered. 'Who are you?' 'Nurses, come to do the patient.' No smile, no lowering of the voice, no names. 'Got to get on with it,' one said. 'Others to get round.' Frances showed them into the bedroom and came out in tears a couple of minutes later. She hated to see how rough they were, hauling Marion up without saying more than the now inevitable 'We're nurses, come to do you.' They were so big and powerful, more like bouncers than nurses, but who were we to criticise and demand some latter-day Florence Nightingale? We felt not just humiliated and brushed aside but curiously ashamed, as though we had let Marion down by allowing this invasion. We should have stood up to them, insisted on some personal contact however short the time, insisted on their approaching Marion quietly and gently. But we didn't. Instead, we simply cancelled that particular service. We said we'd manage, which we did for a little while longer.

When the nights became a problem, we switched to Marie Curie nurses. They were different – quiet, friendly, composed, they slipped easily into the atmosphere we'd established. But even so, Marion didn't want them. When, on the first night, the Marie Curie nurse settled down in the armchair for the night, Marion was appalled and in the morning told Frances to tell the nurse not to come again – 'Say thank you, but don't come back, we'll manage.' Frances, in the most tactful way possible, had to say that no, she could not manage at night, not any more. It was too hard. The broken nights, answering Marion's every call to be taken to the lavatory, on top of the exhaustion of grief, were rapidly bringing her to breaking point. She had to have some sleep. Marion accepted this, as she accepted everything, with a good grace but she was not pleased. She wanted privacy. She hated strangers, however kind, doing anything for her. But, on the other hand, she also hated the idea of having to go into the hospice to die and she had enough commonsense to realise that if Frances cracked there would be no alternative.

It was strange, her deep aversion to the hospice which had served her so well, but she was emphatic: she wanted to die at home surrounded by her loved ones and her own things. She'd always had strong ideas about this. Everyone, she believed, should be able to die at home, and no one should die alone. It had caused her absolute agony of mind when her mother had died in the public ward of a mental hospital with demented cries all around, but no family beside her (even though Marion and I had both been with her up to six hours before). She was passionate about how wrong this was, and we had promised to respect her wishes. But in the first days of November I began to wonder if this was another promise I'd fail to keep, like the promise to my father that he'd never be put into a home. I could see circumstances changing, the strain becoming intolerable if her dying was protracted. I was staying the night by then, sleeping in an upstairs room above Marion's, alert to the sound of the buzzer the nurse would press when she needed assistance (it took two people to help Marion to the lavatory – one nurse could no longer manage on her own). It made sense for me to be the one who got up. Frances, upon whom the burden was by far the greatest, needed more sleep. Sometimes the buzzer sounded only once, sometimes twice. On the nights when, in spite of our help, Marion fell, it could take half an hour or more to get her back into bed. She would crouch in a heap on the floor saying, 'Wait, wait,' and we learned, the nurse and I, not to try to lift her until she was ready. Then, with a great heave and massive determination on Marion's part, it would be done. All this struggle could have been avoided if she had agreed to use a commode (which towards the very end she had to), but she wouldn't. Her wish was to drag herself to the proper lavatory, whatever ordeal it put her through, and we had to support her in this. No one thought of refusing. Force is not something you use against the dying.

But this night-time ritual was endlessly distressing. Distressing and also bewildering. Again and again, at two or three in the morning, watching Marion perched on the end of the bed gathering her feeble remaining strength to try to stand and then walk, I wondered why she was doing this. What pushed her on with this compulsion not to give up? Why didn't she just lie back on her pillows and let go? The room was so quiet. Her breathing was so heavy it filled the silence. Her eyes were shut, the effort clearly visible in her expression. Such determination *for what*? The mattress made little squeaking noises as she manoeuvred herself off it. 'Sounds like a kitten,' she said, smiling. Minutes went by. The nurse was completely relaxed and patient. She didn't speak, just patted Marion's hand, quite content to be directed by her. My hands were cold when, once Marion was finally on her feet, I took one arm and the nurse the other. 'Cold hands, warm heart,' Marion said, and laughed, delighted to be upright, delighted with another of her mother's little clichés. Slowly, very slowly we shuffled across the three or four feet to the door, knowing that if she sank to her knees we would never manage to support her and once she was on the floor we'd have to start all over again from a much worse position. If we did get her to the door without a collapse, she never fell on the rest of the way. A handrail had been fitted onto the wall between bedroom and bathroom and in the lavatory itself there was now a specially raised seat with handrails either side. The relief of reaching it was overwhelming and, oddly, the journey back always passed without incident.

In the morning, each Marie Curie nurse (usually a different one every night) ended her shift at seven o'clock and I got up to relieve her. With luck, Frances, knocked out by sleeping pills, might sleep another precious hour. I am always up by seven anyway, wherever I am, so it was no hardship. Early morning is my best time and I'd positively bounce into Marion's room, all energy, only to be greeted with indignant surprise. 'Good heavens, what are you doing here?' she'd say, and when I replied that I'd been staying the night to help the nurse if she needed me, she'd snap, 'Ridiculous. There's *no* need for it. You should be at home. It's too much.' I just ignored this, made tea, chatted, tweaked at the bedcovers, employed every delaying tactic to keep her in bed until Frances woke. If Marion wanted to get up,

I would have to buzz for Frances, so I did a lot of rapid talking between seven and eight in the morning, anything to distract her from wanting to get out of bed.

It was somehow a sweet, consoling scene, not a sad one, when I left, each of those November mornings, to walk home. Frances would by then be up, sitting beside Marion, in her new tartan dressing-gown, both of them sipping coffee, Radio 4 on low, the dim light coming through the blind mixing with the stronger glow of the lamp, a smell of toast hanging in the air. There seemed nothing tragic about it. It was sometimes as serene as this in the evening too. I'd return about four o'clock and make a meal, and we'd eat it on a tray in the sitting-room in front of the fire. For this great event Marion would be up for an hour or so, sitting in her nightdress in the armchair, and she would sigh with what sounded so like contentment and say, 'Now, isn't this cosy, isn't this agreeable?' and we'd say yes, it was. She'd watch Frances eat proper food – it pleased her that I was making sure Frances ate good food – and sip her own soup (less and less each evening) and say she wouldn't call the Queen her cousin, another of her mother's many satirical sayings. Everything was lovely; she had no complaints. All the previous agitation seemed to have gone and she was drifting with some sort of hidden tide after going against it for so long.

What exactly had changed I couldn't tell, but something had. I watched her closely all the time without knowing any more exactly what I was looking for. There was no need to look for signs of deterioration any longer – we knew she was in the last stages of this terminal illness. We had been told so, even if we hadn't recognised this for ourselves. Still nobody would risk giving us an informed estimate of when Marion was going to die – how could they – but one nurse had murmured she thought maybe there was a month to go and another thought three weeks maximum. But not to Christmas. No, they all shook their heads over that, she was unlikely to make Christmas.

Marion herself had stopped mentioning the troubled subject of how long she still had. Once, this awful speculation had fascinated her, but not now. She was no longer interested. What I thought I saw was a retreat from thought. Other people alleged that she was now confused and hardly knew who she was, or what she was doing – she was surely muddled, no longer of sound mind – and there was the suggestion that this was a blessing. But it was not true. Most of the time, if all was peaceful, if her routine was undisturbed, she was perfectly clear in her mind. Yet at the same time she was also having to concentrate ferociously on being always present – it was as though again and again she pulled herself back from escaping. One night she said very distinctly to Frances, 'Goodbye.' Frances laughed and said, 'You mean goodnight.' 'No,' Marion said, 'goodbye.' The conviction in her voice was eerie. She never repeated this. I imagined that, on this particular night, she had realised that when the time came for the real goodbye she either wouldn't be able to say it or wouldn't realise she needed to. So she got it in while she was able.

There were other curious moments like that. One morning, soon after the nurse had gone, and I was reading aloud to Marion an article from a day-old *Guardian*, about the increase in attacks on social workers, she suddenly leaned forward and put her hand on mine. I thought she was either bored with the article or that she wanted something. 'Tea?' I said. 'I'm happy,' she said. Then she lay back on her pillows. Her eyes still held mine. 'I'm happy,' she repeated; 'got that?' I could just have said yes, or nodded. Probably I should have just said yes, or nodded. But I didn't. I couldn't let this go. I said I couldn't believe it, it was surely impossible actually to be *happy*. Did she mean she was content, maybe? 'No,' she said, very firmly, 'I am happy. And it isn't the drugs, before you think of that.' And again, looking quite fierce, staring at me from her pillows, she repeated, 'I AM HAPPY. All right?' 'All right,' I said, meekly. She closed her eyes, and seemed to go back to sleep for a while, as though exhausted by making herself clear.

I should have been made happy myself by this declaration but instead I was suspicious; I couldn't believe her for one minute. What I thought she was doing, by this insistence on her state of happiness, was to make her 'loved ones' able to face her death more easily; we could all say to ourselves, 'She was happy,' and that would be a comfort. Why be unhappy ourselves if Marion, dying, had stressed she was happy? But maybe I was doubting her happiness when in fact it was real. What right had I to interpret 'I am happy' as some sort of trick, or a noble attempt to be selfless? What did I know about dying? Maybe, so near to it, there is a feeling akin to happiness. Perhaps, I argued with myself, I should respect this. Marion knew something I did not: the serenity that in some cases comes before death.

I'd seen something like it before, after all, and also been disbelieving. My agent, Tessa Sayle, died the year before Marion of a brain tumour, in her own home. Unlike Marion, she had no partner, no twin, and though she had good friends she didn't appear to have 'loved ones' around her in quite the same way. I went to visit her ten days before she died, climbing the many stairs to her top-floor flat in Kensington, heavy with the dread familiar to all who visit the dying. What would I find? How would I cope? But what I found was a cheerfulness which confounded all expectations. Tessa was in a wheelchair, her wig (she'd lost all her hair through chemotherapy) a little crooked, but otherwise as elegant as ever. A nurse was in the background but soon went out to collect a prescription. It was April and the flat was full of sunlight. I admired the views of the trees, all thick with pink and white blossom. Tessa said she was so lucky to have such views. I think she went on to repeat the word 'lucky' fifty times during the hour I was with her – she was so lucky, she insisted, lucky to be at home, lucky to have such good nursing care, lucky to have so many concerned friends, lucky to have such reliable staff running her agency . . . On and on it went, the emphasis on her luck, and she was ten days from dying, unable to walk, unable to read (and almost unable to see at all), unable to eat much. She talked animatedly, sometimes forgetting halfway through a sentence what she wanted to say and, catching herself forgetting, saying, 'My mind is a little affected,' or, if she'd merely been unable to pronounce a word, 'My speech is a little muddled.' She was clearly quite conscious of what was happening to her but she was determined not to give way to misery or fear. This was a process, the process of dying, which she was going to go through with dignity. None of her standards were to be abandoned, no matter how great the pressure. And, as with Marion, it was of supreme importance to her not to inflict on others any of the suffering she was experiencing.

But did they do it to persuade themselves? I couldn't decide if I was right to think it was done for others, this performance – but there I was again, assuming it *was* a performance. Yet surely, I told myself, dying people have neither energy for, nor interest in, performing. At any rate, that statement 'I am happy' was the last thing of any significance that Marion ever said to me. The following week she didn't speak much at all. She was retreating fast into some interior world of her own. In the afternoons she liked to sit in the wing armchair in the sitting-room for an hour or so, wrapped in her tartan dressing-gown, the one which matched Frances's, listening to tapes of Scottish songs. She sat with her eyes closed, smiling, tapping the rhythms with her fingers, singing along with the words she still recalled from her childhood when her mother had sung them to her. Most of these songs were painfully suitable, ballads of lament and sorrow, and one especially was fitting enough to make us, listening, feel raw with the grief of it when she sang the words – *The Four Maries* (about the death of Mary Queen of Scots):

> I ha'e but just begun to live,
> And yet this day I dee;
> Oh tie a napkin owre my face,
> That the gallows I mayna' see . . .

Their Scottish heritage was so important to Marion and Annabel, but neither of them had a Scottish accent, though they had been born in Scotland and spent their early childhood there. It was a way of honouring their mother, whose love of her native land (her family was from the Highlands originally, near Aberdeen) was extreme. As well as Hogmanay being enthusiastically celebrated, so was 25 January, Burns' Night. Marion had organised Burns' Night parties for her mother during the last years of her life, when she came to London to live with her. Tartan ran rampant – tartan tablecloth, tartan napkins, tartan ribbons and sashes, tartan-backed books of Burns' poetry. Not that Mrs Davies needed any books. She could, and did, recite Burns by the yard, once the haggis had been eaten and the whisky drunk. There she would stand, before a propped-up photograph of Burns, her eyes shining, her already thick Scottish accent thickening, and out would come 'To a Mouse' –

> Wee, sleekit, cow'rin', tim'rous beastie,
> O what a panic's in thy breastie!
> Thou need na start awa sae hasty
>     wi' bickering brattle!
> I wad be laith to rin an' chase thee,
>     wi' murdering pattle!

followed by 'Address to a Haggis', 'Tam o'Shanter', 'To a Louse' and all the other favourites. Marion would watch her with such pride and love, encouraging her when she faltered (though she rarely did) and laughing when she paused to explain certain words ('A pattle is a plough-staff' — 'Yes, we know, Mum. Carry on').

A tape of bagpipe music and another of Scottish reels would be played, and when her mother asked who was going to do the Highland fling, Marion would be up on her feet and performing energetically. Eventually, the merriment would die down and, as more whisky was drunk, Mrs Davies would turn a touch melancholy and begin talking about Scottish history. Culloden would be remembered as though she had been present at the slaughter of the Scots in 1746, and the Highland clearances described with heavy sighs. There was something about the sadness of all this which had always appealed to Marion as well as her mother. They were both by nature cheerful people, lacking any trace of dourness, but they could be overcome at the memory of what the ancestors they had never known had endured.

After her mother died, Marion took her ashes back to the ruins of the croft near Bonar Bridge where her family had once lived. She scattered them there and sang to herself one of Burns' songs (though she didn't ever tell me which one). I thought of that now when I heard her singing, and wondered if it had been his 'Lament of Mary Queen of Scots', the last verse of which reads —

> Nae mair to me the autumn winds
> Wave o'er the yellow corn!
> And, in the narrow house of death,
> Let winter round me rave;
> And the next flow'rs that deck the spring
> Bloom on my peaceful grave —

Returning each day around four o'clock, after the few hours I'd spent at home, I'd hear those Scottish ballads again the moment I opened the door. Going up into the sitting-room, I'd find one or other of Marion's close friends blind with tears as they sat in front of her. But Marion herself was never in tears, and she no longer saw that others were, so could not be distressed by their distress. We'd get her back to bed, with great difficulty, always liable to find she slumped onto the floor even with one of us on either side. Getting her up again grew harder and harder, and it was obvious we were approaching some sort of crisis. We had a Macmillan nurse, we had district nurses, we had Marie Curie nurses, and yet we were still on the brink of not being able to manage. The district nurses, who came twice a day to dress the now horrifically deep pressure sore and the wound in the neck (which had opened up further), had begun to murmur that Marion might be 'more comfortable' in the hospice. But we'd promised she could die at home, and besides, what did they mean by 'more comfortable'? What could a hospice provide that we could not provide? Politely, they said that her dying might be far more prolonged than had been anticipated and that during it Marion's requirements would change in such a way that we would be unable to meet them. Such as? Such as the need, once she was completely bedridden (which was imminent), to be lifted on and off a bed pan, which, in view of the pressure sore, would take skilled hands. We, Frances and I, did not have skilled hands. We just had loving ones. Love, it seemed, could not compete with skill in this case. And in the hospice they had hoists, to make lifting easier and less painful, and special mattresses, and ways of administering pain relief. There was the faintest, the very faintest, insinuation that by keeping Marion at home we might be depriving her of comfort.

It was distressing to have to consider this. If only we knew how long there was to go – the reluctant cry of everyone who watches someone die. Miracles could be performed, anything endured, anything arranged, if we knew there was only a week, a month, a fixed time to aim for. But without this information, which no one could give us (though, when pushed now, the nurses were suddenly guessing that Marion had no more than two weeks left), we were obliged to contemplate a stage where we might finally be failing her. Maybe we already were; maybe we just didn't realise it. Then one of the nurses suggested a compromise: why not take Marion to the hospice just for a weekend? During it, Frances and I could both get some real rest, and something might be done to ease the pressure sore and deal with the oozing from the neck wound. Forty-eight hours of respite care might be of benefit to everyone.

It was a delicate situation. Frances was against moving Marion to the hospice. I couldn't bring myself to urge it because, if I did, it would seem that I was saying I had had enough; and if I did say that, Frances could not manage on her own, no matter how many nurses came in and out. I realised that I wanted it to be over, 'it' being Marion's death. I wanted it to be over now as quickly as possible and I had wanted this for at least a week. But Frances did not want it to be over. She wanted life to go on as long as possible, down to the last tiny flicker. If Marion had been writhing in pain then, of course, her feelings would have been different, but since she was not, and furthermore she was happy, or so she said, Frances saw every justification for clinging on to each precious minute of life, whatever Marion's state. Her attitude was that since death was approaching rapidly anyway, why hurry it? Mine was, since it was coming soon inevitably, why delay it? Marion's condition appalled me. I saw in it agonising suffering, even if there was no pain. Frances saw only an infinitely slow drifting away which she wanted to be part of as long as possible. If Marion was moved to the hospice she feared not only an acceleration of her dying but being separated from it — the intimacy we had at home would be destroyed. She didn't want to spend Marion's last days in a sterile white room in an institution, no matter how kind and caring and skilled the staff. She wanted them both to be utterly comfortable amid their own things, enveloped in an atmosphere domestic and lovingly familiar.

She was right. I knew she was right. Quite apart from Marion herself believing that this was how people should die, I could see that dying in one's own bed at home is always preferable to the alternative. But still my imagination leapt ahead, to having to look after a bedridden Marion who would have to be regularly turned and whose sores and wounds would make this difficult to do. If she were in the hospice, the responsibility on us would diminish at once. If she were in the hospice, we could sleep. Instantly, I felt craven and despicable – it was shameful of me to make such calculations. So I backed the braver Frances up. When one of the nurses took me aside and implied that if I said I couldn't go on, or if I suggested that the hospice might be better for Marion now, Frances would have to weaken, I said no, I couldn't do that: Marion wanted to die at home and we must see that she did. The nurse was worried. She, in turn, began wondering aloud how long she and her team could sanction Marion's being nursed at home. She said she would have to consult her superior.

What was very clear was that Marion herself no longer had any say in the matter. She was long, long past being in control of her own life, never mind of her death. Her earlier assurances that she would take all the liquid morphine and finish herself off when she felt she'd 'had enough' had been pointless. All we could assume was that while she was in control she had never in fact 'had enough'.

That, in itself, seemed to me hugely significant.

On Thursday 9 November, Annabel came, but not on her usual weekly visit. She was on her way to Germany to visit her daughter, a long-planned visit which Marion had been very anxious she should make. There were no pretences. Annabel could see what was happening. She knew Marion might die while she was away for those three brief days, but then she might not. She didn't in any case wish to be there when her twin actually died – the grief and pain of it was too great, the need to witness it mercifully absent. It was so hard for her to leave, saying she'd be back on Monday, but she did it cheerfully, as she does everything, as Marion herself did. I thought, as I watched Annabel go, how rarely she and Marion had been on holiday together. When they were children, there weren't any holidays – such luxuries didn't feature in Davies family life – but Hunter and Annabel used to be sent at times of crisis to Cambuslang, to stay with relatives. Somehow, Marion and Johnny never were. They stayed at home, wondering why they were not the chosen ones (and the suspicion was that Hunter and Annabel were the more sociable and easier to have). Later, in adolescence, Marion did go to stay with her Scottish cousins, and was just as popular with them as Annabel, but the twins hardly ever went away together, even then.

The only times they did were when they went to the Royal Observer Corps camps, once they had left school and were both working in offices. The ROC was really part of the Civil Defence Movement, kept going after the war (this was the 1950s) by the RAF in case it was ever needed again. The twins hadn't the faintest interest in civil defence but they were very taken indeed by the stories circulating in Carlisle of the good times to be had at the annual camps and by the fact that they would get paid if they joined. So they joined. The headquarters was in a large Edwardian house in Norfolk Road and here they went every week, wearing a version of WAAF uniform, barely able to keep their faces straight at the sight of each other. They were taught how to plot flight paths and how to identify the various aircraft. Neither of them was much good at this but somehow they managed to pass the annual examination (mysteriously, to them, called 'triangulation'), which entitled them both to a few shillings and to go on what they regarded as a holiday, to a camp.

They went off to one in Kent and one in Lincolnshire, and the experience was every bit as exciting as they had been promised. They got drunk every night, met loads of boys, and loved the company of the other girls in their dormitory. The actual exercises they had to do during the day, the whole purpose of being there, were a joke – much strutting about, saluting, which gave Marion every opportunity for the parodying she relished. She would sometimes get dangerously near being openly mocking and have to be restrained by the more law-abiding but, in truth, no more respectful Annabel. But both of them thought of those weeks at the ROC camps as highlights of their youth and never needed much encouragement to demonstrate their saluting and marching abilities.

As adults, they'd only been on a couple of holidays on their own together, once for a week to Majorca, once to Sicily. Otherwise, their times together on holiday were within family groups. Going off just on their own was always a much-talked of plan, but the organisational difficulties were formidable and now of course it would never happen. Annabel's going off on her own that night seemed cruelly to underline this fact.

That same night, Marion fell twice, at one in the morning and at four. The nurse and I found it almost impossible to lift her up. We spent ages, each time, kneeling on the floor, either side of her, waiting for the right moment to assist her up. 'Wait, wait,' Marion said. We waited. In my line of vision was the morphine bottle, ever by the bedside. I loathed the sight of it. If only, I used to think, she'd drunk the lot a couple of weeks ago and spared herself this agony – because it was agony, crouched on the floor, panting like a dog, struggling to force herself to put her feet on the floor and allow herself to be dragged, literally dragged, upwards. For what? What was the point of subjecting herself to the absolute tyranny of her dying body? I wanted to open her mouth and pour the morphine down. But she wouldn't have been able to swallow it. She could barely swallow anything. It was too late to help death on in that way. I expect it almost always is. Those who want to die while still in control have to do it not when they are ready but while they are still able. And that, almost certainly, will be before they are ready. A fine state of affairs.

Marion was exhausted after that night. She slept through the night nurse's departure and the arrival of the district nurse. All day she was drowsy, though not actually asleep. In the evening, Frances went out for a meal with two friends. She had barely left Marion's side for weeks but had been persuaded to take this short break. The restaurant was just round the corner and she had her mobile phone with her. Two people had to be with Marion, so Hunter joined me. We sat quite cosily in the bedroom, Hunter entertaining us in the way Marion liked, in the best Davies family tradition with all kinds of anecdotes. Marion smiled and hummed a bit and made one or two rambling remarks connected with nothing. I tried to feed her some ice-cream but she couldn't swallow it, and then some jelly, a few spoonfuls of which did slip down. She mumbled something about the Lonsdale and asked what day it was. 'Friday,' I said. 'Oh, a busy night tonight,' she said.

The Lonsdale was one of five cinemas doing booming business in Carlisle in the 1950s, when we were all growing up there, and by far the smartest. Marion worked there as an usherette during the period she was saving up to emigrate to New Zealand. She'd leave her office job at five o'clock, dash home for tea, then rush back into town to be ready for the parade. The manager of the Lonsdale was a military type, a Mr Scott-Buccleuh, who ran the cinema exactly like a military operation. The entire staff had to be on parade by a quarter to six, ready to open for the first house of the evening. The usherettes would go to their respective stations – Marion was usually put in the back stalls – and wait for Mr Scott-Buccleuh to march onto the stage, where he stood to rigid attention and roared out the names of the various parts of the cinema. 'Front Circle present and correct?' he'd bellow, and the appropriate usherette had to shout back: 'Yes, Mr Scott-Buccleuh!' When all the usherettes had responded, the order came, 'Check torches!' Torches would be flashed (Marion loved that bit and could hardly contain her mirth – he made it sound as though the torches were rifles), and then at last Mr Scott-Buccleuh would yell: 'All correct! Doors open!'

Marion used to say that, usually, far from an eager horde of cinema-goers who must be controlled surging in, a couple of old-age pensioners would totter through the doors and everyone would feel vaguely let down. It was eight o'clock before the multitudes arrived and suddenly the usherettes were busy. It was extraordinary how she liked being busy, how she enjoyed this job in spite of having already worked a long day. She loved the power of the torch, knowing exactly where to direct the beam to discomfort the well-known regular raincoat brigade, or disturb lovers seeking anonymity in the back rows. She play-acted through the evening, delighting in the manager's self-importance and using the breaks in the staff-room (while the big picture was on) to mimic him. The usherettes were nearly all smokers and she was comfortable, puffing away with them and swapping stories, even though most of them were much older than she was.

The Lonsdale years were decades ago now, but she smiled at the memory and we all took the chance to reminisce furiously about the ABC minors' club on Saturday mornings at the Lonsdale, and the Beatles coming to give a concert there later on. It was such a comfort for the three of us to be united like that, effortlessly able to communicate through the memories of all those shared times, all of us with the same background, all of us bound together, firmly rooted in Carlisle lore. We never had to explain anything. Then Hunter, who was writing a book about lottery winners, suggested she chose six numbers and he'd buy her a lottery ticket. She thought hard and came up with six numbers, pausing a long time between each choice, but three of them were the same. It seemed so awful to be asking a dying person to choose lottery numbers. Where would any winnings be sent if she were to be a winner? But she was amused and that was all that mattered. There was no possibility, after all, of any meaningful conversation.

This thought was what kept me awake that night as I lay in bed in the room above Marion's – all the time I'd had with her alone in the last two months and yet the sum total of what had been said was pitifully unimportant. But what was it I wanted to say to her that I hadn't said? And more importantly, had she been given the opportunity to say what she wanted to say to me? I think so. But what she had wanted to say turned out to be apparently of very little consequence. It had been a kind of conceit, I decided, to imagine otherwise. I'd looked for messages and she had none to give. I'd looked for enlightenment and, though she had struggled to provide it and had managed to articulate something of how she felt, it was still vague, muted, her new knowledge, of what it felt like to die. She'd told all of us that she regarded herself as having had a perfectly good life; she'd told us she valued us and had felt valued by us; she'd told us we must not go to pieces after her death. Beyond that, what was there to say, except goodbye? All words were useless, helpless to convey anything at all.

Another very disturbed night followed, and then, in the morning, Saturday, we had great difficulty keeping Marion in bed once the Marie Curie nurse had gone. She was agitated, incredibly restless, and kept trying to get out of bed, but I couldn't let her until Frances came down. She sat on the edge of the bed, the covers thrown back, and I sat facing her, my knees jammed against hers, talking frantically about Armistice Day ceremonies. When I had to call for Frances – I could no longer prevent Marion from trying to stand – she was calmer, and agreed to stay in bed until the district nurse came. When she appeared, it took the three of us to support Marion. It was only two steps to the chair she would sit in while the bed was made, but it seemed like two hundred, so agonisingly slow were her movements. The bed was quickly remade but then the pressure sore had to be dressed, and that was best done with Marion leaning against the bed while we held her up, so we prepared ourselves for the ordeal (and I thought how easily this could have been done in the hospice).

Getting her onto her feet from the chair was hard enough, but the moment she was at last upright, Frances and I on either side and the nurse hovering, she collapsed – swiftly, absolutely suddenly, just *down*. The nurse wanted to send for more help but we wanted to let Marion try to get up first. We sank down beside her and talked quietly to her and stroked her back, and told her to take it easy, not to worry, there was plenty of time, plenty of time . . . Her breathing was heavy and we wondered if she had simply fallen asleep, but eventually she sighed and said, 'Wait, wait,' as she always did. And then, as we levered her up, she managed to get onto her knees and, after another long wait, to raise herself further, and we quickly pushed the chair beneath her and lowered her into it. It was easy then to shove the chair towards the bed and half tip her out onto it. The sore was dressed, the neck bandaged and at last she was tucked up, drowsy and still breathing heavily. 'Thank you, now,' she said, and went to sleep, propped up high on her pillows but soon slumping forward.

We were drained and exhausted, and went to sit in the next room, shaken by the drama of it all. The nurse came in. 'This can't go on,' she said: 'Marion needs to be in a hospice.' Frances lashed out, saying she would not accept that the hospice could look after Marion better than we could. The nurse muttered something about a hoist, as she had done before, and a pump to deliver the morphine into the system more effectively, and yet another kind of water mattress. A hoist? Fine, we'd get a hoist, and a pump, and the special mattress: we'd order them all on Monday. The nurse was silent. Then she said that the point she'd warned us about had been reached and that she couldn't accept responsibility for letting this go on. She'd be discussing it with her superior on Monday. We said nothing, still too distressed to argue effectively. We went on sitting there after she'd gone, trying to calm ourselves. Marion's breathing was so very loud we could hear it through the wall. It was laboured and harsh. We went to look at her and saw mucus dribbling from her nose. We had to keep wiping it away, but this did not disturb her. She slept on, and we thought that was good. Perhaps she would sleep all day and make up for her broken night.

Friends and family came and went, tiptoeing up the stairs, talking in whispers. I wasn't scheduled to stay that night – it was to be my first night at home for a week and I was going to try to have a ten-hour sleep to prepare myself for what might be the long haul ahead. A kind friend of Marion's and Frances's was to take my place, and off I went at about five o'clock, reluctant to go but knowing I should be sensible. We all had to husband our resources. I went to look at Marion before I left. There was no change. She was still asleep, as she had been since ten in the morning. She looked awful, all hunched up, nose leaking, face swollen and grey, hair damp with perspiration. I walked home, glad to be outside, though the air was cold and far from fresh all the noisy way until I'd crossed Highgate Hill. I went straight to bed, slept for a few hours, and then woke around three. When the telephone rang just before seven I was ready for it. Even before I answered I knew Marion was dead.

The relief was instant. It was all over, all that horror. She'd died at home, and though only the Marie Curie nurse was with her when her breathing stopped, she had indeed been surrounded by those who loved her, as she had wished, right up to her last moments of consciousness.

The dead body was lying flat on its back, covers pulled up to its bandaged neck, hair neatly brushed. Since I'd seen such bodies before, four of them by then, I had no fear of this one. A dead body was an object, a cadaver, no longer a person, and I'd always found it strangely reassuring that this should be so. Before I saw my first dead body, a cousin's, when I was fourteen or so, my imagination had terrified me – I'd envisaged something repellent and disgusting, something hideously disfigured, perhaps covered in slime, or crawling already with maggots. The reality had surprised me. I felt nothing, confronted with the corpse, which had seemed bloodless and devoid of any ability to scare. But I'd wondered if I'd feel differently when the dead person meant something more to me. If corpses had been loved when alive, would they have the power to be frightening or at least to awe? I found they didn't. Later, when my mother died, my father had exclaimed on seeing her body, 'That's not her!' He hadn't meant that it was the wrong dead body but that this was no longer his wife. And I thought he was right. Death was, as I'd thought since I lost all my childhood religious faith, definitely the end. Even those who believe that a soul or spirit has flown from the body to some other place do not deny that the corpse is a husk, empty and worthless.

Some people want to see the body, some don't, saying they prefer to remember the person alive. Some invest the corpse with feeling and treat it as an object worthy of reverence or even as a still living, but sleeping, thing. Either way, dead bodies have their own mystique and a house with one in it can make people shudder. Frances wanted Marion's body to be seen and could herself scarcely bear to leave its side. She maintained that

Marion looked peaceful and that she had a smile on her face. To me, her face looked grotesque, distorted by the cancer cells packed within it, her smile — a grimace. I looked at it and banished it, replacing it with Marion's face before the disease began. For me this lifeless thing, lying there, had nothing to do with Marion. But for Frances, it did. She didn't want to part with Marion's body and wouldn't let it be taken to a funeral parlour, not yet. She was desperate to keep it, to invest it with continuing meaning.

But on Monday morning it had to be removed. Only the fact that it was mid-November and suddenly cold, and that the bedroom window had been wide open all night, had kept the body from smelling worse than it did. The undertaker's men came at nine o'clock, as arranged. Frances, distraught, shut herself in her bedroom. She begged me not to let these men be disrespectful, not to let them handle Marion roughly. But I didn't need to tell them anything. They spoke in whispers, came in quietly, carrying not a coffin but some sort of black bag. I showed them into the room. They asked if I wanted the dead lady's nightdress removed and left. I said No. The very idea seemed bizarre and made me feel nauseous; or perhaps it was the atmosphere in the room. The body went into the bag. It was lifted as though it were an object so precious and fragile it might break. Carefully, slowly, silently, the bend in the stairs was negotiated, the bundle taken out of the house. The leading man took a quick look up and down the street. No one about. Another man went ahead and opened the doors of the hearse. The distance from front door to car was covered in seconds. The doors were closed, and off they went.

'Thank God that's over,' said Marion in my head. 'Now get me a cigarette.'

Then there was the funeral, just as it had been organised and planned by Marion. A packed church. We sang 'Guide Me O

Thou Great Redeemer', 'The King of Love My Shepherd Is', and 'For All the Saints Who From Their Labours Rest'. Very mournful, hardly comforting. There were readings – Ecclesiastes 3, Verses 1–8 ('To everything there is a season . . .'), and Matthew 5, verses 1–10, 14–6 ('And seeing the multitudes . . .'). I couldn't imagine why she had selected the Matthew verses. Why hadn't she chosen something from Burns' poetry? It would have had more meaning. Hunter gave an address, talked about Marion's life. It provoked some quiet laughter and was a relief to many. I concentrated on looking at the flowers, white lilies and roses, and at the bunches of heather I'd put on the coffin. What a carry-on, as Marion would have said, it had been to get heather in November. I'd tied the bunches with tartan ribbons and we'd draped a tartan sash of Annabel's, one worn for Burns' Night festivities, underneath.

Then we went back to the flat, to which the entire congregation had been invited. The rooms overflowed with mourners, the stairs were jammed with them, and there was soon a queue outside. The people in the downstairs flat kindly opened up their rooms, too, so that mourners did not have to stand on the pavement. For hours and hours Marion's family and friends ate and drank and reminisced. Then at last they left.

Was the ceremony the comfort that Marion had hoped it would be to those who loved her? Do funerals and wakes fulfil this admirable purpose? For most people probably, yes, they do. For Frances and Annabel this one did. But not for me. For me, it was a ritual which had to be gone through, willingly if it would help even one person, and because Marion had wanted it, but curiously empty, in my case, of any relieving emotion. I never felt the least bit moved, though others did. I had never felt less like weeping, though the tears of others flowed plentifully. The slow hymns, the portentous readings, the solemn prayers all helped them. Far more affecting to me was the private cremation next day. Only five of us were present – Hunter and I,

Annabel, Jeff, and Frances — when, in the otherwise empty chapel, the coffin slid silently away. It seemed, in contrast to the church service, simple and so much more appropriate. I said so in my head to Marion. She laughed and told me to keep quiet, I was always out of step, and far too fond of speaking my mind. She didn't want Annabel and Frances more distressed by any odious comparisons I might make.

I felt quite cheerful afterwards. We'd begun talking again, Marion and I. She looked and sounded as she always had. Now she was dead, now the dreadfully prolonged cruel business of dying was over, she lived again in my mind. It was going to be, I assured her, a very safe, secure place to be. I'd look after her.

# VIII

THE DAY MARION died, 12 November, I didn't write my usual weekly letter to my father. My sister telephoned him and told him the news and he said, 'Pity,' as expected. But I wrote the following week, touching only briefly on the funeral and otherwise concentrating on family chitchat, as I knew he would want me to do. And I resumed the regular telephone calls, taking up my place again in the rota. This seemed to please him very much – 'Grand,' he said, 'back to normal now.'

Back to normal. Since it was November, it was normal to be thinking of his birthday. He would be ninety-five on 4 December. Since my brother always 'did' the birthday, he and his wife were going north to be there for it again. In fact, it was a good birthday and my father enjoyed it. The home made a little event of it, with a cake and candles and everyone singing 'Happy Birthday, dear Arthur'. Gordon said that instead of embarrassing him this had amused him and he'd been in high good humour. On his calendar he wrote – 'Got a birthday party. 95.' Two weeks later, Pauline and her family arrived at Loweswater to spend Christmas, going in to see him on all the crucial festive days. They had Christmas dinner with him at the home and reported that he had loved all the nurses wearing paper hats and the place being lavishly decorated, and everyone in exuberant form. 'Smashing Day,' he put for 25 December.

He'd had forty more years than Marion and still he looked forward to the New Year. At least there was no mix-up over his new calendar this time. I'd left it in our Loweswater house, prominently displayed, back in September, all ready for Pauline to take to him for the ceremonial opening on 1 January 1996. Horses this year, every type and colour of horse, beginning with a chestnut mare and her foal. The space for each day was broad enough for him not to have to write too small, but narrow enough for him not to have too much blank square to fill. I remarked on the telephone that I liked the August horse best, a black stallion standing on the top of a hill. He was shocked that I'd looked ahead. He never did, he said. 'Why not?' I asked. 'Bad luck.'

In February, it was my turn to go for a short visit, to help bridge the gap between Pauline's visits at Christmas and Easter. I hadn't seen him since September and expected to find he had deteriorated further. But he hadn't. When I arrived, at two in the afternoon,he was sitting up alert and smart, wearing a new blue shirt and red tie, hands resting on his walking stick, as though poised for getting to his feet at a moment's notice. And he did try to rise out of his chair as I entered the room. 'Don't get up, Dad,' I protested. 'I will if I want,' he said, but sank back, the gesture over. He was animated, full of questions, even if they were the usual questions with which he always greeted me, about the train, whether it was full or not, whether it was on time, and the weather. I put the flowers I'd brought into a vase and the sweets on the cabinet beside him, and for a while there was a sense of bustle and activity which successfully covered up awkwardness. Because there was always awkwardness when visitors arrived. In his own house, still mobile and in control, my father had been able to cover this up with strategies of his own (a lot of pacing about, a good deal of fidgeting) but now he couldn't. All he could do was wait, and he hated it.

Eventually, I had to sit down, on the bed, facing him. He fell asleep, his head sunk on his chest. I studied his calendar carefully. February was illustrated with three white horses drinking at a pond. Very nice, very rural. I could get five minutes' chat out of that when he woke, by considering whether the horses were siblings, by speculating on the location of the pond – oh, a wonderful conversational piece there. I noticed the writing on the calendar wasn't all his. The nurses and carers had added things. 'Andrea and Lynne on holiday' I read for 3 February. He must have told them to jot this down. They wouldn't have dared to do it otherwise. His own words were hard to decipher now, but then what was there to decipher? 'Light drops of rain', and impossible squiggles followed by 'Dry Sunny later'. I scrutinised the missing words and, after consideration worthy of a scholar unravelling a medieval document, decided he'd just repeated 'Light drops of rain', then, realising this, had written over them. That was all right, then. Only the weather seemed to be recorded now. There was no gardening, of course, to merit notes, and no outings to list at the moment, though he had regular visits from quite a variety of people and in that respect was well off. By comparison with other patients, that is. By comparison with Marion, very well off just through being alive. What a silly thought to come into my head, one which showed me only too clearly and unpleasantly the resentment that lurked there. As if the poor old man could help living longer than Marion. When someone young died, my mother used to wail that she wished God had taken her instead; but my father never voiced such sentiments, and I was fairly certain he never harboured them either.

He woke up and looked startled when he saw me there. 'You still here?' he said. I said Yes, for another hour or so, and then for tomorrow too. What a long hour (so long that I was timing it to the minute). The hours I sat with him during the last days he spent in his own house had been long enough, but then I'd been able to break the monotony by making tea, washing dishes, picking flowers – there'd always been some little action to hand. Here, in this one small room, there was none. I'd already done the flowers, trimming each carnation, arranging them with infinite care, a veritable Constance Spry. Going out to fill the bird container with nuts was the only other ploy I could think of. There was a box of nuts in the bottom drawer of his bureau. I asked permission to get them. It was eagerly given. He was as keen as I was that one of us at least should be *doing something*. I spun the task out to a full quarter of an hour by dint of dropping the nuts in one by one, then going in search of water to fill that part of the tray. Through the windows I saw not only my father watching me but all the faces staring in my direction from the rooms which overlooked the garden. I felt I was on a stage, my audience desperate for something dramatic to happen to relieve the unbearable tedium. If only an eagle would swoop down and carry me off, or if only I could be attacked by a Hitchcockian band of smaller birds. Plop, plop, went the nuts. And then I was done, the show was over in all its disappointing ordinariness.

I returned to my father's room, feeling as always that entertainment was expected of me. My function was to distract him, to brighten up his dull days. He was always quick to complain about any visitors who 'just sat' when they came to see him – 'I had to do all the talking. They just sat.' I decided to tidy his cabinet drawers. But when I suggested this, he wasn't enthusiastic. The two drawers in the little bedside cabinet between bed and armchair were his last area of privacy, because he could no longer get to his bureau drawers unaided and so could not secrete things there. But finally, he said he supposed these drawers could do with a bit of a turn-out and I could go ahead while he supervised.

The top drawer was in a terrible mess, one great jumble of things jammed into it. I fished out not one but three salt cellars. Salt from all of them had spilled everywhere. To each there was a history which he relished relating. The most valued was a small, blue plastic item he had brought from his own kitchen and greatly treasured. It seemed this had been accidentally removed on a tray and the other two were substitutes provided by the home when his could not be found. 'I raised hell,' he said, with satisfaction. 'I wasn't going to have it pinched.' I laughed at the idea of anyone deliberately stealing a blue plastic salt cellar, but he glared at me and said I might laugh but I didn't know what went on and he had to be alert at all times, or else. He also had a whole packet of Saxa salt with the salt cellars. 'Don't they have salt here?' I asked. Yes, but not the sort he liked and never enough of it. 'Too much salt is bad for you,' I said. His turn to laugh.

There were pounds of sweets in the drawer, bags of Devon Toffees and Barley Sugars and Mint Humbugs, all broken into, and in some cases the individual sweets had been unwrapped, sucked for a while, then dropped back into the bags. He wouldn't let me throw any away, not even the ones that had picked up hairs. 'Waste not, want not,' he said. Several handkerchiefs of dubious cleanliness lay on top of two pairs of broken spectacles, the lenses of each right eye cracked diagonally. I said these really were useless and made to chuck them in the bin, but no, he insisted on keeping them because the left lenses were intact and who knows, they might come in useful. There was a spoon, sticky with sugar, in one corner of the drawer. 'Careful,' he said, as I took it out and wiped it, 'that's precious.' His grandchild, my eldest daughter, had sent it from Botswana. It had a long black wooden handle, its end carved into the shape of a rhinoceros, and on the back of the bowl of the spoon was engraved the head of George VI. My father stirred his tea with this spoon. No other would do. After each stirring he just tossed it into his drawer, 'for security', and enjoyed trying to find it again later. The remaining contents of his top drawer were letters from me and Pauline. 'What's got into you?' I teased (though since my father didn't recognise the concept of anything as frivolous as teasing, this had no effect). 'Keeping letters now?' 'I have to hang on to something,' he said, defensively.

The bottom drawer had ties in it. Lots of ties, all creased and screwed up, heavily spotted with stains. 'Dad,' I protested, 'these need to be cleaned. Give them to the girls to take to the laundry.' He said he didn't want them washed, washing ruined ties, but when I offered to have them dry-cleaned he said, No, it was too expensive. I said I could stand the expense, for heaven's sake, but he was getting irritated, so I just put the ties back. An hour had almost passed by now. An hour in the company of my own father, whom I hadn't seen for five months, and all I could think about was escape. I didn't dare look at the time again, though with the alarm clock facing me and the large mantelpiece clock he'd been given on his marriage in 1931 ticking away, it was difficult not to be aware of each second passing. Next day, I vowed, I'd bring some sewing or knitting. What a joke. I hadn't knitted anything since I was six, when I managed to knit a dishcloth using very thick needles and rope-like yarn, and as for sewing I had always loathed it. I'd have to buy one of those tray cloths stamped with a pattern and sit decorously embroidering it. It would be a return to the nineteenth century: I'd be a woman silently sewing to fill a void.

It was almost the time when I'd decided I could decently leave – he'd earlier encouraged me to walk the long way, while it was still light, to Jeff's, where I was to stay – when he suddenly said, 'I'm not getting any better,' and shook his head. 'You're better than you were a year ago, when you came in here,' I said. He gave a little snort of derision. 'It's hard getting up from this chair,' he said, 'and I could do that easy when I came here. I could walk without a stick, nearly.' He tried to get on his feet, to demonstrate his lack of strength and, though he managed to stand, he swayed alarmingly. I put out my hand to steady him. – 'No!' he said. 'I have to do it myself. I have to manage. I have to get better.' He said he'd walk me to the front door, which I didn't want him to do. I'd rather have said goodbye to him in his room, where he looked secure. All down the corridors he clung to the rail which ran along the walls. There were gaps with no rail, where doors appeared, and he was obliged to take my arm. I could feel the bone beneath the jacket and shirt sleeves. That's all his arm was, a bone, a thin layer of skin stretched tight over a bone with no flesh to pad it out. Marion might have been desperately thin, but her arm had been much more substantial when she died. 'See, I'm not getting any better,' he repeated as he edged his way slowly along. I said nothing. What could I say, in the face of this evidence that he thought old age a disease from which he expected to get better? How could he not recognise that this was not an illness from which he could recover but the approach to the ending of life?

I went to see him again in March, the same short two-day trip, just so that he would not be too long without family attention before Easter, and Pauline's longer visit. The same routine, the same feelings of depression. He was even thinner and I was told he wasn't eating as well. His breakfast was all he wanted now – no other food all day. When I arrived, the pudding from his lunch was still there on a tray, untouched. 'I told them not to bring it,' he said. Sitting on the edge of his bed, my feet knocked against something. I bent down and lifted the counterpane to investigate. There was a plate full of food – a potato, a piece of meat, some shreds of cabbage and some slices of carrot. He'd fallen into a doze, but when I lifted the plate up he woke and became fully alert and furious: 'Don't touch! Leave it!' It was ridiculous. Nobody would force him to eat anything, nobody would be angry if he didn't want food. I said this to him – 'Why don't you just say you're not hungry?' He shook his head, put his finger to his lips, and gestured that I should put the plate back.

The staff knew, of course they knew, what he was doing, but they played the game he wanted to play. The plates of food were tactfully removed at the end of each day when he was in the bathroom. They gave him less and less, so that his reduced appetite would not be overwhelmed, but he still left most of his lunch and tea and supper, and hid it. But where did he imagine all the full plates were going once he'd stuck them under his bed? Or did he think they were all still there, plates and plates of rejected food slowly rotting underneath him while he slept? He still ate every scrap of his cooked breakfast, especially every morsel of bacon, no matter how difficult this was due to the state of his teeth. He still had all his own bottom teeth, which did most of the chewing, but they were beginning to loosen. When a tooth felt loose enough he pulled it out himself. A dentist had visited him in the home and done his best to make his mouth comfortable, but it was a fairly hopeless task – 'I've got him beat.'

Before I left this time I wrote on his calendar the date Pauline would be arriving, to stay at Loweswater for two whole weeks and coming in every other day. 'Good,' he said. The nights were getting lighter, spring was near, and he was cheerful. He'd survived another winter and now he would get out and about again. I wrote down our date of arrival too. Always a happy moment for him, knowing we would be near, only forty minutes away for a whole five months. 'Let's hope you don't have to go gallivanting back to London again this summer,' he said. Gallivanting? I thought about challenging him on that one but decided to let it go. It was easy to understand how important it was for him to rely on us staying close for an unbroken stretch of time. The summer routine was so much better for him than the winter one. A weekly letter and a thrice-weekly phone call were nothing compared to a twice-weekly visit and a daily phone call.

I don't recall how this daily phone call started. What had been wrong with the winter rota, when I used to phone alternately with Pauline and Gordon? There should have been less reason now, not more, to phone. But somehow I'd slipped into this 'quick call' business at six o'clock and like all such fixtures involving my father it could not be stopped once started. And God knows, it was easy enough to do: only a matter of exchanging pleasantries, giving him reassurance — hardly a burden. He liked to tell any of the staff in his room at the time, 'Watch the clock. When it gets to six, she'll ring.' Such triumph when I did. Now that I was seeing him so regularly there wasn't much to say, but I always found something — the first sweetpea out, a red squirrel in the garden, a new postman . . . It didn't matter. All he wanted was another marker to help him feel his way through time. Duty done, I could relax.

Driving into Carlisle from Loweswater, on our first visit of summer 1996, duty weighed more heavily than it had ever done. Duty sounds such an ugly, cold, hard word, signifying a lack of love or pleasure or tenderness, devoid of those qualities one can feel happy to possess. Doing *only* one's duty towards one's parents smacks of implied resentment, stinks of self-righteousness. I knew that perfectly well. It was awful to be going to visit my father out of duty. I wanted to be going to see him out of anything but that. I wanted to discover within myself feelings of genuine warmth and love, but I couldn't. There was something there, though, which was either not quite duty or which softened it into a feeling less repugnant. In theory, I did not agree that children are honour-bound to look after parents simply because those parents have given them life: I refused to acknowledge that there was an indisputable duty. And yet there I was, identifying duty as the reason I looked after my father and stayed close to him.

We drove through the Lorton Valley and round the end of Bassenthwaite Lake on a glorious May morning. I remembered the long bike rides I'd had with my father, forty miles or more each time, all pedalled in silence, the only stops those at pubs when he'd go in for a pint and bring out lemonade for me. We passed the turn-off for Keswick, where he'd taken me on the bus to cross Derwent Water and climb Catbells. Next the road took us through Uldale and onto Caldbeck, where he'd taken me to hound trails. He'd loved the betting, but he loved, too, the sight of the dogs bounding across the hills, their owners whistling and shouting and banging on tins of food held out for them at the end. They were good memories, but what, I wondered, was I trying to make of them that was relevant to an analysis of my sense of duty – trying, I suppose, to make it more attractive? Was I suggesting to myself that nostalgia meant I was not merely dutiful? But I wasn't nostalgic. I had no desire at all to be back, aged eight, on long bike rides with my father, or aged nine, at hound trails or climbing Catbells. The idea made me shudder. What I actually felt was nothing as sweet as nostalgia – it was gratitude. I was grateful for the time he had devoted to me. Many a child of a working man who had no car and little money never left Carlisle, never knew anything of the beautiful countryside around it. My father had made sure I did. He'd bothered. He'd shown me the glories of the Lake District without needing to say a word, and this was a gift more precious even than ensuring that I was adequately fed and clothed. Duty was distasteful, but gratitude was surely tolerable.

Swooping down from the fells, driving down Warnell towards the Eden Plain, where every stretch of the road held some memory or other of my father, I thought of something else: pity. A word as dubious as duty. Nobody wishes to be pitied. Sympathy is fine; pity, offensive. But it was pity I felt for my aged father as we neared his nursing-home. Worse still, it was not a particular kind of pity, but the common-or-garden sort which one feels for any extremely frail old person, pity nearer to compassion, for their infirmities and the hopelessness of their situation. The very words 'I feel so sorry for you' have always made me want to hit the speaker, but that was what I wanted to say to my father 'I feel so, so sorry for you.'

I wondered, as we came within the city's boundary, about my

father's own attitude to his parents. His sense of duty had certainly been well developed. He'd looked after his parents in their old age with devotion but never, I was sure, with love. Yet he'd not been put to quite the same kind of test his own children were now facing. His parents had both died in their mid-seventies and, in fact, it was my mother who had fulfilled his obligations for him. He believed he had obligations, though. That was true. Unlike me, he firmly believed adult children had to look after aged parents. That was how the system worked: it was natural and allowed for no discussion. During my adolescent years, when I furiously demanded discussion on every banned subject, I'd tried to take this up with him. I'd asked what was supposed to happen, in this natural, immutable order of things, to childless people? Being childless was their own fault, he said. Greatly daring, I also suggested that times had changed and what was once natural no longer needed to be so – children need not be the automatic consequence of marriage and if they were *chosen* by people, not wished upon them, what then? In that case, I said, there was surely no unwritten contract. He said if I believed that, I'd believe anything, and I was talking daft. This attitude of his had never faltered. If he thought at all about why his children were looking after him now, he would see it as his rightful dividend.

At least none of us three children was doing it out of self-interest. Duty might be the prime reason, but there was no sinister motive. We were not hoping or expecting to inherit anything. My father's parents had owned their own house, if a modest one, and had had a few thousand pounds in the bank. My father never owned a house, nor did he have money in the bank. He was much poorer than his parents. In fact, when I came to look into the particular history of his family I realised he was its poorest member for generations. His great-great-grandfather, another Arthur (who lived to ninety-three), had been a wealthy farmer with forty-eight acres of land deep in the

Border Reiver country; his great-grandfather was a prosperous innkeeper (though he started off as a schoolmaster) in the same area; his grandfather Arthur (the one whose grave we visited) had been a successful carpenter who established a thriving business in Carlisle.

Then what happened? This grandfather of my father's left enough money for his son to buy his own house even though he was only a fitter. His comfortable circumstances were due to this inheritance and because he was thrifty, not to say parsimonious; and, never unemployed, he was able to save. Yet what he saved was not enough to leave to my father and his brother anything like the amount that had been left to him. But what he was going to leave them inevitably came into his relationship with them. My grandfather George Forster was an irascible old man and his sons knew he could change his will at any moment if they displeased him. But now my own father had nothing to leave. None of us would benefit financially from his death. He, at least, had no need to be haunted, as so many old people must be, by the suspicion that our devotion was motivated by greed. And his lack of money meant he could never play games, threaten us with being cut out of any will. We were all richer than he had ever been, with our houses, our cars, our standard of living. He, who had worked harder than any of us, was stranded between parents who had had something and children who had a great deal, whereas in a material sense he had nothing. Somehow this made me feel better about being dutiful. The duty, if nothing else, was pure. I liked that.

But even if feeling better about being motivated by duty and gratitude and compassion, unsullied by expectations of financial gain, cheered me up, there was still a piece missing from the puzzle when I tried to understand the power my father had over me. I decided, as we turned into the road where the nursing-home was, that it could only be due to one extra element, to which I had not given enough weight: his own personality. Old people, sick people, who have once been fierce and dominant don't seem to lose their force of character when their physical strength ebbs. This power in them actually seems to increase instead of waning, and as it does so it commands even more respect than it did before. What I was seeing, in these years of my father's final decline, was evidence of some inner power to which it was impossible not to respond. He had no *actual* power any more; he could not make me do anything at all, as once he had been able to, employing physical force if necessary, but he still drew forth tremendous allegiance that was far beyond duty. To be so old, to be so near to dying, and have the kind of determination to live that he had could only excite admiration – this, too, was part of his power.

This admiration always flared up, however gloomy I was feeling, whenever I saw him for the first time each summer. I dreaded walking down the corridors to his room, inwardly groaning at the realisation that all this was starting yet again for another five months, but as I turned into his doorway and saw him before he saw me I felt proud of him. He was visibly doing his best not to be a lump in a chair. But this time he was not as upright, not as alert, nor as smart as he usually was. Since March, there had been a noticeable deterioration. He had lost more weight, especially from his face, which looked suddenly gaunt, the cheekbones now very prominent. There was effort in the smallest of movements and his hands shook.

But he wanted to go out. There was no hesitation about that. 'I've been sitting in this damned chair long enough,' he said, and struggled to get out of it. He had a great struggle to stand and then, when he had managed it, his walking was so unsteady, in spite of his stick and my arm, that he knocked into the door frame. One of the staff, seeing him stagger, said she would bring a wheelchair. 'You will not!' roared my father. 'I might as well give up if I have to get into one of those.' It took ages to reach the front entrance and then there was the usual problem of coping with two doors opening onto each other. This almost defeated us. If a nurse had not rushed to help he would have collapsed, caught for ever between inner and outer door. The same nurse helped us to the car and put my father into his seat, a task which I saw now required considerable skill. 'What a carry-on,' he said, as finally we set off. 'I don't know what's the matter with me.'

We drove to Silloth. The new season always had to open with a drive to Silloth, twenty-two miles away, and for some time now too far to take him because of his fear of incontinence (a fear sadly solved recently by the use of pads). 'Grand,' he said, when we said where we were heading. 'Have you checked the tide?' I had. We weren't catching any boat, but I knew we had to know the tides. His pleasure was complete when I said it would be high at three o'clock, just as we would reach the seafront road. I liked giving him pleasure. (What did that mean? Did it mean I wasn't, after all, merely dutiful? I kept looking for ways to avoid that charge.) He made comments which showed his enjoyment all the way to Silloth – 'That farmhouse has been painted since last year' . . . 'Wigton's by-passed now, we'll come to it in a minute.' When we reached the coast road the sea was crashing against the wall, and no part of the shingle beach was visible. 'Get out, then,' he ordered me. 'You'll want to walk.'

He was right, I did, and not just to please him. The car trundled slowly off, Hunter trying to make the last mile take for ever, and I set off, the spray from the waves showering me if I went too near. We'd done this walk so many times together, my father and I, in all weathers, and I knew he could still do it in spirit so long as I was doing the walking for him. The more the wind blew, the more colour came into my cheeks, the more he would be able to look at me and say, with immense satisfaction, when I joined him again, 'You've had a good blow, then.' I walked quickly, practically running, the wind in my face all the way. It was too early in the summer for many trippers to be in Silloth and the car park nearest the front was empty except for our car. Hunter got out the minute I arrived, all too eager to obey my father's instruction to go and look at the docks. I sat there with him now, facing the wild sea, his binoculars trained on the seagulls perched on the buoys, until Hunter returned and reported a Greek trawler in the docks. We drove there and made a stately progress along the quay. Once these docks had been teeming with ships but now we were lucky to find this solitary boat. 'Pity,' my father said.

After the ritual visit to the docks, there was nothing else to do except creep round the streets so he could reminisce. Not many streets in Silloth, and all laid out conveniently on a grid system, so we were round them all in minutes. Since getting in and out of the car was such an ordeal for my father, and since the weather was still too doubtful (clouds over the sun by three o'clock and rain in the air), there was no question of hauling him out onto a bench. We parked near the Green and bought ice-creams where we'd always bought them and sat licking them, looking at the Green where the donkeys had once given rides. 'Pity,' my father said. 'Everything's gone, it's all come to an end. Silloth was a grand place in the old days.' I said it still was, that it was unspoiled and I liked the emptiness and sense of peace. 'Well, I like a bit of life, like in the old days,' he said. We sat a bit longer in silence and then couldn't put off any longer the return to Carlisle. The treat was over, and it hadn't been as satisfactory as usual. All that Silloth now meant was sitting in a car licking ice-cream.

He slept all the way back, head sunk on his chest, body held in position only by the car's seat belt. When we drew up outside the home, he slept on. We waited for him to waken in his own time. He showed no signs of doing so. I thought how wonderful it would be if he had died peacefully in his sleep on his last outing to his beloved Silloth. But no. He hadn't. No such luck for him. Or for me. I'd fantasised such perfect endings for him for years now. One last heave with his spade in his garden and then oblivion among his newly planted potatoes – that was one. I had variations on this same theme, of his dying while active, doing something he enjoyed before the cruelties of extreme old age were visited upon him. But no, another fantasy was grounded. He woke up. We couldn't get him out of the car and had to fetch a nurse. She brought a wheelchair and this time there was nothing my father could do about it. He had to submit to being put in the wheelchair and he was wheeled away, his eyes tightly shut and mouth set in a grim line of revulsion.

From then onwards we took him to and from the car in a wheelchair. His only way round what he saw as this humiliating capitulation was to rename the wheelchair and treat it as something else. 'Fetch my pram!' he began instructing us and gave to the words a ring of 'Fetch me my chariot!' There was a bitter humour about his attempt to rise above the indignity of being placed in a wheelchair and he whistled loudly, pointedly, as he was propelled along. It was a means to an end, his 'pram', that was all. I suggested one day pushing him in it round the streets outside the home, but his tolerance did not extend that far. 'No! I'm not starting that game.' What game? It seemed that wheelchair-to-car was endured out of necessity, because he wanted to go for drives so much, but being pushed round the streets would make him a permanent not a temporary wheelchair-bound person and this difference was crucial. As usual, no discussion was allowed. He had his own standards and felt no need to explain or justify them.

At least it meant we could now get him to the car swiftly and that he was not exhausted when he reached it. But there was still the problem of getting him from the wheelchair into the car seat. He could never believe he couldn't do it himself. Always, he expected to be able to. There was the same 'Wait, wait' that there had been with Marion when she fell, the same determination that mind should overcome matter. Soon he had to admit defeat, though only for that particular day, and then we tried to manoeuvre him into the car. And failed. Two strong people unable to lift a frail ninety-five-year-old man, who weighed nothing, into a car. The staff could do it with ease. There was one girl, a carer not a nurse, who could do it on her own without any help at all. She was eighteen, tall and heavy, and she simply picked my father up, getting him (very reluctantly) to put his arms round her ample waist. 'Where is it?' he would shout. 'I can't find any bloomin' waist, lass, you're that stout.'

Sometimes, after all the anxiety this induced, he would take a while to recover. The regular loss of dignity was always traumatic and he never got used to it or became philosophical about it. He would sit silently, calming down, and I sat in the back, also in a state, wondering if going for a drive was worth this. But of course it was, there was no doubt about that. He loved those car rides. They were the focal point of his dreary days, and he didn't care where we went. He no longer made any attempt to direct us. He was happy simply to be on the move and out of the home. But then, around the end of July, a strange change took place. He began to say he didn't think he'd bother going for a drive. He looked amazed himself as he said this – 'I don't think I'll bother.' This was hugely significant, surely. Why had going out become suddenly a bother? He didn't plead ill health, he didn't blame the weather (which was good, anyway). I wondered if I should try to persuade him but decided that would be a waste of energy. He had always been oblivious to anyone's coaxing.

If we were not to go out, there was instantly the problem of how to fill the two hours usually spent in driving somewhere. The time had never exactly flown by on those expeditions, but since it had taken fifteen minutes to get my father into the car, an hour to drive to the sea, or some country village he liked, and back (including halts to look at anything remotely interesting, even a sheep with its horns stuck in a fence), the rest of the afternoon had been easily accounted for in settling him in his room again. Now, when we never left the room, two hours were an eternity, just as they had been when I made flying visits on my own. Hunter talked valiantly, telling my father all kinds of things he liked to hear about football and lottery winners and suchlike, but even he was defeated after an hour and took to roaming the corridors restlessly or departing for some imaginary appointment. It was no good consoling ourselves with the thought that my father just liked our company, that in itself this was sufficient and we shouldn't worry about filling the time for him. It wasn't true. Company was an irritation to him unless it was performing. When talk flagged, I had to be doing something he could watch. Otherwise his attitude was that he might as well be on his own.

I took to sewing nametapes on his clothes. Pauline had marked them all hastily, as required, when he came into the home, but she'd simply written his name in ink on plain tape and after all the zealous washing that went on this had worn off. She'd ordered proper Cash nametapes and these had now arrived. I showed them to him. He liked to see his name, A. G. Forster, in bold blue capitals. He watched while I began sewing them onto his shirts and trousers and cardigans, onto every single sock and handkerchief. It was going to take a blissfully long time. I sewed as I always sewed (when I forced myself to sew at all), with large, careless stitches, my aim being to secure the tape to the garment and not concern myself with neatness. For good measure, and to take longer, I crossed back across each jagged stitch. My father glared at my handiwork, frowning fiercely, and said, 'That's a fine mess.' I agreed, cheerfully. 'You're no needlewoman,' he said accusingly, as though exposing some hideous fraud. I agreed I wasn't. If I'd said so in a penitent fashion, he would doubtless have overlooked my abominable sewing, but since I obviously didn't care he was annoyed. 'Pauline is the sewer. She sews grand,' he said. I said Yes, she did, he was right, and weren't her tapestries exquisite, and didn't her— But he cut across all the compliments to my sister. 'If you're no good at it, why are you doing it, stabbing away with that needle and making a mess?'

I thought about saying:

> To give me something to do and you something to watch.
> To relieve both our boredoms.
> To help me feel more comfortable.
> To stop me screaming at the agony of all this.
> To stop me running away.
> To stop me falling asleep.
> To make me feel useful.
> To avoid asking questions you consider daft.
> To do some small thing for you because I can't do any of the things you would like me to do such as wave a magic wand and either have you back digging your garden or else end all this.

But what I said was, 'It's got to be done' – an answer absolutely in line with his own way of thinking. Piously, I continued, as he would have done: 'It's got to be done. The clothes have to be marked properly, or they'll get lost in the wash.' He sighed. 'Well, I won't be needing them much longer. I can't go on for ever.' And what did I say, given this opening? I said, as I always had done when he made this comment, 'I don't see why not.' Oh, how droll, how amusing. And he *was* amused. His mood changed. He snorted with derision, but seemed pleased. 'Good lass,' he said, as I went on with the wretched sewing.

But I knew I wasn't a good lass. I was a cowardly one. Always, I'd resented the fact that my father would never talk about feelings, his or anyone else's, and there he had been, getting as near as he was able to confessing that he knew he was near to dying, and I had chosen to be facetious. Why did I do it? Why does anyone do it? When an old or very sick person says they feel they haven't got long to live would it be better to respond with, 'Yes, I think you're right, you're dying at last.' Or even more brutally with 'That's good.' But evading the issue seems the only kind way of dealing with forlorn statements like my father's. I don't think I'd have been rated a 'good lass' if I'd agreed he wasn't likely to need his clothes much longer. Silence might have been best of all – silence and a pat on his hand (very bold) and a little whimper of sympathy. But would silence have been kind or cruel in a different way from verbal agreement? As for using his remark to launch into a discussion about whether he actually wanted to go on living, that would have been the most interesting way of tackling it. Could I have said, 'You're right, you can't go on for ever, but then perhaps you don't want to?' But I know what his reply would have been: 'No choice. Can't be helped.' Exactly; so it seemed better not to have said it.

We left him fairly cheerful that particular afternoon, and the next time we came he wanted to go out. But from then on we were never certain how we would find him. His favourite carer was concerned. 'He isn't himself,' she said. She thought he might be sickening for something. I could hardly restrain myself from suggesting 'Death?' On Friday 23 July, we visited but he wouldn't go out. We passed the time well enough with me showing him photographs of Carr's biscuit works at the turn of the century which I'd been collecting for a book I was researching. He liked that. It stimulated him to talk about Carr's and my aunt who worked there. On Sunday, when I made my daily phone call, there was no answer. The telephone was right beside him, on the little cabinet next to the chair, from which he could not now move unaided. I rang the nurses' desk. Arthur, they told me, had elected to stay in bed all day. He didn't want to be bothered with the telephone. They'd rung to warn me and to assure me he wasn't ill, just tired, but there had been no answer (we'd been fell-walking all day and came back only at six in time to phone). They said not to worry, they'd report his condition in the morning, which they did. Arthur, they said, was still in bed. He'd had a stomach upset in the night and they were going to send for the doctor to be on the safe side. We went in straightaway, hoping to catch the doctor, but he'd already been. It seemed that as well as a stomach upset my father had a chest infection.

He was in bed, with the curtains half pulled, lying propped up on several pillows, his eyes closed. We crept in, noting how odd his face looked without his heavy spectacles, how exposed. He was very pale, quite devoid of colour, his complexion (always good) wax-like. But he wasn't asleep. He opened his eyes and turned to look at us and said, 'What are you here for? It isn't on the calendar. It's not Tuesday yet, is it? Or am I going barmy?' I said no, he wasn't barmy, it was only Monday and he was right, we'd said we'd come on Tuesday, but when he hadn't answered the phone we were concerned and wanted to see how he was. 'I'm a bit off,' he said. 'I don't know what the devil is the matter with me.' I said he seemed to have had a stomach upset and now he had a chest infection. The doctor was going to call again tomorrow and keep an eye on him. 'Put it on the calendar,' he said. 'Keep me straight.'

I took the calendar off the wall and studied it. The illustration for the month of July showed a black stallion galloping across a field of buttercups. The space for each day had been scrupulously filled in my father's handwriting for the whole of the previous week had become progressively less certain and there were lots of crossings-out. On Friday, he'd noted our visit, without any comment; on Saturday it had been 'a hot day, a long day, no visitors'; Sunday was blank. Now we were at Monday. I took his Biro and carefully wrote, for Sunday: 'A. in bed, so-so' and for Monday: 'Dr called. M & H here.' I showed this to him for his approval. He grunted. Then he said, 'This is no fun.' It was an odd phrase to use. Had his life ever been *fun*? I doubted it. But he hadn't been searching for appropriate words. Those he used were just what occurred to him and it was useless to ponder over whether they were accurate. 'No,' I said, 'I can see this is no fun.' I was sure he was not complaining but trying to express despair. 'This is no fun' also could mean 'this is no life'. He was acknowledging that, at almost ninety-six, he had come to the end of his life but nobody would admit it. Everyone conspired to keep him going, in this state of 'no fun'.

This was the point I had hoped he would never consciously have to reach. He had a chest infection, known once upon a time as the 'old man's friend'. In the days before antibiotics it would have killed him, but now it would not be allowed to.

The doctor came again the next day and this time I was there to see him. He said he'd like a word with me. A nurse showed us into the little staff-room so that we could have some privacy. The doctor explained that my father's chest infection was a form of pneumonia. One of his lungs was already quite heavily infected and the other slightly. He was wondering how the family felt about this. His language was so careful I in turn wondered if he was using euphemisms, but I don't think he was. It then emerged that, apart from the chest infection, there was something else wrong which would need admission to hospital for proper diagnosis. (The home didn't have the neces-sary sophisticated equipment.) At least this was easy to respond to. I said my father emphatically did not want ever to go back into hospital and that he'd said so, loudly and often: he was not going into 'that place' again. So that was clear. The doctor nodded. There was still the delicate matter of antibiotics. A course of these might clear the infection up. There was a pause, perhaps unintentional, and he asked once more how the family felt about this. I said we were all in agreement: we wanted our father made comfortable and relieved of pain if possible, but that was all. 'He says his life is no fun now,' I said. The doctor smiled sympathetically. He said my father had amazing powers of recuperation, but he was nearly ninety-six and very frail and anything might happen, quite suddenly, antibiotics or not. I said I understood.

What I thought I understood correctly was that my father was literally at death's door at last, arriving by a different route from Marion but finally there. I wanted him now to go through that door as smoothly as possible, with no banging on it, no standing in the rain waiting, with none of the hanging about he loathed. He looked so peaceful already, lying still like a good boy, pyjamas buttoned up to his neck, white hair neatly brushed, muscles of his face relaxed. He was ready. He could just drift into death. No more hauling him about, no more bruising of his poor limbs with every assistance given, no more forlorn hours trapped in his chair. I wished I had said, 'Please, no antibiotics.' But I didn't want him to be in pain and a chest infection is painful. It was a Catch 22 situation: deny him antibiotics and he might suffer unnecessarily. If he didn't respond, that was different. And I doubt if the doctor would have permitted me to insist on antibiotics being completely withheld.

I reported all this to Pauline and Gordon. Pauline was about to go on holiday to Italy. When our mother died, she had been on holiday in France. She had ever since regretted not being with her when this happened, so she decided at once to come to say goodbye – if that was what it was to be – to our father. I stressed that the doctor had said nothing was certain, that a recovery was perfectly possible. But she wanted to come, just in case. By the time she arrived, our father was sitting up, dressed, in his chair. The antibiotics had zipped through his system with spectacular results – probably because he'd never had any in all his ninety-five years. It was remarkable to witness his recovery, almost a resurrection, or so it seemed to me. The air of celebration around him was remarkable too, all the staff delighted he had rallied and actually proud of him. They attributed his recovery not so much to the miracle of modern medicine but to his own determination, and treated him as a hero. My sister went off on her holiday amused that yet again our valiant father had insisted on holding on to his precious life and in spite of saying it was no longer fun had certainly not turned his face to the wall and given up.

He was full of awe at his own survival. 'That was a close shave,' he said, and, 'Thought I was a goner there.' The doctor complimented him on his resilience and seemed so pleased himself. 'Is life fun again, Mr Forster?' he teased. My father took this the wrong way. He looked at the doctor as though he were mad and bellowed, 'Fun? *Fun?* You call this fun?' I had to defend the doctor later. 'He was only picking up what you'd said yourself, Dad. He was only being kind.' This drew the retort, 'Kindness is no damned good. I want him to make me better, that's what.' I pointed out that he had indeed been made better. The doctor had successfully treated his chest infection and brought him back from his 'close shave'. This only irritated him. 'That isn't the point,' he grumbled. 'I'm still in a chair, I still can't walk or do any damned thing for myself. I'm helpless. That's the point.'

And by then we were into another month. August on the calendar was another black stallion – the one I'd liked when flicking through – stationary this time, standing on a rocky outcrop above a distant valley. My father started making entries on it on 10 August – just two shaky letters: 'OK.' But it was obvious to him and to me that he was not really OK. He wasn't dying any more but he had lost more strength. He was more frail than ever, and horrified to discover he now couldn't stand up at all, not even when he pressed hard on the arms of his chair. This panicked him. 'Look!' he cried, 'look! Can't get up!

I've had it!' It appalled him to have the last vestige of independent movement taken from him. 'What am I going to do?' he asked. I found myself saying, 'You'll manage.' I meant it to be a soothing phrase, the one he always used himself in difficult circumstances, but it sounded more like an order, you *will* manage, though I hadn't stressed any word. He would manage because he had no alternative. The alternative was illegal. This was the final test of his own pragmatism. He would adapt because he had to, and what he had to manage was being trapped.

Because he was trapped he began using his telephone in the kind of random fashion he had never done. 'If you put a phone right next to his bed and chair he'll be bothering you all the time,' the home authorities had warned me, but I'd known this would not be true. He was disciplined in his use of his telephone, as he was in everything. But now this control broke down. Unable to move without assistance, trapped in his chair and raging with boredom, he began picking up the receiver and pressing any of the call buttons without paying attention to which one it was. They were all labelled with our names, the names of his family, but he had no idea whom he'd called until they answered. He started to do this random calling at all hours of the day and sometimes the night, and we had to be alert and act as though it was perfectly normal to be called at four or five in the morning. We had to do all the talking too – gone were the days when he told us things. Answering his call, I'd say, 'Hello, Dad?' and he'd say, 'Oh, it's you. What do you want?' and I'd think of something to say to satisfy him. He was just playing with the telephone because he felt so isolated and had nothing else to do. But then, by the end of August, there was a new urgency to the calls. He wanted to know where he was, where his kitchen was, and most of all where the hell Lily (our dead mother) had got to and when she would be back. This confusion was minimal – he quickly accepted the truth when reminded of it – but it was real and it upset him. He sighed, and said, 'I'm going daft. That it has to come to this, trapped and going daft.'

Going to see him now became even more of an ordeal. More and more often I arrived to find him not bolt upright and alert but slumped forward in his chair, his head on his knees, as though he had collapsed onto them and couldn't raise himself up. It was a terrible sight, seeing this abject figure as I entered the room, and then when I spoke and he struggled to sit up, it was even more terrible to see his spectacles dangling from one ear and his look of absolute weariness. He had no energy to talk and barely enough to listen. He didn't seem to care about anything – the birds no longer caught his attention, he wasn't able to tolerate television, and he stopped chatting up the staff. All he wanted to do was sleep. He asked to be put to bed earlier and earlier and was only comfortable when there. They weighed him and found he was only six stone but this was no surprise. He was visibly a skeleton, his face sunken, his hands ridges of bone. But he tried so hard still to respond to my presence, struggling to remember what I was working on and never, ever, moaning about his fate.

Early in September, he picked up a little and said, one beautiful day, when the sun was streaming into his room and he could see the sky was a cloudless blue, that he'd like to go out for a drive – 'A breath of sea air might do me good.' It took an army of us to get him ready and into the car. He needed a jacket on top of his cardigan and I couldn't even manage that without help – it was extraordinary how difficult it proved trying to get his arms into the sleeves as he sat in his chair. I thought they might snap as I tried to manoeuvre them. I couldn't do it. I had to go for a nurse and she in turn had to go for another and at last he was clothed in tweed with his cap firmly secured on his head. Two nurses and I picked him up and put him into a wheelchair and then we were off on stage one of this laborious journey. He became quite cheerful as we trundled along and when he saw one young carer coming towards us he was ready with some of the old banter – 'Oh, it's you, is it? What have you been doing with yourself? You've a barnacle on your chin again.' The girl laughed, taking his rudeness as they all seemed to, as a mysterious sign of affection. 'You are awful, Arthur,' she said: 'it's only a small spot,' and then, to me, 'What was he like when you were young?' and she rolled her eyes in mock horror.

What was he like when I was young? As we went through the next stage of getting my father into the car I thought about how I could have answered her. He was a nightmare, I could have told her. My appearance, while I was growing up, was endlessly commented on and always critically. I was getting fat (though 'fat' was a euphemism for 'developing') and it didn't suit me; my hair looked as if a mouse had chewed it and it made me look like a lad; my spots were all barnacles (though, in fact, I hardly ever had even a small spot) and should be covered up if I didn't want to scare people; and, worst of all, I didn't look like my mother. Everything I wore was given the same treatment. Why didn't I wear nice frocks/high heels/nylon stockings/a decent coat? Why did I wear trousers/boots/polo-neck sweaters/duffel coat – and all in black or grey instead of pink and blue? I learned to rise above all this. I learned how wonderfully effective it was merely to smile condescendingly and say nothing. But the carers and nurses didn't need to learn how to do any such thing when my father was offensive. They didn't care what he said. He was very, very old and allowed to say anything. Personal remarks made to them were taken as a sign that there was a spark in him still and they liked that. He was harmless, and at least he noticed them and their barnacles, their hair and earrings. The closer he got to dying, the more outrageous he could be and they would go on admiring his spirit. It suddenly struck me that this might be the only advantage of old age I had ever identified, and I said so as finally we drove off in the car. 'One thing, Dad, now

you're a Grand Old Man you can say what you like to anyone.'
He snorted and said, 'I always have. Nowt special about being
old.'

Sitting in the back seat, I realised my father had shrunk in the
last few weeks. His head wasn't anywhere near the head-rest.
He had withered away to such an extent that it looked like a
child's body curled up there. He looked like a rag doll, merely
a bundle of clothes, limp and loose. I realised he could hardly
see out of the windows – he had sunk so low in his seat – and I
longed to pull him upright. Then when we had meandered to
our favourite stopping place, Glasson Point just before Port
Carlisle, there was another sign of his weakness. He simply
couldn't hold his binoculars up to his eyes. They were old-
fashioned big heavy things (he'd refused to let me replace them
with a small, lighter but just as powerful pair) and his arms were
no longer strong enough to lift them. 'Damn,' he said, then,
'Here, you look. Tell me what you can see.' I took them and
focused them and reported I could see seagulls and some drift-
wood floating in and the tide beginning to surge over the grey-
brown sand bars and some cows a long way off, bunched on the
marsh grass right on the edge of the sea. 'Here,' I said. 'You
look, I'll hold them,' and I put the binoculars in front of his
eyes. 'It's no good,' he said, and I took them away, thinking he
meant the focus was wrong for his eyes and he couldn't see. 'It's
no good,' he repeated, 'I don't know what's going to happen to
me. It's got me beat.'

'It'? Did he mean the riddle of life? Or of death? The
meaning of the universe? The point of existence? Was this 'it'
that had got him 'beat' that deep, dark force he had always
believed ordered things? Should I say 'it' had got me 'beat' too?
But then 'it' meant something different if clearer to me. What
defeated me was why we, meaning the society in which we live
and by whose rules and laws we are governed, allow no escape
for people like my father whose life had gone on so long that its

quality was eroded to the point where it was no longer precious, either to him or to those who cared about him. It was wearying and wearing, this agonising, long-drawn-out descent into death. Why did my father, or anyone else, have to go through this hideously slow process of disintegration? What purpose did it serve, when he was in his ninety-sixth year? He didn't believe in God, so it would be a nonsense to say to him that this torture was God's will. He didn't believe in an afterlife either. He was tired, he was trapped, he was beat. And yet, because his heart and lungs were still functioning his body was not, in fact, beat. He was dictated to by what was left of his body. His wishes counted for nothing. Even if he had wished it, no one could help his body to be brought to a standstill.

We sat there in the car, facing the sea, a little longer while Hunter planted sticks in the sand so that we could see the tide overtaking them one by one. I had still said nothing aloud. What was there to say, in reply to that forlorn 'I don't know what's going to happen to me.' I could dodge the real issue as I had done so many times and say, 'Oh, you'll be well looked after, Dad.' I could be enigmatic and sigh and say 'Who knows?' What I couldn't say, as always, was what I wanted to say – 'Have you had enough, Dad? Would you like to be put to sleep for ever?' If such an option had been available it would still have been an impossibly hard question to ask, implying as it did that *I* thought he'd had enough. But I might have asked it, and I firmly believe the answer at that moment would have been 'Yes'. Unlike Marion, he was mentally fully alert and knew exactly what was before him if the infinitely painful waning of his strength went on. He'd soon be one of those comatose bodies in the home, one of those zombies whose rooms he passed every day and whose plight had always appalled him to the point of shuddering and averting his gaze. But I couldn't ask him if he wanted his life ended because to end it was against the law – and we were both infinitely law-abiding. Every effort was being made to keep him alive and no effort at all to help him die. No wonder he was beat.

So I said nothing. Hunter came back to the car. 'Ready, Arthur?' he said. 'For what?' my father said. 'Leaving,' Hunter said. 'Oh, I'm ready for leaving all right, don't you worry,' he said, with a sad little laugh.

Soon our five months in the Lakes would be up. The security for him of having us so close, constantly visiting, would end. I dreaded telling him the date of our departure even though, at the same time, I'd tell him of the usual winter arrangements, of how Pauline would come for a week in early November and Gordon for his birthday a month later and then Pauline again at Christmas, and we'd keep the rota of daily phone calls going and I'd write every week . . . I dreaded it. Wrap it up how I liked, the message was depressing: we are abandoning you. I took the calendar down as soon as we got to October. A chestnut mare trotting along a beach. Good. I'd had enough of the black stallions. For Sunday 13 October, I wrote the fateful words 'M. and H. to LONDON', and then the cheering ones, 'Pauline arrives at Loweswater' two weeks later. There. It was done. I showed him. 'Good lass,' he said; 'you've been a grand help.' No resentment, no requests for me to stay. He considered we'd done our bit and that, of course, we must go. No self-pity, no attempt to make me feel guilty. He made our approaching departure as easy as he could and this was more touching by far than any tears or distress.

Our last visit was on Friday 11 October. Mercifully, he said he would like to go out, though he hadn't wanted to for some time previously. He endured the usual performance which getting into the car involved, and we set off in surprisingly good spirits. We'd discussed where we should go and he'd elected to have one of our city tours – the weather wasn't good enough to go to the sea, where he predicted we'd see 'nowt but mist'.

He was intrigued when I said I wanted to go to the castle first to pick up a photocopy of a document which would be ready for me in the record office there. He loved driving over the moat (empty for many years) and through the arched gateway where once the portcullis had clanged shut, and into the old parade ground of the Border Regiment. The castle always pleased him, though he had never felt the need to discover its history, about which he had only the vaguest idea. He approved of its very existence, though he would have preferred to have it still bristling with soldiers. He'd taken me round when I was a child without being able to answer a single one of my irritating questions. He didn't know when the castle had been built, or why, or by whom, or anything at all beyond the fact that Mary Queen of Scots had her head chopped off here (which, of course, she did not, though she was imprisoned there for a time). As far as he was concerned, he didn't need to know its history to appreciate the castle's attraction. It was enough just to look at it, to walk its battlements and peer into its dungeons.

I was out of the record office quickly, with the copy of a will I'd wanted. I showed it to him – it was Jonathan Dodgson Carr's will – and he was puzzled. 'What are you going to do with it?' he asked. 'It's no use.' I said it would be of use in the book I was going to write. But he had no interest in it and said no, he didn't want me to read it out as we drove along, why would he want that? We did the tour of the streets he liked and then drove past the cemetery and the crematorium to go to Dalston. 'Don't forget,' he said as we passed the gates of the crematorium: 'take me straight to the crem when I go; no church, no parsons, no messing about. And quick.' I said, 'Right you are, squire.' We crawled through Dalston and looked at the river and then came back into Carlisle by another route. Near to the home, we stopped at a florist's. I'd heard that it was his favourite carer's birthday that day and I wanted him to give her some flowers. He chose pink carnations and I had them wrapped in pretty paper and tied up with pink ribbon. Once he was back in a wheelchair, I put the bouquet on his knee and told him not to forget to say Happy Birthday when he presented it. 'Do you think I'm daft?' he asked. 'Do you think I don't know what's what any more? Of course I'll say Happy Birthday. What do you think I'll say, Happy Easter?'

I wheeled him into his room and by good luck the birthday girl herself was waiting there to transfer him to his chair. He thrust the flowers straight at her and said, 'Here. Happy Birthday to you. Please accept this, my gracious gift.' We all burst out laughing – 'gracious gift' indeed! Where on earth had he got that from? 'Oh, Arthur,' said the carer, 'how lovely, how kind. Thank you. Can I give you a little thank–you kiss?' 'If you must, I suppose,' my father said, gloomily, and with the air of a martyr closed his eyes and held up his face. More laughter. We left with everyone laughing, including my father. The fuss over the business with the flowers had not been deliberately stage managed to help us get round the moment of departure, that awful 'last time' atmosphere, but it had succeeded perfectly in doing exactly that. It was easy to leave him, surrounded by carers and nurses who had come to see what the laughter was about and stayed to admire the flowers.

I calculated on the way home that it was probably the twen-tieth time I had parted from my father in his old age with the realisation that I might very well not see him alive again. This time I didn't think it. I felt resigned to another summer, the following year, during which he would become bed-bound. Maybe two more summers. The episode in August seemed to me to have demonstrated how very gradual his dying was going to be if he was so well looked after, if antibiotics were used to combat infections and he was hauled back time after time from the brink of death. To wish someone dead is a terrible thing, but I'd grown so used to wishing it that it didn't seem terrible any more. Usually, I felt relief when I left him, the simple relief of knowing I need not actually witness his decline for the next few months. But this time I didn't feel it. I felt that leaving him like that I was letting him down, a feeling quite different from guilt.

I saw later on that my father had filled in his calendar for the first half of November and then after that the eight horses thundering over a snowy field were doomed to gallop over blank spaces. On the eighteenth, there is the entry 'Nothing Doing. Bad', and that was the last time he had the heart to write anything at all. The evidence of his accelerating decline was there in every phone call. It was agony trying to have any sort of conversation – he could manage 'Hello' and that was about all, he who had always been avid for family news and expert at cross-questioning. The only thing to do was master a new art, that of talking without expecting a reply. I took to ringing the nurses' desk as much as I rang my father so that they could tell me how he was.

How he was was 'quite comfortable'. He'd had a few falls, but nothing serious, though in his fragile state they'd shaken him badly. He kept falling out of bed but if rails were put up round it he tried to climb over them and when he succeeded the falls were worse. Once he fell on the window side of his bed, where there was only a small gap between the bed and the radiator under the window, and he stayed jammed there until the next check-up during the night. The radiator was hot and an hour was long enough for his arm to be slightly burned. The indignities and miseries seemed to accumulate daily and little could be done to protect him from them. The matron wanted to change the position of his bed, but he wouldn't have it and she didn't want to upset him more, so the bed stayed and night-time vigilance was increased. She advised removing his telephone too, as she had done before, but I still vetoed that. True, he was ringing us frequently in the early hours of the morning, but it was worth putting up with this to let him retain at least a feeling of control.

December 4 arrived and Gordon went as usual, with his wife Shirley, for his birthday. It was not the jolly, happy occasion his ninety-fifth had been. He couldn't be bothered with even the smallest of celebrations and refused to leave his room to be wheeled into the dining-room where his cake awaited. He wasn't interested in presents or cards, or anyone singing 'Happy Birthday, dear Arthur' (though the carers sang it anyway). He said he just wanted to be better. Everyone who visited him now found him slumped in his chair, bent over double, visibly struggling to stay awake. Often, he stayed all day in bed. Nobody forced him to get up, but after a couple of days he would say this was no good, he had to 'get going' or he'd never get better, and then the nurses would go through the ordeal, for them as well as him, of dressing him and putting him in his chair. They were careful, they handled him tenderly, but they dreaded touching his limbs, seeing that the slightest pressure bruised him and caused him discomfort. But it was better for him to be up, if he himself wanted to be, because it was better for his chest – it kept it clear of the mucus which could gather, if he contracted another infection, when he lay prone. Better to be up, better to move a little. Why? To stay alive.

I was not at home when the matron tried to reach me on 11 December, so she rang Pauline and told her our father was 'really poorly'. Pauline correctly interpreted this as dying and left immediately to go to him. She rang me from his bedside that evening and said that it was impossible to assess the situation yet. Yes, he was indeed 'really poorly' but it might be August all over again. Would he rally, as he always had done? Would the antibiotics once more have a miraculous effect? At any rate, she and David would stay at Loweswater and come in each day. They had been due to come for Christmas the following week anyway so might as well just stay. How lucky, we agreed, how lucky, because one of us would have had to go to be with him. The next day, Pauline rang to say that our father seemed brighter. He was still in bed and his breathing was laboured, but he was talking and objecting to various things she was doing in mistaken efforts to please him. I said I'd come up and help, but she said there was no need. I could come later if necessary and give her a break, but that it was a waste of our resources for me to come when she had just arrived. This might be the beginning of a long decline and we might need to alternate with each other again for weeks, so that one of us was always near him.

Pauline was there to give me a daily report throughout the following week. She began to realise that 'really poorly' did mean dying this time, but that still no one could estimate how long it would take. Could be weeks, even months. Or could be days, even hours. On Monday 16 December, she rang me mid-afternoon and said she thought our father would like me to speak to him. He wouldn't be able to speak to me, because his breathing was such an effort, but if she held the telephone receiver next to his ear then I could speak to him. I heard him breathing heavily, each breath almost a whistle, but not like Marion's breathing had been that last day – he had more energy and the breaths seemed to come quicker and be noisier. I didn't know if that was significant or not. 'Dad,' I said, 'you must be so tired. What a struggle you're having – you must be so fed-up with all this, thank heaven you're being well looked after and that Pauline is with you. Just try to sleep till you feel better. I'm sure that's the best idea.' He made some sort of sound, hard to describe – a grunt, not words, as though he was trying to say something but couldn't. Pauline took the receiver and said he was being put to bed now and that she'd be leaving after she'd tucked him up. She went on to say there was no real change, but that the antibiotics were having some good effect, and that he seemed easier.

To go or not to go, that was very much the question. I told Pauline before she rang off that I thought I'd pay the kind of flying visit she'd paid in August and we began to discuss when I should do this. But during the night, while I lay awake thinking about it, I decided to go the next day. I'd get an early train, be with my father that afternoon, stay at Jeff's, and spend another day, giving Pauline two days off. I slept then, relieved to have made up my mind, but was awake at six, ready to ring the home and tell them I was coming, so that they could tell him, and let Pauline know so that she need not come in. I knew the night shift ended at seven o'clock and that this was the best time to ring, when the nurses did the handover in their little room. The nurse who answered was silent when I said I was coming and would she tell my father. 'I'm so sorry,' she said, 'but your Dad passed on about two o'clock this morning.' They'd rung Pauline to tell her and she hadn't rung me, I imagined, because she saw no point in waking me up then.

I rang her at once. We both agreed we felt absurdly shocked – absurdly, because this death had been expected for so long. Expected and wanted. But still we were shocked and disbelieving. He *couldn't* be dead at last; it seemed impossible that this torment had ceased for him. Then there was the regret that one of us had not been with him, actually there holding his hand (if we'd dared). Pauline would've stayed all night if she had known the end was so near, but nobody had predicted that death would come quite so soon. It didn't really matter, of course, since he was said to have died in his sleep, as Marion had done, and Pauline had been with him when he went to sleep – there if not at the literal end then at the end of consciousness. The phone calls went on all day, backwards and forwards between the three of us, Gordon as amazed as we were that this incredible life-force had finally stopped. Whatever our feelings about him, none of us could deny that our father's death removed a powerful influence over our lives.

What fascinated me, as the day went on and we discussed funeral arrangements, was the absence of that relief I had expected and which had come so quickly when Marion died. The whole horror of my father's final ghastly two years was over and I'd anticipated feeling light-headed with relief. But I didn't. Did this mean I wished he were still alive? Good God, no. Yet still I felt this amazement and with it some kind of peculiar agitation, as though something terrible had happened. My father's death was the end of a long, long tough march, but I didn't seem able to rest. I was still on that arduous march with him, still going through the motions of keeping him company. It was as though, because he was so very old, he had come to seem immortal. I had despaired of death for him. The grim reaper had kept passing him over, constantly rejecting him, and I'd lost faith in him ever being chosen. It would never be his turn – and then it was, and the shock was all the greater for being deferred.

I thought the relief I looked for might wash over me once I'd seen him dead. Maybe I didn't really believe, on one level, that he was. Maybe I needed to see his dead body to be convinced this was not a trick. I went to Carlisle that afternoon, stayed the night with Jeff, and then walked to the funeral parlour in the morning. It was a bitterly cold December day, the air raw and harsh with an east wind scudding in from the Pennines, blasting right across the Eden Plain and bringing flurries of snow with it. How appropriate the weather felt as I battled across the city, bright with Christmas decorations, and over Caldew bridge and up past Carr's factory, past my old primary school, onto the Wigton Road. The cold, the bleakness, the biting wind, all pleased me. I didn't dread going into the funeral parlour. I was intrigued, because though I'd seen dead bodies before I'd never actually seen one in this sort of quaintly named place – a parlour, indeed. As I stood waiting for the door to be opened I wondered inappropriately why it was called a 'parlour'. Because bodies traditionally lay in their coffins in the parlour of the house, I supposed, that formal, largely unused room so characteristic of Victorian houses. Nobody had a parlour any more and yet the name had not been changed.

I was shown into the small room where my father lay and was invited to spend as long as I liked there. I could see there were lots of small rooms along a corridor, presumably all ready to be occupied, a hotel for the dead. The atmosphere was hushed, the light dim and the man who showed me in spoke in whispers. I found myself tiptoeing, as though fearing to wake someone up. Left on my own in front of my father's body I thought what a very good-looking corpse he made. His face looked quite relaxed and even healthy, and I realised this must be due to the undertaker's art — surely, the cheeks were padded somehow, banishing that awful skull-like appearance his face had taken on recently. His hair, a surprising amount of it for a ninety-six-year-old man, was beautifully brushed. It looked very clean, but I couldn't believe the undertaker had gone as far as to wash it. He looked so fine, lying there, quite unlike poor Marion who had been so disfigured by her disease and who had not, when I saw her, received any attention from an undertaker. This, too, my father's corpse, was just a *thing*, but the illusion that it was more than that was strong and entirely due to the way his body had been laid out. It was quite dangerous, I thought, to make dead things look living.

All that detracted from the general impressiveness of what had been done to my father's dead body was the strange garment he'd been dressed in. It was a ridiculous black silk affair, vaguely Chinese in style. Where was his good suit, the handkerchief peeping out of the pocket, and the sparkling white shirt? He would have been outraged to be so garbed, but this garment had been put on him without Pauline knowing and it had seemed silly to make a fuss and insist on the robe being changed for his suit. His hands were lying on his stomach, not quite touching each other. I suddenly had a desire to hold one, not out of any surge of emotion or sentiment, but in a woefully clear-headed spirit of scientific enquiry. Would it be cold and stiff? No, it was warm and quite pliable, more evidence of the undertaker's work, or was this normal? There was so much I didn't know about these things called corpses. He hadn't approved of hand-holding. The last time he'd held my hand had been when I was a child and we were crossing the road. The moment we were safely over he always dropped it quickly. He had such big hands but they were never clumsy. His hands had worked well for him, proving adroit and nimble in the handling of his precious tools. I laid his hand carefully back on his stomach, just as it had been placed, all neat and tidy, just as he liked things.

I couldn't go on standing there much longer. Daft, as he would have said. Time to leave. I stared at his face, quite noble in appearance. He had never approved of kissing either but I decided to kiss his forehead. I did it. I didn't feel remotely distressed, but on the other hand I did feel something unexpected – a certain tenderness and sadness that there had not been between us what there might have been. Then I left, knowing his body would now be put into the coffin. I noticed as I left the funeral parlour and began the walk to the crematorium that I felt calm. The agitation had ceased and the relief I'd looked for had at last arrived. Seeing the body had reassured me; touching it had proved a strange release from tension. I stepped out smartly, enjoying the cold, and when I met someone I knew coming down Wigton Road I beamed at them, as they offered their commiserations, in a manner they clearly considered inappropriate. Yes, I said happily, he's dead, it's all over, it's all over. The funeral? Oh, today, but it's private.

We were, of course, going to carry out his instructions – 'Straight to the crem. No parsons . . .' It was in fact odd, his insistence that there should not be, in the accepted sense, a proper funeral such as my mother's had been. Then, he had been most anxious that every attention should be paid to detail – he'd wanted 'the lot' for her: the best wood with brass handles for the coffin, a hearse and several posh cars, and most important of all a funeral tea for the family mourners. He had been deeply satisfied that St James's Church was packed, that the hymns had been sung lustily (though not by him) and that the vicar had waxed most eloquent about his wife's sterling qualities. It had been 'a good turnout' and this had mattered. The church he hated had done her proud; the religion he despised had provided a framework for grief, which had helped. But he hadn't wanted what he called 'that kind of daft carry-on' for himself. His respect for convention and tradition was not as strong as his contempt for the church. Funerals involving 'the lot' were only for the faithful and he would not pretend to be one of them. His was to be absolutely simple and, most important of all, was to be paid for by himself.

The cost of my mother's funeral had shocked him. It came (in 1981) to £455.12 and he hadn't been able to pay it. They had both been in a Death Club since the 1930s, paying a penny a week at first and then their contribution rising gradually to sixpence, but when this was cashed in the sum total, by some miracle of arithmetic I didn't understand and couldn't begin to explain, came to only £88. His distress was dreadful and only partially relieved by my suggestion that since she was our mother as well as his wife we should split the bill equally and all pay a quarter. Agreeing to this was a bitter moment for him – 'Can't even pay for my own wife's funeral!' Clearly, he saw it as an indictment of his failure in life that he didn't, at the age of eighty, possess £455.12. He saw himself as disgraced and humiliated and resolved to make sure this would never happen again: he would pay for his own funeral and need help from no one.

I took care, when I reached the cemetery, to go round by the grave of my great-grandfather (the one my father was called after, the one who died at ninety) and then to visit, in strict order, all the other family graves. The last one, my grandparents', was right at the top on an exposed hillside from which there are magnificent views of the northern fells. These had snow on the tops and all along the skyline thick grey clouds pressed down hard, though the sky above was a brilliant blue. I stood looking not at the ugly black marble stone with its flashy gilt lettering, but beyond, to that view. My father, even though he never put it into any words beyond 'grand' or 'champion', loved such scenes. 'Look at that!' he would say, confronted with some vista of glorious landscape, and then no more. Words were daft. Words were inadequate. Eyes and ears were all that mattered. In his head, he knew what he felt and that was enough.

Pauline and David, and Gordon and Shirley, and the faithful Nixons, his old neighbours, were waiting beside their cars outside the crematorium. Others would have come but we had explained this was not to be a funeral in the sense they might expect and that they shouldn't feel obliged to attend so basic a ceremony. There were to be no hymns, readings, psalms or addresses by vicars. Straight in, straight out, no messing – embarrassing, really, for the average mourner. We'd been asked if we wanted any music played and had decided to have a couple of carols (hoping this did not exceed our brief) – 'Silent Night' on the way in, 'In the Bleak Midwinter' on the way out. Very seasonal. The coffin, when it came, had a wreath of red roses and holly upon it, and a pretty posy of freesias, the wreath from us, his children, and the posy from his youngest grandchild. We walked behind the coffin into the chapel, the smallest available and yet still seeming much too large, and sat down in the front row. The coffin was now resting in front of the curtains behind which it would soon slide.

Silence. A cough from the undertaker. What now? No

messing indeed, but there had to be *something* before the coffin disappeared. I got up and stood in front of the other five mourners and spoke for a few minutes about my father. It was an attempt at summing up a life, that was all. I said we, his children, were regretfully aware that we had not loved our father, but that still we had admired his good qualities and especially his particular kind of courage during his last years. We had, finally, been proud of his lack of self-pity and his determination to do his best. It was easy to go over his life, and remind myself, and them, of how hard he had worked for little reward, and without achieving the material comfort we had all achieved, but more difficult to find some note to end on. I said, something more than duty had probably bound us to him, but maybe we shouldn't try too hard, as I myself had tried, to divine what it was. He was dead. A long life had ended, and we should be glad because the last two years had put our father through a process he should never have had to endure, making, as it did, a mockery of all that had been precious about it.

We went to the Crown Hotel at Wetheral for the funeral tea, one of our father's favourite places for a bar lunch. The hotel stands above the river Eden in a lovely village five miles from Carlisle. He used to bring us out here to walk through the woods when we were children. Since it was only five days before Christmas there were several office lunch parties just ending when we arrived, but we found a relatively quiet corner in the lounge, and tucked in to sandwiches and cakes and tea. It was not at all like a funeral tea and we were relieved. We thought we should all really have whisky to toast our father in the manner he liked, but it was four o'clock and everyone except me had a long drive ahead of them. We swapped anecdotes about him, all well known to us, and repeated some of his more famously outrageous sayings and doings. By the time we were ready to part, we were all surprisingly cheerful. The job had been done, with 'no messing' as instructed.

The following day, I went back on the train to London. Plenty of time to think, and what I thought about, obviously, was my father's death. I stared out of the window at the snow-covered tops of the Lake District fells on the right-hand side and wondered what my father would have thought of his own death, of the way he died. 'Pity,' he would have said, for sure, and, 'Can't be helped.' He'd have shrugged, and if I'd said maybe it *should* have been helped, what would have been his response? 'Don't talk so daft.'

I couldn't decide whether he was right. He'd suffered much longer than he need have done, than he would have done if everything possible had not been tried to extend time for him. His life, at ninety-six, had been considered so precious that it was fought for by others to the bitter end. Splendid? He may have thought so. Nobody asked him. Nobody knew his views on dying.

Suddenly, as the train left the fells behind, I found myself thinking of a boat trip when I was aged ten. It was the time when I'd had jaundice badly and was convalescing. My father thought I needed some sea air 'to perk me up', as he put it, before going back to school and he proposed taking me to Silloth. My mother was not at all sure that this was a sensible idea – it was only February – but the weather that week was unseasonably (for Carlisle) mild and even sunny, and she weakened. I was wrapped up in layers and layers of clothes, and off we went, my father and I.

I know it was a weekday but I can't remember how on earth my father managed to get the day off. At any rate, because it was a weekday, and because it was February (and Carlisle folk did not normally start thinking about going to Silloth until, at the earliest, April), the train was empty. We had a whole compartment to ourselves and it felt odd. My father read the racing pages in the *Daily Express*, pencil in hand, marking the runners he fancied, and I read the *Girls' Crystal* which he had kindly bought me. 'Here's a book for you,' he'd said, and I'd managed not to show off and point out it was a magazine and not a book. Illness had definitely softened me. Neither of us spoke to the other on the journey, of course.

When we got to Silloth we didn't, as we would usually do, go straight to the sea-wall across the Green. We turned left outside the station and went into the docks. We walked right round them to where a boat smaller than all the others was tied up at the quayside. My father told me to wait, and he went ahead and entered into negotiations with the boatman, who was sitting smoking above his boat. I didn't hear what was said but I saw money change hands and then he turned to me, positively triumphant, and told me to get into the boat with him. 'Grand,' he said, when we'd clambered down. 'This is just what you need.'

It wasn't a very tidy boat. There seemed to be a lot of clutter in it, ropes and nets and waterproofs and fishing tackle everywhere. We were the only passengers and sat close together on a slippery plank seat without a back. The boatman started the engine, which made a tremendous noise, and we spluttered our way out of the docks and began chugging along the coast, until we were roughly parallel with Skinburness, where we changed direction and began to veer out into the open estuary towards Annan on the Scottish side. Our progress was slow but it was impossible for it to be slow enough for my father, who was relishing every minute and wanted our voyage prolonged. The sun was shining obligingly and, apart from a few clouds, the sky was mostly a weak blue. The breeze was stiff, though, and my face was soon stinging. 'Doing you good!' my father yelled above the noise of the engine.

There was not a great deal to do in Annan when we got

there. The boatman said we had an hour, so we followed the usual routine for family outings: my father found a pub and brought me out some lemonade and crisps, then he went back in and had a pie and a pint. After that we walked up and down Annan's main street until it was time. The clouds were growing by then and I could sense my father was a little anxious about the return trip. But the boatman was punctual leaving, which was a relief, and in fact we made quicker progress this time. When Grune Point, the tip of Skinburness marsh, was visible, my father said, 'Good. Nearly there.' The sun had vanished by then. Thick, grey clouds covered the sky and the wind had strengthened. The sea, which had been as calm as the Solway Firth ever is, was becoming rougher and there were white tops to the waves. We were just edging our way past the Skinburness itself when the engine stopped. It gave what sounded like a little cough and then another and then it stopped. The boatman tried to restart it and failed. He tried again, failed again, and then sat back on his haunches, saying it would be best to wait a while, this engine often played up. He seemed quite unconcerned, and indeed we were so close to the shore there seemed no real reason to worry.

But I could tell that my father was worried, though he said nothing. He was worried about me. The waves were slapping against the rocking boat quite violently and spray was coming over the side occasionally. It was suddenly bitterly cold and we were sitting unprotected. A few drops of rain fell, which at first we thought was spray, and my father swore (though only a 'damn!') and took his own coat off to put round me. Then the boatman tried again and this time the engine caught and we began moving safely towards Silloth and the docks before the rain became heavy. My legs felt quite wobbly when I was lifted onto the quayside. I was glad to get to the warmth of the train. 'It's done you good,' my father said firmly, once we were settled.

Had it? All I knew was that I'd been frightened. I could see we were not far from land, and I was a good swimmer, but still I'd been frightened. I'd imagined the boat drifting the other way, out into the open sea. I'd imagined a storm hitting us — the sky looked full of storm clouds — and the boat capsizing. I'd imagined drowning however hard I tried to stay afloat. And in the middle of all this imagining I'd felt the strangest tremor of a fear I'd never experienced before, the fear of dying. I'd thought about death and the dead often enough, with my morbid pre-occupation with the subject, but never of the actual *process* of dying. It was the first time.

All those years later, sitting in another train, speeding south, I could only assume this little memory had surfaced because I'd been wondering whether my father ever felt that tremor himself. I don't think he did until the last few months of his long life. That was his strength: his lack of fear, his acceptance of whatever was going to happen happening. He might not be religious, or even like Marion 'spiritual', but he had confidence in the natural order of things. And he didn't necessarily even see that this natural order was being interfered with, that in fact for him it had become highly unnatural. Was that good, or bad?

I wished he could have had the option of escaping the worst part of dying, the apprehension, the absolute certainty that his life, once so precious to him, had been devalued because he was no longer living it, he was living death. But few people can do that. It's all a matter of luck, how the dying will go. That's the part which dismays me; the part that comforts me is witnessing how the human spirit in perfectly ordinary people adapts to it.

These have been two stories not of life but of dying. They have been about two people for whom life was precious in quite different ways and who approached death with quite different attitudes. Both died bravely, in that neither made those around them suffer. They had no self-pity and made it as easy as possible for their loved ones to witness their decline. One, my sister-in-law Marion, was, in effect, given the means to end her own life whenever she chose. She could have overdosed on liquid morphine and shortened the time she had left. But she did not choose to do so. Under no circumstances would euthanasia have been acceptable either to her or to anyone involved with her. If she wanted to go on living no matter what state she was in, then we wanted it too. She had made her choice and it was absolutely respected. But my father was never given the choice. He was the one who had come finally to regard his own life as no longer in the least valuable. He was tired of it. But he was obliged to go on. There was to be no cutting short of his dying, inevitable though it had become. It is as though we take a pride in seeing how long we can prolong a life which is clearly over.

It seems odd. It seems wrong.